THE CULTURAL BARRIER

The sun has a splendour of its own,
the moon another splendour, and
the stars another, for star
differs from star in
brightness.

1 Corinthians 15:41 (*New English Bible*)

Do not dislike a man on sight if
you do not know anything
about him.

The Instructions of 'Onchsheshonqy 6.20
(trans. S.R.K.GLANVILLE)

The Cultural Barrier

Problems in the Exchange of Ideas

NORMAN DANIEL

at the University Press
Edinburgh

© Norman Daniel 1975
Edinburgh University Press
22 George Square, Edinburgh

ISBN 0 85224 249 2

Printed in Great Britain by
Western Printing Services Ltd
Bristol

Preface

THIS BOOK BEGAN as a study of mutual benefit in academic exchange. This led quickly to an examination of the facts that hinder communication between cultures. The question that next arose was: what can, and what ought to, be exchanged? A final problem then set itself : is this an historical problem to which experience may provide an answer? Now this book tries to do three things.

The first is to define the cultural barrier that inhibits communication.

The second is to identify a cultural filter that can distinguish between technical and cultural borrowings.

The third is to test judgements made about situations of the present day by historical parallels.

These three are closely connected. Each leads to the others, and no one of them is fully intelligible without the other two. 'Communication' is a subject still currently popular. I have tried not to write about ephemeral aspects; failure to communicate between cultures is my subject. My main theme is that effective communication requires an acceptance of differences which is often unhappily reluctant. There is nothing esoteric in my problems, or in the facts which I use when I look for solutions. I have used simple, and, as far as possible, accessible source material. Indeed, many of the facts that bear on the problems seem obvious; but even obvious facts have to be assembled in a useful order, and this is what I try to do. I hope by arguing carefully each step of the way to interpret the facts about communication between cultures on an acceptable theoretic basis that has useful practical results. It appears that even the barrier serves a useful purpose. Some things easily pass it, while others are held back, so that it is not only a barrier, but also a filter. It is of the 'barrier' that we are first conscious, when we are prevented from communicating. Later we realise that, granted certain conditions, communication after all continues. Some process of selection is at work. It may not be what we would prefer; it is emphatically not everybody's selection. Still, there is a selection, and it serves a purpose; I argue that this also is a useful purpose.

I have tried to approach these questions simply; first I define my terms; then I summarise the background attitude common to most people who have felt themselves the victims of imperialist exploitation. I go on to illustrate the actual difficulties of communicating, and so to approach the study of what it is we are trying to communicate. The whole subject has been so inadequately analysed that historical parallels are needed to clarify the issues involved, and two in particular: the nature of cultural arrogance and the choice of what to communicate. Such parallels help us to judge the effectiveness today of cultural resistance to intrusion from outside. What results from my study is not a firm prognosis, nor even a complete diagnosis, but we learn something about passing across the barrier, and perhaps through the filter. Our conclusions can only be tentative, but they have a practical bearing.

Would it have been possible to treat my three questions separately? Need I have written about them all at the same time, after all? To write about academic exchange without exploring the problems underlying it is possible only at the relatively frivolous level of personal reminiscence or professional experience. To write about the bases and background of cultural tolerance without reference to practical points that arise from day to day would be to rob the subject of its salt. More than that: individuals can only be expected to make the effort to overcome cultural differences if they clearly see their meaning and value; and, on the other hand, only a practical application clarifies the theoretical position. Within our own culture there is no 'alternative culture', only some development or reshaping of that which we inherit, and what is commonly meant by an alternative culture is more what we may call an 'anti-culture', that is, the same culture expressed in reactive terms. When we come to communicate with people of different traditions it is essential that we should not deal with them exclusively or intolerantly, still less aggressively, in our own cultural terms, whether these be traditionally conservative or traditionally radical or revolutionary.

That is why I do not believe that it would be right to take any of these questions in isolation. I have related contemporary problems, not to recent history, but to attitudes of the more distant past, because I am convinced that we can best understand the small failures of mutual understanding which occur in ordinary experience by taking them out of the nearer historical context into a longer perspective. In this way history may even make a contribution to sociology as sociology has added to the content of history.

ACKNOWLEDGEMENTS

I have discussed this book, or parts of it, with a number of people who are responsible, not for its faults, but for suggesting or stimulating improvements: with my son, Gerald, before his death, with my wife, Ruth, throughout, and with Sir Robert Fowler, Fr Gervase Mathew and Sir John Richmond, who were kind enough to read the typescript. Conversations with many friends have helped me, as have their recommendations of particular books. I am grateful to the President and Fellows of University College, Cambridge, as it then was, for the opportunity to work in Cambridge; in particular, to the President, Mr John Morrison, for his encouragement; and, equally, to my employers, the British Council, for making this possible. Everyone who has used Cambridge University Library is indebted to the Librarian and staff. I benefited greatly from opportunities to discuss aspects of this book at seminars and meetings at (in turn) the Institute of Commonwealth Studies (University of London), at the Department of Islamic and Arabic Studies at the University of Edinburgh, at the Middle East Centre at the University of Cambridge, at the University of Bradford, at the Middle East Centre at St Antony's College, Oxford, and at the University of Wales, Aberystwyth.

NORMAN DANIEL, *Cairo, April* 1973

Contents

Part One

THE PROBLEM

Conditions of Cultural Exchange

I SET OUT my argument in this book in historical terms and in the language normal to a traditionally trained historian. More recently developed techniques, such as social anthropology and linguistics, have used a special vocabulary, and this sometimes tends to an esoteric result. In ignoring such techniques, I am not indicating that I despise or dislike them; far from it, I believe that the historian is free to take, and should accept, whatever help he can get from disciplines which, after all, are technical forms of history itself; but I do not want to say anything that is not intelligible to any reader, whatever the discipline in which he was educated. I suggest that it is useful to try to discuss contemporary problems from some little distance, and to avoid the phrases and patterns of thought of the day, if we can. I hope I have not invented a jargon of my own; we tend to do this, and I have tried to reduce it as much as I can. It is easy enough to fail to be intelligible, without adding to the hazard. My use of 'barrier' and 'filter' is meant to refer specifically to functions. It is metaphorical only in the sense that all language is metaphorical, as when we speak of thinking 'deeply' or 'highly'.

I borrow the anthropological use of *culture*, to include all the customs and attitudes, as well as the artefacts, evolved by any human group. Even this is given different shades of meaning by lay writers, but the old dictionary definition, 'the intellectual side of civilisation' is no longer useful. We are not sure what is a civilisation, or what is intellectual; but we realise that the most characteristic art of any society is the way it lives, its 'manners and customs'. I cannot use 'culture' just to mean 'artistic and literary', but equally, of course, that is included in the total definition. The arts, education, science and research, religious practice, economics, finance, commerce, politics, amusements, are all of them aspects of a culture; we must use the word sometimes as a common noun, just as we speak also of 'a civilisation', and sometimes generally, as a quality: culture; but even then it will carry with it much more than the narrow sense the old dictionaries gave it.

I am concerned with cultural exchange, give and take between different cultures. To judge this at all, we have to distinguish what is 'culture free' (at least notionally) from what is 'culture bound'. If the subject of an exchange, or an object to be exchanged, can only be transmitted together with the culture in which it originates, then certainly it is culture bound. If in that case the receiving culture rejects the cultural accretions, the object will take no root. Probably no one would argue that there is anything in the world that is entirely culture free; grass, for example, has quite a different cultural part to play in the Scottish Highlands, in the Syrian desert and in Equatorial Africa — the sparse grazing of the crofters, the will o' the wisp that nomads must follow seasonally with their camels, the hiding place of animals and even soldiers. A car is culturally different where it is the possession of every worker, and where it portends the rare arrival of a senior government official. Yet if 'culture free' is nothing more than the notional antithesis of 'culture bound', there is a third and very practical alternative, the 'culture transferable'.

A radio is culture transferable: it will talk English or Russian, Arabic or Swahili, Hindi or Chinese, with equal facility. The car is culture transferable in the example I gave above; so is all machinery, and any technique. Most artefacts are common to the whole human culture, for example, a weapon, or something to drink from; but the shape they take varies with the culture, and can be borrowed and often adapted from culture to culture without losing its original character. A computer, or a harvester, or a tractor, like a car or a radio, will work for anyone, though of course adopting them will affect the culture that does so, and cause it to develop itself in a new direction. It is neither harder nor easier to do this than it was for a neolithic culture to adopt the use of metal; at least, in principle it is no easier, though it may be in practice. But many different cultures in the ancient past learned new techniques, and learning the same techniques they still did not develop alike: Scythians and barbarians, Jews and Greeks; there was always room for cultural variation, and for the adaptation of whatever was culture-transferable. The great universal human ideas, religious ideas like 'spirit' or 'sacrifice', and moral ideas like 'murder', all have their cultural varieties, and change more or less subtly as a culture develops. There has always been room for variety, *at least up to now*; one of my main themes is to ask what room remains for variety of cultural divergence today.

The characteristic symptom of any cultural situation is that we do not recognise it. It is like what seeing our own faces must have been before the days of good looking-glasses; or like trying to imagine how our personalities appear to others. So we cannot see our own culture clearly. Also it is like being in a room made of glass. We cannot see that we are enclosed; and we do not realise that the glass is subtly coloured, or subtly shaped, so that it distorts the appearance of what we see. At least, the same thing looks different from another viewpoint in another culture. Can even anthropology, which by hypothesis is cross-cultural, be culture free? The sociologist or anthropologist is interested in a particular range of information, and he has a particular technique for elicit-ing the information. A review of a study of kinship in the English Middle Class says that 'If a Trobriand (or a Chinese) had been a member of the research team, we might have got some fresh insight'. Is this true? If it is true, it is likely enough that the new insight would have been unwelcome to us of the English Middle Class. Be that as it may, the technique is fixed, so that any new contribution must come if at all in the process of interpretation. Is all the interpretation of anthropology culture-bound? I. M. Lewis, who on behalf of anthropology holds out an olive branch to history, quotes writers who say 'that anthropology is an epiphenomenon of colonialism, and as such old hat', and adds that this roughly coincides with an African nationalist opinion that anthropolo-gists are tribalists, opposed to modernity.[1] This view, which he believes to be declining in popularity, has certainly seemed justified by the way some anthropologists have talked, but we can all reasonably hope to be given the chance to modernise ourselves, whether we are tribesmen, or anthropologists, or historians. Still, it seems clear enough that inter-pretation and the use to which a technique is put will be affected by the changing ways and ideas of a culture, and certainly the anthropologist too belongs in his own culture.

The interpretation of the results of a technique is the product of the culture; and that culture is not represented by one man alone. We can recognise three stages in the working of any 'scientific' technique. There is the critical method, designed, for example, in the case of history, to penetrate beyond the meaning intended or understood by the original author of a document to new meaning, not necessarily, and preferably not, incompatible with his own, but elucidating a complex of facts in-accessible to him. The connection between the facts is interpretative, and this is the imaginative achievement of the historian. Finally many people working over the same subject constantly, and reworking it, must produce something which is even more the product of their cul-ture than any single man's contribution; and what they produce will differ according to the character and aims of the society to which they belong. There is room for cultural eccentricity in one man's work, but no room for it at all in the formation of a consensus. Not the technique, but the use of it, will inevitably change from culture to culture, and in each culture will correspond to the trend there prevailing. If we want to speak across cultures, we have to watch ourselves very carefully for what is most culturally marked in us; at least we should try to recognise it, and allow it to be picked out by a reader or a listener who comes from the next culture. We shall also realise that there must be something, perhaps much, that we have not recognised in ourselves as culture bound. Those things in which we have most cultural support, which seem most certain, because unquestioned or firmly maintained by our society, are likely to be those which are most bound to our culture.

It will already be clear that the techniques that can be transferred from one culture to another are of many kinds. These are physical techniques like shoeing the horse or cleaning the plugs; there are abstract methods of keeping accounts, or of historical, or literary, or linguistic criticism; there are good methods and bad methods, methods of making, doing, judging, and evaluating. Theoretically any technique at all can be transmitted and put to a new use by a new culture, without adaptation of the culture itself to the ideas of an alien culture. If the borrowing culture does not like the use that the originating culture gave the technique, and can put it to some other use, of course it will do so. When the technique is transferred, whatever is interpretative or purposeful in its use, and therefore cultural, is liable to be changed. It will not necessarily change, of course, because cultures may resemble each other in a number of points, and still differ in enough to be recognisably distinct. Any kind of knowledge whatever can be transmitted between cultures to the same extent that knowledge is transmitted between individuals. The way the facts known are understood may be peculiar to a culture, and this may impede their transmission, but mainly it is the use to which knowledge is put that is characteristic of a culture.

CULTURAL BARRIERS

Some people will deny that cultural barriers exist, still more that they are themselves affected by them. Not only do these barriers exist, but they affect every human being to greater or lesser extent, and those least aware of them are often those most affected. Those who deny them do so because they do not perceive them. By a cultural barrier is meant everything that the individual derives from the community in which he is brought up, and which he does not share with individuals brought up in other communities with different ways. What is not innate, but acquired, is in principle cultural; but it may be acquired in the case of different individuals from outside sources, perhaps from other cultures. What an individual picks up from another culture may prove to be a link between his own culture and that one; but everything part of the furniture of his mind and will that belongs to the community to which he belongs, and is not shared with another community, is a cultural barrier. Language is often a part of the cultural barrier, and within a single linguistic group, accent and dialect may be culturally divisive. Anyone who lives abroad, and is at all sensitive to the society of the country in which he lives, will slowly and over years notice new little differences, and later blush for early errors of behaviour of which at the time he was quite unaware.

People usually hate to have to overcome the cultural barrier. This is why national clubs are so very popular overseas. British people like to relax together, so do Americans, so do French; they do not really like it if any stranger is invited in. Of course, they are used to, say, the club servants, who may in fact be government spies, but this not a rational matter at all; rather it is a question of what is familiar. In the same way, overseas students like to form national associations in European countries. If an Englishman cannot relax only with English people, or a Frenchman with Frenchmen, and the alternative to mixing with each other is to mix with people still more different, the chances are that English and French will prefer to relax with each other. Englishmen and Americans, with no real language problem between them, will manage even more easily to relax together, though there are a number of social and political ways in which the Englishman is closer to another European than to an American. This is probably because of a combination of the language factor and of a certain similarity in kinds of relaxation. There seem to be occasions on which a white American will feel more relaxed with an Englishman than with a black American, but in fact the two Americans obviously have much more in common than either have with the Englishman; the behaviour of the white American must surely here be the effect of a doctrine about race. Race itself is really cultural; I discuss this further later.

Every divergence of background to some extent inhibits communication, because people are deeply attached to habits and customs, to particular ways of doing things, and greatly exaggerate their importance. If people visibly do things in a different way, how can we trust them in anything? We do not know how to expect them to act in any respect; certainly it would be folly to trust them. Secondly, any failure to realise that simple everyday things are done differently in different cultures often leads to misunderstanding; an action receives its meaning from custom, and so has a different meaning where the custom is different. If one culture requires a great deal of handshaking, head bowing or other formality for politeness, people from another culture who act differently may regard such behaviour as ridiculous at best, and effusive, and so insincere at worst; while the other side consider their opposite numbers brusque, ill-bred and barbaric. Actually no one code is other than accidental, so none is more meaningful or more really polite than another. I speak there of conventions. All societies can agree that the purpose of politeness is to facilitate social relations, so that some sort of expression of good will is essential to all; what differs is the convention that expresses it. All this may seem very obvious, but it is likely to be the source of misunderstanding at any given moment within a mile of any reader.

This can lead to very harsh judgements. The tendency of most people to think that people whom they do not understand, because they come from another culture, are dirty, is a case in point. Slight differences in the habit of washing may lead to the conviction that the other man is dirty. Cultures that differ about methods of cleanliness in the lavatory are particularly apt to think each other dirty. Different sexual conventions also lead to serious misunderstanding, and again to harsh judgements, although the basic behaviour may not be different. All these differences limit communication because of the hostility they engender, and because of the misinterpretation of ordinary actions to which they give rise. The fundamental weakness is the failure by most people in this world to accept that it is quite normal that other people should be different. Why should not people in one place do things one way, and people do them another way in another place? It is common to all cultures to dislike what is not common to them; the unfamiliar is a source of fear, and xenophobia is a basic condition of humanity.

The fact that people see each other every day does not necessarily lead to their becoming friendly and familiar; it may only be the external appearance that is familiar. There has been great mutual intolerance and lack of understanding between classes, although they may live within a hundred yards of each other. In the Middle East, where for long centuries Islam tolerated the existence of other religions, provided they were organised separately, the members of these religions have lived countless generations side by side without really communicating in the culturally important matters. Sometimes there is personal friendship, and sometimes when that happens it sadly disappears at moments of stress or pressure. In any case there is no understanding. An example is the way the two religions, Christianity and Islam, have regarded each others' fasts. A Muslim who has suffered the absolute prohibition of anything at all passing his lips throughout the heat of the day, cannot see that there is anything serious at all in the oriental Christian, who for very long periods goes without nutritive foods like sugar and fats. The Christian who is debilitated by this sort of fasting thinks the Muslim who can 'eat as much as he likes' from sundown to sunup is doing nothing difficult, although in fact the absolute fast for twelve hour periods is very difficult, and the night does not really allow 'feasting', because the alimentary system adjusts to a totally new timetable only with difficulty. The point is that these two fasts have happened side by side for fourteen centuries, over a large area of the world, and the failure to understand and to feel mutual respect continues.

Cultural differences can of course be acquired very easily, and may amount to little more than a habit of mind. In Britain people sometimes adopt an attitude to the police which is appropriate to quite a different society; they play at activist 'resistance', knowing that they incur no serious danger, and seek to provoke a police force which they also expect will continue to help and protect them (often in situations needing real courage); they would hate to do without it, or to do with the kind of police they are pretending to have. They act a part borrowed from another sub-culture, and this may or may not produce an actual cultural change in due course. When a change occurs, often not the thing, but the attitude to it, changes, as, to take a new example, to cosmetics. Puritanical and irrational condemnation in the earlier part of this century gave way to an equally irrational absurdity of indulgence, under the pressure of the manufacturers and their advertisers. The cultural stimulus has turned one and the same action from non-conforming to conforming; and a different culture, which has not passed through the same experience, may judge ours, which has changed, by the standards we have left behind. The quickest and most often recurring cultural reversal is that of the motorist who, having hated pedestrians, steps out of his car and begins to hate motorists. This is one way in which most of us switch our sentiments and even patterns of behaviour. Not only a new experience, but the acceptance of a doctrine or orthodoxy, may lead to a misjudgement of what someone in the other orthodoxy thinks or does or says. It is not only that by accepting a doctrine we have joined a different group or culture, but also that our understanding of words changes. This applies not only to Christianity and Marxism, but also to liberalism, or 'permissiveness' or progressivism; and not only to general doctrines, but to the special languages (or, if we want a pejorative sense, 'jargons') of particular disciplines and techniques, and even the fashionable use of words ultimately deriving from special disciplines, such as (currently) 'restructuring'. It is possible to judge the meaning of what someone says only if we know his presuppositions, which change with the environment; the environment may change while the man is part of it, or he may move from one environment to another. The objects with which we are concerned themselves change with the environment. At one time it used to be said that 'primitive' peoples, in their ignorance, would part with objects of real value in exchange for cheap beads or other trinkets mass-produced in Birmingham. Whether said with approval of the European trader's smartness, or with disapproval of his dishonesty, this was always said patronisingly; yet by the laws of supply and demand which these same critics presupposed, the criterion 'cheap' was meaningless. We are thinking of a time when what was cheap and common in Birmingham could only be carried with great expense and trouble to central Africa or remoter Polynesia, and so rightly became expensive. Nowadays the tourists from Birmingham pay fancy prices for articles of local manufacture which would be locally worthless. Behind, and determining, the economic laws of the market lie the variable and local judgements of different cultures.

Unfamiliarity creates misunderstanding, and misunderstanding, suspicion; and hatred and suspicion grow rapidly from small beginnings. We generally understand the actions of other people, so long as we are familiar with the sort of people they are, and confident of their background and pattern of behaviour. The same action seems ambiguous when we distrust the doer of it, and distrust, perhaps, only because we are unfamiliar. We judge unkindly in a stranger and the representative of an alien culture behaviour that in a friend and a member of our own world we can explain and immediately excuse. Drunkenness and other forms of debauchery are often thought to characterise an alien culture, just because we notice every recurrence of a fault among others that we dismiss as untypical of our friends. It is this that creates the double standard of judgement, harsh for 'them' and understanding for 'us'. This relationship subsists between all separate groups; not only between those that are distant from each other and enemies, but, as we have seen, between those that live side by side; and not only between closed communities, more or less hostile, living side by side, but also between allies, come together for a common purpose. This has been true since long before the Crusaders, for example, came into conflict with the Christians of Eastern Europe whom it was their original motive to help; and much more recent examples will be familiar to many people living.

COLOUR PREJUDICE

'Colour' is not my subject, but it is worth saying that, as I define cultural barriers, colour prejudice is just one kind of cultural prejudice that has accidentally got latched on to the pigmentation of the skin. Prejudice in this country against West Indians or Pakistanis is called colour prejudice, because the unwilling host culture denominates alien groups it dislikes by their most obvious and recognisable characteristic. In America, Griffin's description of his experience when he artificially coloured his skin and travelled as a member of the black minority in the white South shows how much of the sensitivity alike of the victims and of the perpetrators of hatred is centred on the pigmentation; but even so it reveals all the characteristics of cultural hatred, some of which I have already described (especially the associations of dirt and sexuality).[2] If we compare the feelings of English 'racialists' towards Irishmen, especially forty or fifty years ago, and towards West Indians today, there is little difference in the degree of feeling, and none in its quality. The cultural dislike is made up of the usual elements: pure xenophobia, that is, 'these people are different, they are not our people, so fear and and hate them'; and applied xenophobia, the dislike of the actual customs of the newcomers. For example, they may have emigrated because they were poor, and they may be forced to live in overcrowded conditions, and the consequences of poverty and overcrowding are then attributed to the culture (or 'race'); nearly always also there will be real cultural differences, such as different degrees of attachment to music and dancing, which may result in one side seeming noisy, and the other unfriendly because less addicted to parties. All groups (including the Irish) are often accused of being too prolific.

The intellectual adventures of Malcolm X, surely a great and good man to have overcome his disadvantages of birth and upbringing, illustrate well that the colour is only a sign of the culture. His interest in the history of 'black civilisation'— the Pharaohs, for example— was less a boast about colour than a violent rejection of the pretence that black people's culture is inferior; his was a very sophisticated improvement on Elijah Muhammad's crude myth. He puts it very fairly: 'In that day the black man in Egypt was wearing silk, sharp as a tack, brothers. And those people up in Europe didn't know what cloth was.'[3] The impact on Malcolm X of making the hajj seems to have been decisive, and to have clarified this point in particular. 'The color-blindness of the Muslim world's religious society and the color-blindness of the Muslim world's human society: these two influences had each day been making a greater impact, and an increasing persuasion against my former way of thinking.' In Mecca there were 'no segregationists— no liberals'; indifference to colour was spontaneous, and for Malcolm X this was evidently a shattering experience: 'I shared true, brotherly love with many white-complexioned Muslims who never gave a thought to the race, or to the complexion, of another Muslim'. He was able to agree with a white American ambassador to an African state that they were both immediately colour-conscious in America, but not in Africa.[4] The same point is illustrated by the situation of the Hindu, at once a victim and a perpetrator of colour prejudice— 'heir to the oldest conscious tradition of superior colour'— because the same society can despise at the same time as it is despised.[5]

Colour prejudice is only a symptom or 'irrationalisation' of a group conflict, that is, a conflict of cultures; but it is natural that the point of actual colour should be dominant in the minds of its victims. It is intolerable to carry with you the mark of belonging to a separate culture, wherever you go, and without the possibility of hiding it; worse still that a culture should be defined by an external sign of fortuitious biological origin. A physical difference may easily come to be seen as a deformity. A white man, in Africa, even though living in privileged conditions, may begin to see his own skin as unnatural; it must be very much worse, not only to feel cut off, but also to be despised, because of this accident of physiology. It is not only that this must inevitably be resented, but that any deviation from a normal human relationship, including kindly discrimination, must be. The attitude of the Black Muslims, that they must force respect by self-help, and even of Black Power, that they must force respect by violence, is very understandable. Those who are nice to someone because he is black do not begin to understand the problem; it is characteristic of inter-cultural relations that respect is never given until it is forced. A volume called *Disappointed Guests* consists of a series of essays elicited from Afro-Asian students in Britain, and they tend to be concerned very largely with colour, no doubt because this absurd kind of discrimination was forced on their attention during their stay. In one of the most interesting of the essays, Francis M. Deng writes: 'Most of these exaggeratedly friendly people, whether they are aware of it or not, believe that the African is a destitute who will rejoice to see a white man friendly to him, however impolite the method of contact. Their approaches are therefore often very impudent despite their good intentions.'[6] An African dislikes being treated as different because he is black, whether or not it is kindly in intention; kindliness is rejected, because patronage is only another face of contempt.

All the same, 'black' is only a sign of something else, or it would have no more meaning than any other physical accident, black hair or blue eyes, a scar or a squint or baldness; it is the cultural separation that makes it different. The same writer illustrates the cultural significance of the contempt of one society for another (which he, like me, identifies as the basis of racialism) from his own memories, as a child, of the Southern Sudan. 'I saw the reactions of one tribe to another, of one ethnic group to others, and of course, the attitude of foreign races towards our own. . . . Some tribes looked down on others and would not inter-marry. . . . Where races differ, each race takes itself as the standard with all the others as abnormal cases. . . . Note that the names of most Nilotic tribes in their traditional languages, literally translated, mean "the people", with the rest generally referred to as "the others".'[7] This last point is true in many cultures, for example in Welsh; all these observations are true and acutely observed. All the attitudes of one 'race' to another, one culture to another, one society, or one nation to another, are the same. As between the Dinka and the Shilluk, between the black and the white American, between English and French, between West Indian, Pakistani and native of Wolverhampton, the differences are the same, and it is the same differences that unite them all, in the least attractive side of their common humanity. Xenophobia, which divides people in fact, unites them notionally, because it is the common weakness of the human race.

Another essay in the same collection illustrates the cultural nature of the conflict, although the author gives the facts a different interpretation. He argues about mixed marriages on the assumption that this is a question of 'colour', because it is known that this very often is the case. But there are good reasons to approach any mixed marriage with care, not one of different 'colours' more than one of different nationalities or religions, or even perhaps of classes; all of them may be difficult, because the differences of background will require one partner or the other to sacrifice his or her own familiar culture. This leads to 'cultural shock', which I discuss in more detail in chapter 3. African parents may be clearer that their objections to their daughter's marrying an Englishman, or even their son's marrying an Englishwoman are cultural, than the English parents in the same situation; but although the ideas of the latter may be confused by imaginary problems of 'race' and 'colour', the cultural difficulties remain. Successful mixed marriages of any kind are nearly always of remarkable personalities capable of surmounting the problems of crossing the cultural barrier. The same essay very rightly objects to the indiscriminate character of 'discrimination'; the rich man is despised like the poor. This is not my experience; I have found only too many people willing to accept a person of social distinction. Colour prejudice disappears for the Maharajah. Then the same writer says that the 'advantages' in colour discrimination are dishonest advantages, for example, to avoid a parking ticket by pretending not to understand English well.[8] This is plainly exploiting the cultural situation. I am afraid that I used to take comparable advantage of being foreign, when I was young, in countries of Europe, and I see Europeans taking the same 'dishonest advantage' of their poor English (or their ability to persuade a policeman that their English is poor) in England constantly. I will not continue to labour these points, which all to my mind illustrate the same thing: colour prejudice is only a specialised form of cultural prejudice. The basic problem is the conflict and the mutual contempt of any two distinct societies set apart by their different ways — 'very different' or 'slightly different' may not be important.

CULTURAL AREAS

We have said that we can use 'culture' like 'civilisation', but 'culture' is more nearly neutral; 'civilisation' has an implication of achievement in civic skills. We do not imply greater or lesser development, either economic or intellectual (and those two might be in inverse proportion), when we speak of a culture. In this way 'culture' in general is the expression of any community, and 'a culture' can be used almost synonymously with 'a community'. Cultures, therefore, like communities, can be infinitely divided, sub-divided, or cross-divided. Within national cultures there are class cultures, lesser geographical cultures, and minor communal cultures. A middle-class Methodist in London is divided in three points from a working-class Roman Catholic in Glasgow, from a middle-class Roman Catholic in London by only one. We cannot attempt a taxonomy of cultures, and I doubt if such a thing would be feasible in any circumstances, because there are so many possible cross-cultures and interconnections and conceivable combinations; and everything is changing all the time. Different generations are different cultures, and there may be a greater difference in one period of a few years than in another period of many years.

A main cultural area has sometimes been called an *ecumene*. This, from meaning the inhabitable world, in Greek, came for the Byzantines to mean their own Byzantine inhabited world, and so is used for any more or less well-defined 'world', such as ancient China or ancient India. It can be extended to mean one of the heirs of the old ecumenes, Europe/North America, or the Arab world or the Islamic world, or India, or China, but these are no longer clear and definable entities; on the contrary, they have all extended beyond any frontiers there may once have been, and now they all overlap. If we use the word ecumene, we must do so realising that it refers to large cultural areas with marked characteristics, but many cross-divisions and connections with other cultures. National cultures are themselves sub-cultures, and even over-cultures, without taking cross divisions of class and religion into account. Britain is a sub-culture of the Western world, and of European culture and of English-speaking culture. Welsh culture in English is a sub-English sub-culture, and in Welsh, sub-European. Even this sort of division has its exceptions: African literature in English or in French belongs to European literature, as well as to the African cultures.

The terminology of the 'third world' to which we have been driven is absurd, but inescapable. There is no third world. There is only one world. All sorts of problems are common to the whole world, first, second, and third; for example, the generation gap and student 'revolt'; the crisis of morale; trade union actions and attitudes, and class reactions; technological change and its effects; rural and urban attitudes; clerical and administrative attitudes; forms of corruption; doubtless there are many more, but these are enough to exemplify what I mean. They all have a slightly different appearance in different cultures, and cultures in similar situations show more closely similar reactions, the more closely similar their situations; but all cultural differences occur within a very wide common area which is human. There is an infinite range of differences. There is either one world, or there are as many worlds as cultures; there are not by any count three worlds.

Yet the division is inescapable and the phrase 'the third world' is convenient. It means something as long as it means only the countries that receive aid—bilateral or multilateral economic aid. This is a definable distinction, but not more than merely convenient. In fact the phrases 'developing' and 'developed', 'undeveloped', and 'under-developed', and so on, are also mere conveniences. We do not mean to claim that the developed countries are not developing, or that developing countries are not underdeveloped; but 'there is a real danger in dividing the world between developing countries and developed countries'.[9] To some extent the constantly shifting terminology has been the product of a desire not to cause offence; but in fact it has resulted in the idea that there really is a hard and fast division across the world. The world is less like hills and valleys than like a long range of ever-shifting sand-dunes; there is no absolute division between kinds of countries. They are ranged in an infinite variety of poverty and development; and, as we shall see later, intellectual and educational development is not correlated with economic development directly, although of course there is some relation. We do not use the word 'poor' as a description, lest it give offence; the idea that there is disgrace in poverty is morally primitive, but one that fits into modern economic thought. All these divisions, therefore, are conveniences that represent no exact divisions, but merely relative and approximate groupings that may shift from time to time and according to the aspect under consideration.

Of all the factors that I mentioned as common to the whole world, only technological advance can be positively attributed in its origin to one particular cultural area. The culture that we call the Western is itself hard to delimit. 'Western' is inexact; its cultural origin is in Western Europe, but its current axis of strength is in North America and in the USSR. Wealth lies in the Northern countries of the world, or at any rate poverty tends to lie between the tropics, and the nearer the tropics the poorer. The only point in saying this is to remind ourselves of the difficulty there is in defining this culture geographically. Even the proposal to substitute North for West is inexact. Nor does it seem possible to define it by the technology which it has created and which makes it dominant, because the technology itself is 'culture transferable'; the use we make of it is cultural, but we cannot define the culture by what we are trying to find out about it. It is difficult also to define this culture by its Christian origins. The view that it shaped its own Christianity, though exaggerated, is true enough if carefully defined; and the shape it has given to its present post-Christian condition is also its own creation; it bears some relation to the peculiar emphases it gave to the Christian religion, and some relation to the essential character of that religion itself. Certainly we cannot define the culture by an origin that is not the sole determinant of the contemporary phenomenon we are defining. What are sometimes called 'Western values' are also useless for this purpose; democracy and liberalism may be characteristic of the culture at the present moment, but they are essentially momentary characteristics. Democracy was a pejorative in my great-grandfather's day; and it means quite different things in different parts even of our non-tropical North. Western values are always changing.

The crucial question is whether the 'West' is only the state of the whole world of the future. Will everything go the same way, and will that way be the way that things have gone in the more highly developed areas? If so, we need not talk about West, or North, or any geographical area but just of 'modern'. This does quite often happen. Whether it is right or not is one of the main themes of this book; and in the meantime the 'Western world' will have to stay undefined. We all know pretty well what we mean by it.

CULTURES AND RELIGIONS

At no point do I talk about religion, although I talk very often about the cultural effects of religion, the actions that religion stimulates and the use made of religion in different cultures. I am sure that the difference between a religion and the culture that is attached to it is quite clear. The teachings of the Apostolic age, of Anglo-Saxon Christianity, of the mediaeval popes and of the present World Council of Churches really are astonishingly similar, and it is only their similarity that makes it possible for us to talk about their differences. On the other hand, the practices, the emphases and general approach of all these are as different as their doctrines are similar. If we compare the Latin church with the Greek Orthodox Church, the distinction is even clearer: the differences in point of doctrine are insignificant, the differences in customs and attitudes are almost total. The same distinction can be applied to Islam. There are no differences in belief between Sunnis in Kano, Beirut, and Lahore, but the differences in attitudes and in customs in their respective societies are considerable. The differences in actual belief between Ja'fari Shi'a and Sunnis is much less than the cultural conflict between them. There are considerable doctrinal differences between Ahmadiya and other Muslims, but Pakistani Ahmadis and Sunnis belong obviously to the same culture. There is a big influence of religion on culture and of culture on religion, but the two are quite separate, and I am making no comment anywhere upon the actual religions whose cultures enter into the argument of this book.

CROSS-CULTURAL INFLUENCES

We have seen that it is difficult for anyone to take a detached view of his own culture, because he can only use culture-bound ideas to judge it. This difficulty of recognising one's own cultural characteristics is nothing to the difficulty in recognising due proportion in cultural differences, after they have been identified. Uncorrected perspective is general; the little difference seen from close to looks larger than the big difference seen from far off. This is true on all scales. Two neighbouring

villages may be rivals and not altogether friendly; a man from another
region may see no difference worth noting, but the inhabitants of the
villages may consider the tiny differences created by minute accidents
of geography and history in their customs to be crucially important. It
is normal, or was so until very recently, even where neighbouring
villages were on the best of terms, to talk about marrying into the other
village as marrying a foreigner. So too the differences which may be a
constant irritation to adjacent nations seem negligible to an observer
from another ecumene. The various nations inhabiting the British Isles
tend, however good-humouredly, to take a more serious estimate of
their differences than outsiders do. We have also seen what difficulty
there is in defining the 'Western' culture, although we can all recognise
it when we see it. The visitor from outside that culture can also recognise it when he sees it, but he will probably see it quite differently from
the way we see it, and visitors from different areas may see it differently
from each other.

The difficulty of seeing differences in due proportion complicates the
problems of intercultural influences. The foreigner who rates the differences between Scots, Welsh, and English low in his scheme of importance may be quite right from the point of view of his own country,
where perhaps these three have never appeared in any separate or distinct situation, or where they have in fact constantly appeared in the
same situation (for example, as administrators working together, as
commercials trading together, and, above all, taking their relaxation
together). As making an estimate from within the United Kingdom, he
is wrong, because the differences are there, and on the local scale they
do matter. Similarly the Scot or Welshman makes a mistake if he
fancies that his own differences with Englishmen bring him closer to
the cultures formerly imperially ruled by undifferentiated Britons. In
fact his experience of feeling exploited by the English (whether true or
imaginary is irrelevant) does give him a common experience with the
African or Asian whose fathers his father ruled. His mental experience
should enable him to understand the experience of his African and
Asian friends, but it will not in fact bring the cultures any closer together. Americans twenty years ago used to believe they could find a
common bond with Afro-Asians in terms of their own inheritance of
what they called anti-colonial sentiment. At the present moment an
Englishman can try to find a common bond in the same way, on the
ground that he is another victim of American expansionism. In a few
years' time this too may be quite out of date. Both attitudes seem unreal
across the barrier which separates the 'West' from the rest of the world.
There may in both cases have been, indeed, a situation common to the
man from the West and the man from outside it, and a situation strong

enough to create a genuine bond of understanding or sympathy. That is a true cultural link; but it is far, far less than any one of the countless links between the different people who make up the total 'Western' culture.

We are primarily concerned with individuals. An individual can in certain circumstances, for example, when he is isolated, learn to live in a new culture. This creates a link between cultures, such as I shall discuss in a moment, but unless the number concerned is beyond measure — and the problem ceases to be one of individuals — the link each makes between cultures is small and its influence slight. It is in other ways that cultures have been influenced on a large scale, and in the past by far the commonest means was conquest. However, there is a possibility that technological advance may cause 'Western' culture to sweep over the whole world, without military conquest. Is what we call Americanisation the inevitable development of all cultures under the same technological influence? It is obvious that there are some, perhaps many, local influences that make America what it is; obvious also that some 'American' characteristics are the effects of technological developments. The same can be said of the USSR; and we cannot even assume that what is common to these two is the product of the technology, because there may be other factors common to both. Speculation on such a scale, if possible at all, is at any rate not my business; but the extent to which the technology creates the culture, and the extent to which the technique may carry cross-cultural infection with it, is one of my themes.

ACADEMIC OR EDUCATIONAL EXCHANGE

I could not talk about 'cultural exchange', as meaning exchange within an educational system, without reverting to the discarded sense of 'cultural'. In the sense we are using the word, all exchange is cultural, and the importation of new ways by immigrants is as important as any other movement of ideas or customs. It is not my subject. I am concerned with foreigners who come to take some part in academic life in Britain, and with Britons who take a part in academic life overseas. This does mean that we must discuss the relations between whole cultures, because these go to make up the state of mind of the individuals who travel abroad and live in cultures alien to their own. Ideas are transmitted between individuals, and it is the transmission of ideas, and the barriers that shut them out, that I am going to write about. In this connection the question of perspective is important. To the overseas student in Britain (or America or any European country) ideas which to his teachers appear to have universal validity, and 'facts' which they believe unquestionable, may seem simply the product of the 'Western' culture, an artificial creation and culture bound; and the teaching of these ideas or 'facts' will seem to him to be cultural imperialism.

Similarly the ideas and 'facts' taught by a Briton overseas may be rejected by the people of the country where he is teaching, for the same reasons. These are examples of a failure of communication for cultural reasons.

Of course, there must be some acculturation in the case of any student from overseas; not necessarily in the case of a Briton teaching abroad. A Western university education is not difficult for an overseas student to achieve to the same level as the Western native, although he is 'playing away', and is at a cultural disadvantage. There are no statistics to enable us to isolate the additional difficulty introduced by the possession of a different cultural background, though it is obvious that there must be some; and problems of adaptation are the subject of my fourth chapter. The overseas student normally succeeds in spite of this, but, succeed or fail, he has acquired an alien culture to a substantial degree; not only the literary side, but a knowledge and experience of the total culture. He may perhaps want to suspend or suppress this knowledge in part, or visibly, if he wants or needs to at home, but in fact he will never be free of the understanding he has acquired. Communication between the two cultures concerned is open in his person.

This, of course, is only true if he has not fallen a victim to cultural imperialism; that is, to be of any use to either culture, his new knowledge of the host culture must be added to, and not substituted for, his own culture. If the latter is weakened, he has lost more than he has gained; and his hosts may have acquired a new citizen they do not need, at the cost of a link with another culture which they might have had, and do want. Cross-cultural contact is harmful unless it conduces to communication, and this can only happen if the visitor retains full sympathy for his home culture. There is another source of weakness; exchange is least valuable when it is unequal. This is true at all levels, for example, politically; obligation of any kind, moral or legal, is always resented; and an appearance of superiority is also always resented. We are only concerned with the educational level, but here the same thing is true. The best communication will always be achieved on a basis of perfect reciprocity. In education, for the moment this is often not possible, though the gain to the donor—in appearance, sole donor in the partnership of giving and receiving—already exists, without always being recognised. Unfortunately, it is sometimes the main recipient who realises least clearly that he too is donor. However unequal exchanges may be at present, the objective is equality, and because exchange is unequal, the objective must never be allowed to drop out of mind. No single effort in educational interchange ought to be undertaken, unless it is geared to this end, which in practice is far too often forgotten. Whatever we do, we should plan that it lead to reciprocity;

and if we do that, it is all that is needed, and as much as we can do. In the meantime, while equal exchange, which is the same as true exchange, is often not feasible, we are forced to think and speak instead in terms of two-way traffic. Two-way traffic is the nearest we come to exchange.

It is to nobody's advantage to impose his culture on the stranger; it is very much to his advantage to allow the stranger to understand that culture. The stranger may, indeed, condemn something of what he sees, and approve of other things which seem to be wise in the context of the host culture, but unsuitable for export; finally, he may also see something that he can effectively adapt for use at home. Most of such things will be techniques, techniques of all kinds, which by definition, are 'culture transferable'. There may be a few predominantly cultural elements which are transferable. This is not so important. The value of borrowing, even if it is confined to techniques, extends beyond the acquisition of those techniques, when it creates the necessary conditions for communication — knowledge, sympathy — and this is what all 'cultural' relations are about. It is also what this book is about.

Is it possible for a country to modernise without borrowing the culture of the most modernised (or 'advanced') countries? The next chapter argues that at least there exists a strong resistance to the cultures which are economically the most highly developed; it dates from the early days of the Western technological overspill, it is normally expressed by variants of the doctrine of anti-colonialism, and this constitutes a more or less effective defensive mechanism. How does academic interchange happen at all in these conditions of cultural conflict? The two subsequent chapters describe summarily, first, the cultural situation of the academic traffic which passes in and out of the developed areas of the world, and, secondly, the cultural element in individual reactions to it. In the fifth chapter I speculate about the possibilities of successful resistance to domination by a single culture, and argue that at any rate we cannot take it as proven that modernisation is incompatible with separate cultural identities. All this part of the book has set the problem: what are the conditions of communication between cultures, and what barriers stand in its way? The second part of the book explores the possibilities of an answer from historical experience. Does the historical evidence allow us to evaluate cultures, and so to justify the idea that our own, or any, particular culture is likely, as the fittest, to prevail? If so, all other cultures would have to assimilate to it. Can we learn about the other cultures of the present day from what we know and feel about our own past? The transmission of ideas between cultures has a long history. In the past, have cultures succeeded, when they borrowed, in picking and choosing what to take and what reject? Has there ever been successful cultural resistance, and, if so, has it been combined with productive borrowing? It is in the light of these reflections that I approach the third part of the book, and try to apply shortly the historical considerations of the second part to the present-day problems of the first.

Suspicion of the West

THE GREAT ISSUE of the modern world, as seen from outside Europe and America, has been imperialism. The most powerful idea in the mind of the overseas academic, teacher or student, at home in his own country or abroad in ours, has been his anti-imperialism. Anti-imperialism means suspicion of the motives and intentions of the West, and this suspicion is the background of all cultural interchange today. Beyond it lies another conflict. The anti-imperialist suspects the West of trying to prevent his enjoying the benefits of material progress, but sometimes he is suspicious of concomitants of progress because they are concomitants of Western culture. His dilemma is, and has been since the beginning of the nineteenth century, to discover how to modernise without Westernising; to equal or surpass the West in its own technological field, without accepting its culture. How much of present Western culture is tied irretrievably to its techniques I shall discuss in another chapter; now I want to look at the resistance which has been and is still being put up to Western influence, and I shall begin with a quick glance at the classic theory of anti-imperialism. Some supporters of this theory have begun to see it as an over-simplification, but it is not important only for understanding the recent past. It exerts as much influence as ever, either in classic form, or in revision.

If we count the USSR and its Marxist orthodoxy in with our own culture, as we must, we can say that anti-imperialism is a great part of contemporary Western culture, too. For the Marxist, imperialism is part of capitalist expansion. Others have seen no real difference between Russian and American expansionism (or old-style European colonialism). Russian socialism has seemed too European to some Arabs and Africans, and they have wanted to create an 'Arab socialism' or an 'African socialism', the chief distinguishing characteristic of both being their greater humanity. After the last war, the Americans saw themselves as anti-imperialists, because of their feelings about George III, but they have since learned to put up with being identified as the spring of colonialist aggression. In both Europe and America many sincerely fight both imperialism and racialism, and everywhere these two are seen as one. Black Power talks American, and its culture seems to be American; it was this that Malcolm X came to oppose, when he wanted 'the black people of the Western Hemisphere' to 'restore our African cultural roots and heritage; we must re-establish contacts with our

African brothers'.[1] It is natural that those who, in Africa and Asia, resent the old colonial intrusion and fear the neo-colonial threat, should assimilate all forms of racialist oppression. Really what they most dislike is the continuing dominance of 'Western' culture.

Using the terms 'colonialism' and 'imperialism' as interchangeable (this is a pity, because they ought to refer to foreign rule respectively with or without foreign settlement, but it is now the usage), we shall find a definition rather in Marxism than in Marx. Marx's articles in the *New York Daily Tribune*, collected with other material of his and of Engels by the Foreign Languages Publishing House in Moscow, show flashes of insight, and are often amusing, occasionally witty ('there is to be another civilisation war against the Celestials' he says of China) but are hardly more socialist than radical. Engels lets slip a conviction of European superiority, when he writes, 'The countries inhabited by a native population, which are simply subjugated . . . must be taken over for the time being by the proletariat [that is, European proletariat] and led as rapidly as possible towards independence', an attitude not very different from that of the later imperialists, at least in terms of the dominating culture. 'In time', says the Director of Studies of the Overseas Development Institute, 'it will be possible to see British imperialism — certainly during the first half of this century — in a more balanced way'. Perhaps this is too modest a claim; already scholars from the former empire give credit even to earlier imperialism, and Marx himself said, 'whatever may have been the crimes of England, she was the unconscious tool of history in bringing about . . . a fundamental revolution in the social state of Asia'.[2] It is useful to clarify in our own minds what we think about the history of imperialism, and about the different analyses which its critics and defenders put forward; but the actual problem with which we are concerned now is anti-imperialist sentiment and doctrine. This belongs to a totally different order of reality; it is a thing that exists in its own right: anti-imperialism is a political atmosphere, not a critical study of an historical process. It is the political atmosphere which across so much of the world everyone breathes; people grow up to take it for granted, just as we in the West are brought up to breathe the idea that democracy is the right and normal framework of our lives.

The idea that gives inspiration and a genuine sense of moral indignation to millions of people all over the world, and to increasing numbers as more become educated to the point of political consciousness, is that the 'colonial' countries exploit the rest. The old-fashioned nationalist of conservative tendency, in the Arab world the Muslim Brothers, and the New Left, all think that the USSR is as 'colonialist' as Britain, Germany, and America (France, the most colonial of all in the old sense, has successfully diverted attention from itself). Nevertheless, the language as well as the theory of anti-colonialism owes very much to the constant support and reiterated utterance which the publicity machine of the USSR has given it.

Effectively the theory is not so much Marx's as Lenin's, and Lenin in fact took it over from the English radical, J. A. Hobson. As Hobson saw it at the end of the nineteenth century, the investor in the home market did not expect the public to protect his capital from loss; and the investor in consols did not expect a right of political interference with foreign policy; but the private investor in overseas enterprises did expect interference with foreign governments such as 'will lead to annexation of territory as the only security for the lives and property of our subjects'. At the time that he was writing it doubtless seemed that this very process would never end. He foretold that it would have a disastrous effect also at home, 'the gigantic peril of a Western parasitism, a group of advanced industrial nations, whose upper classes drew vast tribute from Asia and Africa, with which they supported great tame masses of retainers, no longer engaged in the staple industries of agriculture and manufacture, but kept in the performance of personal or minor industrial services under the control of a new financial aristocracy'. If, for example, it were to prove feasible to subject China, he said, we would be 'draining the greatest potential reservoir of profit the world has ever known, in order to consume it in Europe'. The key idea here, 'Western parasitism', 'draining the reservoir of profit' in the outside world, 'in order to consume it in Europe',[3] is the idea that has survived and become an article of faith with a great part of the world. The effect on European society, though not finally disproved, is clearly not proved either; and economists in the Free or capitalist West would mostly deny that this was happening; perhaps economists in the socialist 'West' might find it difficult to prove that it is happening. However, this is not really the point at all; if it is a myth, in the sense of untrue, it is also a myth in the sense of an article of faith, and important because of those vast areas of the world where it is believed.

It was Lenin, of course, who made these theories into a clear-cut revolutionary issue: 'What is the most important, the fundamental idea of our theses? The distinction between oppressed and oppressor nations'. The characteristic feature of imperialism as he saw it was the division of the world into a large number of oppressed nations, and an insignificant number of oppressors, commanding 'colossal wealth and powerful armed forces'. This no doubt is a gross over-simplification, but it has its appeal for that very reason; and one point that Lenin made is a good one. 'The age-old oppression of colonial and weak nationalities by the imperialist powers has not only filled the working masses of the oppressed countries with animosity towards the oppressing nations, but also with distrust of them in general, even of the proletariat of these nations.'[4] Allowing for the fact that in such a context as this the word 'masses' should always be qualified as 'such of the masses as are politically conscious', there is truth in this. Certainly the 'oppressed masses' who were victims of colonialism have as good reason to be suspicious of the oppressor proletariat as they have of the oppressor ruling classes. The important dividing line comes between whole cultures. Lenin saw that this difference was greater than class differences, and the orthodox Leninist today must try to assimilate the cultural conflict to the class struggle.

The great champion of the theory of neo-colonialism was Kwame Nkrumah, who believed it to be the final and most dangerous stage of imperialism; he said that 'the State which is subject to it is, in theory, independent and has all the outward trappings of international sovereignty. In reality its economic system and thus its political policy is directed from outside.' Nkrumah saw this neo-colonialism as much worse than direct colonialism; and it is true that it shares some of the qualities of indirect rule. Neo-colonialism means for the neo-colonisers 'power without responsibility' and for the neo-colonised 'exploitation without redress'. His argument was simple and clear, and it is convenient to quote it because it is a fair expression of the anti-imperialist sentiment of so much of the less affluent part of the world. A good deal of suspicion is sometimes attached to the support of neo-colonialism by cultural agencies (this is to use 'cultural' in the old-fashioned and narrower sense). Is 'cultural imperialism' a useful concept? If we can argue that educational aid is more to the advantage of the donor than of the recipient, the answer will be yes; but, though this can happen, it does not happen much, and it is not a considerable problem. If it is only said that it is being used to camouflage neo-colonialism, it is not said that it is a form of aggression in itself. The value to us of remembering, and thinking about, the anti-imperialist theory is to measure the degree of hostility that actually exists. Imperialism is a part of reality so long as people think it is; and it is pointless for anyone to question it whose cultural origin identifies him as a possibly interested party. We can just say that it is possible for educational influences to be exploited politically — Western diplomats do exist who see opportunities for patronge in educational aid; and alternatively it is possible for them to be disinterested, in the sense that good will and understanding are in the interests of all. There is an important difference between the Nkrumah theory and the Lenin-Hobson theory; the former allowed that there are 'instances of support for liberation and anti-colonialism inside the imperialist world itself',[5] and he did not, I think, just mean members of revolutionary parties.

The key is the independence of a culture. The characteristic attitude of the classic age of imperialism was secondarily, no doubt, that of master to subject, but it was primarily that of the more developed to the less. We can see the situation then, and we can see the situation now, only in terms of exploitation; we can see the situation then, and the situation now, in terms of a helping hand to the less fortunate. The two concepts meet in the idea of paternalism. The affluent know what is best for the 'underprivileged' and decide, whenever possible, what is to be done to improve their lot. The affluent resent that the poor should insist on their rights, or prefer self-dependence to efficiency. This last, more than anything, the donors do not understand. The affluent are often more competent; their competence has made them affluent, and their affluence has made them more competent still. They can understand that the poor should dislike being exploited; but why do they dislike being helped— for their own good, and by someone more competent? On their side, the under-privileged would rather have the second-best in order to have what is their own. In any case, they are unlikely to believe that their own is second-best; any inferiority can be explained as the result of exploitation. That is one reason why the two sides disagree about how much exploitation there has been. Cultural independence is obviously connected with the recent discovery by various oppressed groups that you gain respect only if you are strong enough to take what you want, and that it is an error to accept it as a gift. The group 'developed' and the group 'the privileged' are conterminous; and those who are oppressed, by which we mean those who have few privileges or none, are trying to even privilege out; they are trying to wipe out a donor class, and do not want to be beholden to the donors for doing so. Paternalism, privilege, the attitudes of the ruling class to the working class, of the colonialist to the colonised 'native', of men to women, of an older to a younger generation, are all similar within each pair, and, within each pair, the dominated partner is trying to follow Samuel Smiles' principle of self-help, once the mark of the capitalist and colonialist. Of all the intercultural contempts, the most obdurate is the colonial; the other sub-cultures have been too willing to forego their own struggle in order to take part in acts of cultural aggression, as, for example, when English ladies, or the English working class despise Arabs, Asians, Africans, Frenchmen, Italians, and so forth. The famous occasion when the English dockers supported Powellist racialism is a case in point; and as the class structure is gradually modified, the dislikes of the dominant group or ruling class are accepted by all. In intercultural attitudes there is consequently no change. It follows that we ought to respect anti-imperialism. Whether its arguments are valid or not, it truly reflects the natural, and even heroic, resistance of dominated cultures. We must not be reluctant to accept that an opinion can be important, when the only reason we can see for its importance is that people hold it, and not that it is true. We must understand that others find our preconceptions as unacceptable as we find theirs.

A great deal of the tension, and of the positive disagreement, between the poorer part of the world and the richer part, between the dominated and the dominant, between the 'developing' world and the 'West', is about just this transmission of an aggressive Western culture. We are not talking here about the influences which we shall see may be brought to bear on the overseas student while he is away from home. It is not a question of how the individual can resist pressures. We are talking about the total impact of an outside culture. This is much more than an affair of intellectuals. Fanon, committed to a Marxist definition of cultural imperialism, says of Algeria that 'the intellectual throws himself into the frantic acquisition of the culture of the occupying power'; this contrasts with the behaviour of the mass of the people who 'maintain intact traditions which are completely different from those of the colonial situation'. Then the popular culture dies off: 'becomes a set of automatic habits, some traditions of dress and a few broken-down institutions' until re-inspired by revolutionary fervour.[6] Fanon wrote in a direct revolutionary situation. He had no experience of neo-colonialism, and what he writes sounds a little old-fashioned; it was simplified by Marxist theory, with its emphasis on the period of struggle.

Soper, in the paper that I have already quoted, talks about the dilemma of the left-wing intellectual in England, who discovers that overseas aid can be neo-colonialist, for example that it 'is making rigid, social structures that should be changed'. This, of course, is part of the great anti-colonialist thesis; cultural interference freezes, rather than promotes, change which ought to be organic, spontaneous, indigenous. Soper continues: 'the relationship seems to result in western cultural standards being injected into overseas societies, standards which many intellectuals are ashamed of'. It is not clear to me just what is here referred to, or why the intellectuals should object, if they do, to the injection of their ideas into other cultures; but the other cultures may and do object. It is precisely this that is so often a problem.

Neo-colonialism, as defined by Nkrumah, is an attempt to introduce a consumer orientation into a society innocent of many of the desires which advertisers have created in Europe. That is not the motive, but it has some part in the profit-making which is. It will certainly tend to overbear the local culture. 'The logic of the international corporation is based on the need to find huge markets. . . . It will tend to make decisions based on the economic benefit to the corporation as a whole'. That is not Nkrumah; it is the Chairman Designate of the British

Institute of Management in November 1969,[7] but his description, except that it is naturally devoid of emotive colouring, would be perfectly satisfactory to the anti-imperialist. His advice is that 'the international company must take account of the local environment', which of course does not mean that its local culture will be left untouched. In fact, a taste for some luxuries, for example, for a transistor radio, is readily acquired even in the most ideally neolithic community. The people of Western Ireland, it used to be said, would always export one member of the family in a generation to America, in order to keep them supplied in little luxuries that their subsistence farming could not supply. The fact is that any society, whatever its stage of social or economic development, may indeed wish to escape consumer exploitation, but will also want a fair supply of consumer goods.

Prima facie there is no necessity for any culture to adapt itself radically just in order to raise its standard of living, or as a result of doing so. This does not mean that anyone is going to reject the benefits of technology, or of improved techniques of doing things. The suspicion is of Western culture, not of Western manufacture. The wireless is culture-transferable, as I said, talking Arabic or Swahili or Hindi as well as it can talk English, French or Russian. Its adoption will no doubt cause some change or development in the adopting culture, but it need only be a parallel, not an identical, change to that which has occurred in Europe or America. If the adopting culture had invented the radio, there would have been the same change. If an industrial revolution had happened somewhere else than in Europe, the chance of inventing the internal combustion engine would have been the same wherever it had happened. All cultures, being human, have the same need of transport; and non-Europeans find nothing alien in the motor-car, although they did not invent the machine that satisfies the need. If they had invented it, it would not have been a radically different article. A distinguished Sudanese educationist, who died at the age of ninety-four in 1954 was asked by his son and editor whether life was better in his early days or in our day, and he replied simply that now we press the wall and we have light, we turn a bit of the wall, and we have water.[8] No one questions the need of the world for the benefits of technology. The car and the radio represent exactly the same thing in Africa and Europe, in America and Asia, in that they everywhere represent the modernisation of the receiving culture. That is not the problem. The problem is whether it is possible to modernise without Westernising; to develop, without acculturation to the dominant societies; the problem is to discover the cost of modernising. Must all people pay the same price? Is the culture attached to the technique? Among the cultures which felt the full impact of the manufacturing West in the nineteenth century are

those of Africa, the Middle East, and south and eastern Asia. Something
of what these people thought, and think, about it is easily available in
English. I propose now to glance at this literature, not to substantiate a
contention, but to illustrate an idea.

To take the Arab world first, it was natural to concede only technological superiority to Europe, not moral or religious; although Northern
Europe had been Christian about as long as Arabia had been Muslim,
Europe had moved further from its religious origins as well as deeper
into technological advance. The sense of the uneven division of ameni-
ties between the developed and the undeveloped was already acute:
'They decorate the streets with millions of lamps for the sake of their
passage there once in a while, without thinking of the millions of the
poor living in darkness in their homes'. This certainly is an inter-cultural comment. There is a contrasting attitude; Rifa'a al-Tahtawi
(born 1801) admired European civilisation. He would not blame Islam
for its economic backwardness; oriental Christians were as far from
being French as Muslims were, and so he inclines to a secularist conclusion. Had he been consistent in this, he would, as many Arabs have
done since, have deserted Islam for the sake of vindicating the Islamic
culture. The nub of the question was well stated by Jamāl al-Dīn al-
Afghāni, when he said, 'If someone looks deeply into the question, he
will see that science rules the world. There was, is, and will be no ruler
in the world but science'. The imperialist victories of France and
England in Afghanistan and Tunis were victories not of Europeans, but
of science.[9]

The same point was made by Khayr al-Dīn al-Tūnisi in 1867. He
argues that it is 'necessary to keep up with one's neighbours in all
aspects of progress, military or non-military'; the Holy Law requires
Muslims to be prepared: 'Can we today attain such a level of preparation without progress in the skills and bases of growth to be seen among
others?' European progress was not caused by the Christian religion:
'Europe has attained these ends and progress in the sciences and industries through secular reforms (tanzimat) based on political justice', and
later he says 'the European progress in the field of civilisation . . . has
come through encouraging the sciences and arts and facilitating their
use'. He has no patience with those who reject modernisation, yet compete with each other in buying clothing and home furnishings of
Western manufacture. 'Anyone devoted to his religon should not be
deterred from imitating the commendable actions related to worldly
interests of one religiously misguided. . . . Wisdom is the goal of the
believer. He is to take it wherever he finds it.' Hourani points out that
Khayr al-Dīn's originality lay in his determination to identify exactly
what it was that constituted the strength of Europe. His final answer

was that 'liberty is the basis of the great development of knowledge and civilisation in the European kingdoms'. The lesson this teaches is that it is not only necessary to take the techniques that are directly useful, but also those that make it possible to use them. At the same time he envisaged nothing contrary to religion; he believed that all this borrowing was not only compatible with Islam, but something, neutral in itself, that it would be quite normal to take and make Muslim.[10]

The idea of taking the whole of Western technology, the idea that it is possible to do so while retaining Islamic culture, and a sometimes fierce criticism of European ways, have all survived into the present day. Anwar al-Sadat condemns the European moral system. 'The East, the cradle of Christianity, knows that the basis of its message is not to separate men, but to urge them to love one another for all time . . . the West wallows in the materialism that penetrated all its principles and shames the letter and the spirit of Christianity.' The Muslim Brothers, of course, have less sense of 'East', as distinguished from 'Muslim'; but they have seen as pre-existing in Islam the virtues of both the 'democratic' and the 'socialist' worlds, and they have seen Islam as free of the defects of both. The Arab socialists distinguish their beliefs from those of Eastern Europe by their greater warmth of human feeling, perhaps the same point as Anwar Sadat's in his comment on Christians of Europe, but applied to its socialists. Alternatively, we have the idea that civilisation belongs to all the world, and not to Europe; this, although it does not excommunicate Europe in the same way as the other views, is probably also a way of taking techniques without cultures: 'The present civilisation is that of all humanity, and although Europeans have played a considerable role in its creation and have stamped it with their seal, that does not imply that it can be considered as basically European'. A non-European who is convinced that there must be one single human culture wants to ensure that it is not just European. These are all different ways of trying to ensure the survival of Arab culture: it must contribute something to the world culture, or it can recognise the best of the West already in Islam; or it can borrow culture-transferable techniques.[11]

The rejection of Western capitalism or socialism is at least equally characteristic of African criticism of the European social attitude. The disruptive impact of European cultures, quite distinct from the effects of urbanisation, is a frequent theme of African novels, themselves the use of a Western technique to express African cultural ideas. 'The only virtue in technological advance is to make life easier and better', says a well-known Ghanaian novel: 'as the drum says:

the path was cut to meet the stream
the stream is there from long, long ago.

Technology does not teach ideals; our ideals are our love of freedom, our love of music and dancing and our concern for each other's welfare.' K. A. Busia associates the African rejection of Western or Eastern 'ideologies, technology, materialism, or social and political systems' with a search for 'modernisation and for new political and social institutions' behind which lies 'an interpretation of the universe which is intensely and pervasively religious'. He quotes with approval Nyerere's African socialism: 'In our traditional African society we were individuals within a community. We took care of the community and the community took care of us. We neither needed, nor wished to exploit our fellow men'. It is not our business to enquire whether or not this is true; what is certainly true is that the belief exists that Africa can retain a more humane culture than ours. In another West African novel a boy who is going to study in France is saying good-bye to his mother, who cries: 'Have they no mothers, those people? But they can't have mothers, of course. They would not have gone so far from home if they'd had mothers'.[12]

When we come to look at the literature in English left by the great Indian leaders of the first half of the present century, there is a difference of style from the Muslim and African comments we have just glanced at. The Indian Muslim seems to the Western reader to be more specifically critical than the Hindus, but less eager to grasp Western technology than the Arabs. 'It was hoped that education would bring leisure and prosperity. No one knew that it would also bring atheism with it.' So Muhammad Iqbal. 'This knowledge, science, politics and commerce, whatever there is, is the invention of imperialism.' In Gandhi's autobiography (first published in 1927) there is no comparable criticism of the culture of the West, and it was of course Gandhi's pride to reject nothing good from any source. Because of his total self-confidence and unassailable personal stature, his description of cultural conflicts becomes a matter of personal comedy in the highest sense of the word; for example, there is his account of how he was tempted to meat-eating by a friend: 'The English are able to rule over us, because they are meat-eaters'; and of his eating the legal dinners necessary to keep term, to be called to the English bar. Gandhi can never perhaps have realised the difficulty that so many people have in discriminating, in knowing what to take and what to leave. The gap between European culture in any form and Gandhi's Hinduism, with all its correction of what he disapproved in it, is almost unbridgeable. What he says of the imperial system in the time of British rule might be applied to the wider cultural complex. 'I felt then that it was more the fault of individual British officials than of the British system, and that we could convert them by love. . . . Though the system was faulty, it did not seem to me to be intolerable, as it does today.' Much of Nehru's *Glimpses of World History* is perhaps self-consciously non-Indian in its rejection of the West. Yet he reflects the same ideas as we have already seen among Arabs: 'Christianity . . . is the religion of the dominant peoples of Europe. But it is strange to think of the rebel Jesus preaching non-violence and ahimsa and . . . to compare him with his loud-voiced followers today'. Nehru had in fact accepted secularist values from the West, and yet he saw himself as a revolutionary within his own tradition: 'I too', he said solemnly in his will and testament, 'am a link in that unbroken chain which goes back to the dawn of history in the immemorial past of India. That chain I would not break.'[13]

Much of the Indian reaction against the West was particularly and even virulently against Christianity. The missionaries were hated also by Muslims, and there were special reasons for hating them in China, but for the moment let us just glance at the Indian attitude. Professor Panikkar, himself no mean critic of Christianity, wrote: 'It might appropriately be said that while political aggrandisement was the work of governments and groups, and commerce the interest of organised capital, mission work was the effort of the people of the West to bring home to the masses of Asia their view of the values of life'. It may well be that Christianity was hated during the Imperial period because it was felt to be a total cultural assault on local cultures, a summing up of the aggression, in a way that technical progress was not. As I have said, no one rejects technical advantages; and no one admits that the modern is not as suited to his culture as to any other. A culture that is relegated to a reservation is finished, and the Christian missions attacked the cultures themselves, in a way that military conquest attributable to technological superiority did not. The Indians (and many others) knew that they were inferior in military fire-power, and even in organisation; that is why they were beaten in battle and reduced to political subjection; but they had no reason to admit to any further inferiority, and so the religious attack was the one that was most resented. When Hinduism was venomously attacked by missionaries from Serampore, Rammohun Roy replied in 1821 : 'It seems almost natural that when one nation succeeds in conquering another, the former, though their religion may be quite ridiculous, laugh at and despise the religion and manners of those that are fallen into their power'. Nirad Chaudhuri describes well and entertainingly the fundamental resentment of and contempt for the British felt by all levels of Indians, quoting nineteenth-century examples, and the delight taken by Indians in British defeats, not only in the second, but also in the first world war; but, sensitive to the defects of Hindu culture, he condemns, with Tagore, the 'ready sneers and voluble lectures, in the best Hindu style, on the bankruptcy of European civilisation, its spiritual poverty, and its moral iniquity'.[14]

In fact the Hindu solution was just like the Arab solution; to want the skills and leave the cultural setting. This too goes back to Rammohun Roy : 'We did not want government money', he said in 1823, 'to be spent on giving us a school of Sanscrit studies; we wanted European instruction in "Mathematics, Natural Philosophy, Chemistry, Anatomy and other useful Sciences, which the Nations of Europe have carried to a degree of perfection that has raised them above the inhabitants of other parts of the world".' He combined resistance with missionary aggression, a moral revival in Hinduism, and a desire to acquire modern science, to use the English to create something very un-English. In our own day, President Radhakrishnan believed that Indian philosophy could be 'one of the great formative elements in human progress, by relating the immensely increased knowledge of modern science to the ancient ideals of India's philosophers'. The wisest thing is no doubt to take it for granted that we can transmute whatever is useful to use into a form that is truly our own; but of course there is conflict. A leader of the revival of Hinduism, Swami Vivekananda, said in 1899 : 'On one side, new India is saying, "If we only adopt Western ideas, Western language, Western food, Western dress, and Western manners, we shall be as strong and powerful as the Western nations"; on the other old India is saying, "Fools! By imitation, others' ideas never become one's own; nothing, unless earned, is your own".' In 1951, Chaudhuri said that those who turned back to an ancient India with which they had not living contact 'were being as imitative when copying ancient Indian ways as they were in copying the Western'. All this criticism seems valid to me; what the other cultures want to do is not really to have and eat their cake too. They want desperately to modernise, but they want to modernise in their own way, not in our way; to 'earn' not to 'imitate'.[15]

We return to the same conclusion if we look at the quite different situation in China. It was different in two ways: China had practised a more sophisticated technology than Europe, but, lacking the will to expand, had failed to develop a technology of expansion. According to one's point of view one can say that China was not interested in exploiting technology for aggression, or that China lacked the necessary energy and creative urge. On the other hand, China maintained its traditions and techniques of scholarship alive, changing and intact, without interruption; in this the Chinese culture is unlike the Hindu, which was in eclipse during the period of Muslim and later British domination. It was therefore logical for China to expect only to have to adapt new material to existing methods. 'Hereafter', said Lian Chichao, 'the sciences of Europe and America will flow in steadily and our countrymen, applying the excellent scientific methods which they have inherited to these rich materials and using them as a basis for exhaustive study, will undoubtedly become one of the first-class "scientific peoples" of the world.' He objected to any suggestion of 'the wholesale transplantation of the thoughts of another society'; and it is wholly consistent that those who object to the cultural invasion by Christianity should equally object to liberalism. Since the day of Lian, who thought that 'Sovietism' was dead, but who died himself in 1929, Mao Tse-Tung has introduced a Western system attributed to Lenin. Mao has replaced classical methods by a Wordsworthian simplicity of diction, and revolutionised scholarship as much as land tenure and the means of production. Yet no one doubts that Mao has proved that he meant what he said: 'We stress regeneration through our own efforts', and 'we stand for self-reliance'; or that Chinese Leninism has adopted a distinctive form.[16] There seems little doubt that Leninism in China is already as Chinese as Christianity in Europe became European. All Communist cultures, being committed to the culture of the folk, are committed to some local continuity; but more, there is an obvious sense in which Russian Communism is shaped by the Tsarist and Orthodox past, and Chinese Communism by Confucianism, in spite of the explicit rejection in each case of the earlier phase of society.

An interesting collection of papers about Indonesian historical writing illustrates problems of adopting techniques. Some contributors felt that modern critical technique conflicted with Indonesian source material and traditional attitudes. On the European side, one Dutch writer was quoted as thinking Western Europe peculiarly trained for historical thinking, and the bearer of a 'world historical view'. Both sides seem to see an inherent rather than transitory opposition between the modern technique and the traditional ways. 'If historiography develops from the main body of culture, then can a pattern of life which has already broken up produce a historiography?'[17] There is a real problem here, but it is wrongly stated. I believe that both the Dutch assertion and the Indonesian fear are unwarranted; that modernisation is not made specially Western by having developed largely in Western Europe. It is just that all change, in Europe or in Indonesia, brings problems of adaptation.

In the last few pages I have tried, not to prove anything, but to illustrate by a variety of examples the reaction to Western technology that is almost universal among the nations of the outside world; as anyone familiar with them knows, it has also been characteristic of them since they first experienced the Western impact. Their feeling is expressed largely in terms of anti-imperialist theory, which is often and quite naturally over-simplified. It becomes more attractive when we extend it to include the imperialism of the socialist powers, and define it to include the total tendency of the West and North to dominate the rest of the world by means of technological advance, sometimes with bad intentions (political advantage or excessive profit), sometimes with good intentions (aid for development), and sometimes with no intention at all. Any sensible theory of anti-imperialism must take into account that much imperial motivation has been both in origin and in practice an urge to improve other people. The objection to it is that people do not like it; they say 'we want to be improved; we must learn methods of improvement from you; but we do not want you to improve us, we want to improve ourselves'. The struggle is consciously directed against political and economic exploitation, whether real or imagined; but this is only part of the total resistance (less regularly conscious and less systematic) to cultural domination. It is the total resistance of a culture that lies at the root of all the problems of imperialism and development, whether the large problems of politics, or the more modest problems of educational exchange.

There are some, both in our culture and in the dominated cultures, who on the contrary are convinced that the same technological conditions must everywhere and always produce the same cultural changes. A European or American may say 'these people are just not prepared to give up their muddled traditional ways, as we have done ours, for the sake of efficiency' — efficiency which constantly creates new benefits. Some among the victims may think that the struggle to command the technology is enough, without adding to it the burden of cultural resistance. We have noted that there is a compromise view too: that before a single word culture is established, it can be modified by contributions from the other expiring cultures, and that the present dominant culture is inadequate because only the West has contributed. This would immediately concede that the culture is not the product of the technology alone; but even so the view is unnecessarily pessimistic. We still cling to the variety that survives in the subcultures of the West. It is as natural to put up a bitter resistance to cultural change as it is to be avid for technological benefit. People rightly admire scientific achievement, but they simply want to make their familiar way of living more comfortable; they neither foresee nor desire a different way of living altogether. Why should they? It ought not to be so difficult to exploit new methods and manufactures in a style to suit the genius of each separate culture.

We in our Western culture esteem profitability, and we have all felt impatient with the impoverished peoples of the world who prefer empty ideas to their plain interests, and the freedom, not even of the individual, but of their nation, to profits, wealth, security and progress. Of course, the anti-imperialist does not see it like this. He will think that there can be no progress until the plots of the neo-colonialists have been finally frustrated, and their hope of profit eradicated for ever. Eternal vigilance is the price of freedom. 'I gave my mother the slip', says a boy in a story about Sudanese revolution, 'and joined a demonstration and we went to spit on the US Embassy'.[18] This seems close to purposeless xenophobia. In fact it may be a normal exercise of the cultural filter and a valuable function of the defence mechanism. The Spartan envoys to Persia were shown the splendours and comforts for which they might exchange their independence and replied, 'Only he who does not know how sweet freedom is can speak like this'. We are the ancient Persians, and the romantic young nationalists are the Greeks. Naturally their sentiment only stimulates counter-sentiment in us. We relish an opportunity to discredit their claims, and our resentment at being criticised as violent is evident in our attitude to each case of African or Asian violence. They often succeed in annoying us, but do not always do themselves much good. Anti-imperialism, expressed politically as neutrality between two blocs, may create dependence on the culture that is common to both blocs. The possibilites are complex. We need to examine the effects and the possible usefulness of hostility much more closely.

There is some evidence that the early seventies are witnessing a dilution of the classic doctrine of anti-imperialism in some countries where it has flourished, and it is not yet clear whether this is a temporary fluctuation or the beginning of a consistent tendency. The complexity of 'imperialist' motivation is more widely understood, and perhaps the impression of absolute right and wrong is losing its once clear outline. Suspicion remains, even when old forms of expression pass out of fashion. Disillusion with what nationalism can accomplish is a normal phase of decolonisation, but, although it may result in a more sophisticated theory, it is most unlikely to lead to a recantation. National feeling still looks desperately for expression. In some countries the appearance as well as the essential character of anti-imperialism remains unchanged; in others, it is tempered by weariness and disappointment.

Academic Traffic

I PROPOSE NOW to look at a few of the ways in which hostility prevents communication in practice. I am not going to consider all the areas in which it happens, and this chapter is about the problems inherent only in academic interchange between different cultures. One difficulty in discussing the different kinds of traffic in either direction is that there is an ideal, which should always be the aim in the minds of those concerned with educational aid, and there are any number of passing phases which mark a gradual approach to the aim, but which are still far from it. In countries where there is an over-production of graduates, there are very few foreign staff. If the pressure of the graduates is too strong, there may not even be the minimum of foreigners which will help to stimulate any university anywhere. When we talk about the aim and the ideal, we are taking this into account. In countries where still not enough are trained to the post-doctoral stage necessary for a university concerned with research as well as teaching, communities of expatriate teachers still survive. In the ideal, so far as it is practicable, there will be a stream of short-term visitors from foreign universities, but those teaching permanently will be rare or almost unknown. There is another distinction, which I have already mentioned, between equal and unequal exchange. Here we again find an aim and an ideal in contrast to a series of approximations. There are few exchanges in the sense of exact exchanges — as when two university teachers of the same rank and seniority, teaching the same subject, simply change places for a time. The system by which short visits between European universities take place is an equal exchange between cultures (or sub-cultures), each giving and deriving approximately the same benefit, even if it is not equal as between individuals. Outside the Europe-America ecumene this sort of equality is rarer.

On the whole, the two-way traffic in academics still consists of Europeans who go abroad to teach, to advise about teaching, or to examine; and overseas students who come to Europe to learn, and especially to take advanced degree courses, or special courses calculated (well or ill) to suit the needs of development. There are exceptions; I hope that the exceptions are increasing, and I believe that they must increase until they cease to be exceptions. The old pattern is essentially a stop-gap pattern, created by the colonial and even pre-colonial situations, and by the predominance of the 'West' in technology. In many parts of the

world, few European staff are employed: in some there is a preponder-
ance, and there even still exist European Vice-Chancellors and senior
administrators. Where this occurs, it can be accepted as a passing phase;
everyone is aware that 'cultural imperialism' is dangerous. The ultimate
aim must be to see a constant flow of visits between all parts of the
world. Most Universities will accept the proposition that they can only
benefit from new ideas. I do not know what the optimum proportion of
foreign passports permanently on the staff of any university would be,
but it may be reasonable to suggest something more than 5 per cent and
less than 15 per cent. For the time being, the number of students training abroad to become academics at home is determined by the number
of places to be filled, and as long as rapid educational expansion continues in developing countries, the number is likely to be maintained.
As training facilities are improved in every country, students will tend
to go abroad for courses that are more and more advanced, until finally
equal exchange develops naturally. Between roughly equally developed
countries it already roughly obtains.

   In the present chapter I want to discuss the traffic out of Europe first,
and the reverse situation second. From the present point on, I shall be
talking normally about Britons overseas, and about overseas students in
Britain; but everything that I have ever seen leads me to believe that,
mutatis mutandis, the same applies equally to Americans and continental Europeans overseas, and to students from overseas in America
and on the continent of Europe. I shall be seen to be primarily interested
in the cultural barrier to exchange, and least interested in those people
who overcome it without difficulty; I may seem to be concentrating on
the things that go wrong. This is not an innate pessimism or a hyper-
trophied critical faculty. Our best means of assessing what makes for
success is an analysis of failure. In the next chapter I shall be discussing
some problems of individual adaptation to a strange culture; here, the
general and inevitable difficulties of adjustment between the cultures.
The distinction is a fine one, and I may sometimes seem illogical; I hope
that its main lines will nevertheless stand out clearly.

   The most important fact about an Englishman, or any foreigner,
teaching overseas is that he is there temporarily. It is not his home and
he will not stay there more than a few years. He will not expect to
acquire the culture of his hosts. On the contrary, he will often expect
to live his own life in his own way, because he sees clearly how impermanent his position is. This is not only a matter of political uncertainties, though they do interfere with the tranquillity of foreign teachers,
perhaps inordinately and unnecessarily; it is still more a question of
having no permanent place, either in the social or the professional
ladder. Economists tell us that, with developing countries as it has been

with individuals, the rich get richer quicker than the poor do, and that the gap between 'developing' and 'developed' increases all the time. In education, although of course it cannot be divorced from the development of the economy, almost the reverse is true. Quite a poor country can raise its educational level very high indeed. We find the development economists complaining in fact that there is overproduction of graduates, and educationists questioning the economic value of education.[1]

The width of the gap between educationally developed and developing countries can in principle be measured by the numbers of foreign staff whom an overseas university has to employ, but this is a rough and ready system liable to be modified by other considerations. For example, a concentration of expatriates on one particular subject need not measure the general level of university staff; it may only imply a new department or faculty, staffed initially by expatriates. A general run of expatriates scattered evenly, but not in great number in any one department, is likely to indicate that a university is expanding faster than staff can be found. There can often be no reserve of national staff already teaching at a slightly lower level (such people often make a better job of it than in theory they should) to promote into higher jobs, in a country where every educational level is expanding fast and simultaneously. In such a case, there is no harm in a high proportion of expatriates, if it is not too high and if counterparts are training. The sort of situation that would be seriously detrimental to the interests of both donor and recipient universities would be one where there was a high proportion (even a majority) of expatriates in all or most subjects, without adequate provision for counterpart training. In that situation no progress towards a position of equality, towards one in which both sides can benefit from exchange, could be made. A foreign language department, where native speakers of the foreign language will always have something to contribute in excess of foreign staff in other fields, is a likely exception. Even there, foreigners would not constitute the whole of a department, or its administration, in a normal situation.

ACADEMIC RESEARCH OVERSEAS

The teaching of most subjects will everywhere benefit from the visits of outsiders, who will in turn benefit from the local knowledge, as well as the individual skills, of their temporary colleagues. The importance of the contribution made to any joint project by local knowledge is obvious in such fields as agriculture or veterinary science. In history and similar subjects the situation is more complex; at any rate, less obvious. No scholar, whether historian, sociologist, political scientist, or anything else, will mind being dependent on local sources of information. A document has only to be read, a stone or sherd lies in the ground for the scholar to interpret. The complications are introduced when human beings are the source material. To varying extents, the historian, the anthropologist, the sociologist and the political scientist must seek information from human sources, and it is to be hoped that they will respect the cultures they are studying; they will do bad work if they do not. In three of these cases the human source material will always be more accessible to the local colleague than to the visitor, and the latter must submit his researches to the expert eyes of his colleagues of the country. Unless he does so, he cannot tell whether he has escaped the danger of researching into the obvious, of 'discovering' facts well known to everyone in the country and new only to the foreigner. It is not unknown for a university at home to acclaim as original work that could not be taken seriously in the country where it was done. The anthropologist may be investigating a special group, as foreign to his colleagues of the country as to himself; but the other three foreign scholars must always, other things being equal, be under a disadvantage in comparison with local fellow-workers. They must know the language less intimately. They must know the society and background less familiarly. They must be less competent to assess the facts against the known background, or to understand the nuances of what is told them. There is a danger of their claiming a greater expertise to counterbalance the natural advantages possessed by the person born and bred on the spot.

At the very least the foreign scholar in such a situation should borrow the skills and talents of his colleague to check his results and to give him guidance upon the line of his investigation. If so, and this would be a sensible but humble attitude, he is adopting the most practical means to overcome the cultural barrier. Why is it possible to find the opposite; scholars, sometimes quite young scholars, who make no attempt to obtain the advice and even the co-operation of colleagues whose local knowledge is in every way superior to their own; sometimes, older colleagues, with equal 'Western' paper qualifications, and greater experience? The only explanation that I have ever been able to see is that the junior and less qualified European in this hypothesis must, whether consciously or not, believe that he has an innate or acquired superiority in techniques that originate in the culture of which he is a native. He does not see or does not really believe that a technique of learning is wholly culture-transferable. This is conscious or unconscious racialism, a sense of cultural superiority arbitrarily linked to accidents of birth.

This problem is related to that of the kinds of research available to the expatriate university teacher. In some fields there is no problem at all, for example, in zoology. The individual worker may not be familiar with aspects of his subject which can be studied in the local fauna, but in principle there is no problem. A more problematic case is exemplified in a book by a Swedish author entitled *Sudanese Ethics*.[2] This is a work in the field now known as descriptive ethics, not in social-anthropology, and is liable to arouse opposition in specialists from the latter discipline. It makes for inter-cultural misunderstanding, and may provoke a good deal of local hostility, on the ground that the evidence is inadequate and the methodology at fault. Yet it is an interesting attempt, and worth looking at a little more fully, because it may point a way to more useful inter-cultural work.

Descriptive ethics makes no startling claim for itself, and it seems for this very reason to overlap the anthropological field. It is 'a non-evaluative discipline the object of which is to map existing ethical systems rather than to investigate the conditions which a good system ought to fulfil' and 'which describes and analyses the ethical norms, values and ideals which individuals and groups actually have'. It overlaps, however, with 'metaethics', the 'essentially valuative discipline'. One difficulty in practising this science is that we are all better able to recognise the deviations from the norm to which we are brought up than we are to evaluate the norm itself. A second difficulty is that 'description' is harder than 'evaluation', in that evaluation can hardly pretend to be culture-free, whereas description has to be culture-free in order to be itself. The describer has to ask the questions and his choice of questions must be governed by his own cultural limitations. The work we are now considering has some elements of the overseas syndrome; its background of Sudanese society is defective, and so is its background in Arab history, in Arab ideas generally and in Islam. Its author is conscious that a total of ten and a half hours interviewing time with three informants is by sociological standards not good enough. He becomes aware at the last moment that much of what he is describing in the values of the Northern Sudanese is close to what others have recognised in the Mediterranean.[3] Sociologists and descriptive ethicists seem to be toiling painfully along behind what we have all known for a long time. Standards of morals at one particular period in the history of any society, or under certain conditions, the tendency of patterns to recur and persist, the elements in all our minds which we inherit from our ancestors, all these complicate a complex question further, but, all the more, the subject is one in which we must welcome the beginnings.

There remains the question of the inter-cultural utility of the study. I do not myself believe that anyone is capable, or any discipline can give the ability, to 'describe' without cultural bias. What anyone can do is note how a description is different from what we are accustomed to. There is an obvious danger in this. People whose grandfathers were 'discovered' by nineteenth-century explorers have always resented the ideas that a country already inhabited by a large African population should be 'discovered' by a visit from a European. What that means, of course, is that the European visit put it on the European map. There is still a danger of some kind of 'explorerism'. It is only equivalent to writing for the parish magazine, when a European in an overseas university produces a study which is informative for universities at home, but adds nothing to the knowledge or self-knowledge of people of the culture studied. There is a possible cure for this. Collaboration between colleagues of different cultural origin ought to be very fruitful. The questions put to informants in order to elicit the material of the 'description' would not be framed from inside a single cultural framework. The informants would be taking part in a discussion and would have to deal with a team, or at any rate not less than two, to represent both their own and an outside culture. This responds to a double need. A scholar belonging to the culture being studied can most easily distinguish deviations from the local norm, and an outsider will naturally be quicker to see the differences between the local norm and other cultural norms. In addition, if the culture studied were compared, at all points that arise, with at least one other culture, the tendency to appear to sit in judgement, to which descriptive ethics may be more liable than anthropology, might be lessened. The interrogators might themselves be interrogated. It has yet to be proved that anyone can be dissociated from cultural bias, and a total scholarly impartiality probably cannot exist; but a system of comparative descriptive ethics, through the collaboration of scholars themselves originating in all the systems compared, might be achieved, not only in the methodology of fact-finding, but also in any study concerned to evaluate the results.

THE POSITION OF EXPATRIATES

These are forms of research possible and useful for expatriate university staff, and of course they are relevant irrespective of the state of economic development of the country to which the university belongs, and apply to staff of a 'developing' nationality, teaching in European or American universities, as well as in the reverse case. This situation is not part of a temporary phase, but of the ultimate and permanent aim of university exchange. Visiting staff from abroad, whether they come for a few days, or weeks, or months or years, will increasingly be justified by the additional contribution they can make by virtue of being foreign, and giving an outside stimulus; the temporary situation is where they merely fill a gap for which no national is available. The former situation ought to be a meeting point of different cultures; the latter is one where the visitors are most tempted to regard themselves as in some way set apart. All visitors ought to try to deculturate themselves, and to treat people, and hope to be treated, just as people; but by a curious irony it is those who are standing in for nationals of the host country who are most apt to rely on their own supposed cultural superiority. It may not sound credible, but there often arise situations where English teachers resent having to treat a senior of the host nationality in the same way as they would treat a senior in the equivalent position at home; situations, too, where they have to be told neither to condescend to nor to patronise a junior. The fact of not belonging to the host culture dislocates the human relations of some expatriate teachers; they adopt attitudes either of excessive hostility or of excessive enthusiasm, in any case an abnormal and unnatural attitude. I discuss the effect of these situations on individuals in the next chapter. What makes a successful resident in a strange culture is as difficult to recognise as it is to define. There seems to be no method of selection or interview which will pick out from among the candidates for posts overseas those who are capable of just behaving naturally, and as if they were at home. People who in their own background seem almost indistinguishable turn out abroad to vary between extremes of gentleness and arrogance, of adaptability and obstinacy. Often a man or woman cannot recognise his or her own capacity for cultural — often 'racial' — discrimination, especially if it is disguised. Self-deception easily occurs, especially when discrimination is contrary to the conscious principles of the discriminator. The man who will get on best with his colleagues at home will be the most likely to get on well abroad. The conceited young man, especially when there is relatively little to justify the conceit, will be intolerable in the overseas situation, but he will cause trouble anywhere, and is never really at home, even in his own country.

Every inter-cultural encounter is likely to increase either dislike or co-operation. In the long run every cultural exchange has had something valuable to include among its consequences; but we must try not to make the process unpleasant. The Norman Conquest was a nasty experience for the Saxons, and we do not want to impose a comparable shock. Even 1956 is a long time ago now, especially for educational development in Africa; but in that year Sir Christopher Cox made some public remarks which are valid not only for the day and the context in which they were delivered, but also for our situation now. He was speaking before the independence of most formerly British-controlled African territories, and he said, 'Our help will be greatest if we recall that our problems and theirs, despite many similarities, are not identical; that our assumptions at any given time, about which we can be so very confident, may not have a universal validity; and we can work with and for a people not our own only through intimate understanding and partnership'.[4] This is an excellent recipe, not only for the decolonisation situation of which it was said, but for any other overseas teaching. Britons, Americans, and other Europeans teaching overseas would have little professional difficulty, if they could seek the intimacy and understanding of their overseas colleagues, and still realise that the principles of our older and our younger generations alike, our revolutionaries and our reactionaries, all belong to our culture. Sometimes there is no wish for intimacy at all; sometimes it is marred by the inability to meet the other fellow on his own ground; but most often what lies behind these and other difficulties is the assumption that the principles springing from one aspect or another of our own culture are good for everyone. The assumption is widespread, and often can be recognised and partly shed only after long personal experience. The case of the foreign 'expert' (from a country of European stock) whose expertise consisted of looking up (and expecting to apply) the regulations governing his particular field of government in his own country, as though they must be equally good and valid everywhere, is only a *reductio ad absurdum* of a tendency which is common enough.

The greatest trial for the overseas teacher is a system into which he cannot fit, because he has been trained for a situation altogether different. A common complaint is that local ways are set and unadaptable. The European wants to deviate from the set syllabus, in order to make his lesson more interesting, and finds to his rather simple-minded surprise that his efforts are frowned upon, not only by the alien administration, but also by the students themselves.[5] This is a fair summary of a situation that occurs in many different parts of the world. It is a situation about which absolutely nothing can be done, unless the foreign teacher is willing to put up with it. We may be sure that current educational fashions in England and America are the last word in a progressive discovery of the very best ideas. If others do not agree, and if we have perfect faith, we have only to wait a generation or two till things go our way in their parts of the world also. If in our hearts we have our doubts, we have no right to insist. In the meantime, we have to put up with things as they are; and we may be helped to do this by observing what good results a 'bad' system may have. Where the system can be worked at all, expatriates can work it too; where it cannot, it is useless for them, or for anyone to take part at all.

Expatriate teachers are going to see problems that exist at home in a new light, and often in forms that bring out inherent inconsistencies, which at home are masked. We find complaints of an Education Ministry which makes it easy for as many students as possible to pass their examinations, and yet demands that standards be raised.[6] In our own country we should define the same phenomenon as giving less emphasis to the stultifying effect of examinations, while constantly raising the quality of the teaching. I do not want to sound satirical; it is a genuine problem that occurs in a slightly different form all over the world. The solution must be embedded in local custom, that is, in the culture, and this may be incomprehensible to the outsider. The people in authority will certainly not have the time or take the trouble to explain it all to him, especially if he does not make the effort himself to step over into the culture surrounding him.

There are other situations which really do call for tolerance on the part of the foreigner. There may be a real inefficiency resulting from the imperfect assimilation of a foreign model, for example, something like 'a very rough poorly-administered Secondary Modern School in Britain': students who come and go at classes at their whim, who 'forget, lose, mutilate or sell their books', who ignore the teaching and join in private conversation, who are subject to favouritism from their teachers, and whose examinations are 'farcical', with alternate papers set to preclude cheating, while candidates shout the answers out across the room. This sounds a pretty exaggeration; if all these things have at one time or another occurred, they may not occur regularly or in so concentrated a fashion. Even so, there must be some occasions where the condition of society at a given stage of its development precludes fruitful exchange of ideas.[7] Even when this is not so, we cannot expect from everyone the imaginative effort to understand the preconceptions of other cultures; most people are too tired, and others are not interested, to make the effort. A little gentle grumbling will see most people through. In the last resort, they will cross the barrier if they have a genuine love of their job and of their students; about that sort of thing there is rarely any mistake, and it is at the personal level that those who are not imaginatively endowed can sidestep every obstacle.

SHORT-TERM VISITS

The problem of the short-term academic visit is different from that of 'temporarily permanent' staff, but we are still dealing with the same type of cultural barrier. Personal failures do exist, but they are relatively rare, because a short visit requires no lasting adjustment. The non-resident has less opportunity to adjust to a strange culture, but he neither expects to, nor is expected to by his hosts. If there are still failures, the reason may lie either with the adaptability of the visitor, or with the purpose for which he is sent. The short-term visitor needs to understand the distinction between culture-bound and culture-transferable. He is not at all expert in the ways in which a technique can be put to use in a different culture. He would be very ill advised to express an opinion on this, other than in the secrecy of unofficial talk with his hosts in a confidential, a hesitating and humble way.

Professor Ree of York was discussing education in Pakistan in the course of an advisory visit; he said about this later: 'I found myself sometimes refusing to give them advice which they asked for, or doing so only on condition that they would not take it, because it came from someone who did not know their problems or their culture. The most I felt I could do was to get them to look at the dangers and difficulties which we had found or foreseen . . . and to examine the solutions which we had tried, in order to see if they were relevant'.[8] Education is a matter more than ordinarily subject to cultural modification. Whether any one solution is relevant to any one situation must always depend on the accidents of history and everything else that goes to make up a culture. Most countries know what to do with expert advice, and that is not necessarily, as the cynics would say, to ignore it; but they are often selective in the use they make of it, and only they can choose the right time to make use of it at all. On the other hand, the donors, whether bilateral or multilateral, are haunted by the fear that the recipients' inefficiency and inexperience, or even the recipients' corruption, may nullify the value of aid, and so they sometimes attach conditions which really do detract from the help they give. Usually this is because they ignore cultural difference, and sometimes also because their conditions imply a different standard of judgement from those that obtain in their own countries. To answer to this that he who pays the piper calls the tune is to go to the very heart of the problem of aid. It is not just that charity is bitterly resented all the world over, one factor common to every culture; it is more that in proportion as help given does not allow the recipient to help himself, it is help wasted. These questions can easily take us into the whole problem of aid, and that is beyond my subject; here we need only note that the short-term academic visitor who does not heartily accept the example so admirably set by Professor Ree will be wasting his time. A remark of a colleague of the present writer's is memorable: 'We ought for once to be seen to be doing what they want us to do, not what we think would be good for them'.[9]

Even with short-term visits, anything from a few weeks up to an academic year, the problem is how to communicate. The least successful are not even aware of it. Difficulties of the more obvious sort arise where no large local expatriate community exists which could help the visitor, difficulties of unaccustomed food, ways of washing, and so on. No one at all finds it easy to adapt quickly and completely to quite a new rhythm of life, and it is not easiest for the middle-aged academic. The visitor often has little resistance to infection carried by food and water, and there is nothing so apt to shorten the temper as trouble in the bowels. The visitors who are most successful are those whose temperament allows them to relax and to follow the customs of the country. Certain minor problems constantly recur. For example, many Britons are slow to realise that most other languages agree to a negative question in the affirmative, and not, as English does, with a responding negative. This small point can result in irritation and misunderstanding, and it is strange that it often takes long to be recognised. Perhaps the highest point of the cultural barrier is the natural and inevitable preference that most people have for the company of others of their own culture.[10] This is not just that Englishmen may like to prop up the same bar together. A short-term visitor may learn more about conditions where he is staying from a fellow-traveller of his own or a closely related culture (and the closer, the more he learns), than from any number of people born and bred up in the country, whose actual knowledge is, of course, much more accurate and much more profound, but with whom he does not find it natural to communicate. Also, most Western visitors find it much easier to establish social relations with those of their hosts who are already familiar with Western cultural pre-occupations; this is only natural, but without experience of the country they can hardly tell how closely those they talk to remain themselves attached to their own culture. Some visitors, intelligent and well-meaning people, will find social relations, except on a very restricted scale, very difficult. Sometimes the reason is plain, for example, inability to talk about unfamiliar subjects, imaginative failure to see our own cultural interests as less then universal. There remains an element of mystery. It cannot always be explained why particular people fail to make real contact.

Sometimes visitors are tempted to make their own cultural interpretations, although those that are new to their host culture might do better to cultivate a complete agnosticism in this. It is sometimes clear that a visitor has accepted the cultural explanations of his hosts, and nothing could be more sensible. He is not there to make a scholarly assessment of a society or culture (in most cases at least), but to open up maximum communication in his own field. Where one academic (and often scientific) visitor may do so, the next, for example one to a country of the Asian land mass, naïvely complains that the people are pleasant and happy in disposition, but there is 'no sense of enthusiasm for progress'; he himself does have a sense of the gap between the cultures, and the conjunction, 'but', marks the low level of communication. Perhaps there is more than a hint here of Arcadian nostalgia in what is ostensibly a scientific reproof; but it is very unlikely, as we have seen, that the people of Arcadia would refuse any of the advantages of modern manufacture. When travelling scientists and others from the West make unscientific analyses of a strange cultural situation, it is often, I suspect, as a result of listening to foreign residents and taking various expatriate myths too seriously. One very common mistake made by visitors to Muslim countries is to attribute the learning of passages of dictated notes to the teaching methods of the Quranic schools. This is the purest speculation, which no scientist would tolerate in his own subject, and it circulates among expatriate communities like an old wives' tale. It happens that our current educational theory is opposed to learning by heart by quite young children (and defensively sensitive on the point). When we find children learning by heart, and also find adults doing something very similar, we attribute the second to the first. In fact, this is just one hypothesis; other hypotheses are easily made, for example, that rote-learning of notes is the result of trying to absorb a large body of alien teaching too fast. Victorians who had learned a great deal of Latin and Greek poetry by heart, and some of them much of the Bible also, were not only able to think scientifically; they initiated the lines of thought on which we are still living intellectually today. Moreover, Quranic study led on in due course to discussions on a rational basis, and in times past did so in fields other than jurisprudence and theology; there is nothing in it contrary to constructive thinking, except to the eye of prejudice. The constant repetition of this easy explanation of some bad science teaching (and for that matter, bad history and bad Arabic teaching) in schools in Muslim countries is nothing more than an intrusion of our cultural hostility into our own rational thought. We simply want a reason to express an emotional antipathy, of which we often fail to recognise even the existence.

This would be a depressing note on which to leave the cultural barrier that can intervene in short-term visits overseas by academic staff. It would be to ignore the generous appreciation by many scientists of the work of their colleagues in developing countries, countries where scientists are often isolated by distance, by poverty and by its concomitants of poor communications, poor supply of equipment and even of learned periodicals, and yet manage to keep techniques acquired in the West alive and healthy. Such visitors will praise, for example, the pattern of concentration upon urgent development, and the applied research that this has required; they will note the idealism and dedication which characterise so many of the scientists and technicians of a developing country, or the great faith, as well as determination, which goes to develop a new university in an adverse physical environment. Sometimes they are struck by a higher standard of research than they feel they have been led to expect. We also find criticism that is freed, so far as reasonably can be expected, of cultural intrusion, by the recognition that faults are common to situations both at home and abroad. This is the right way to criticise: for example, a visiting scientist may want to combat the idea that sophisticated equipment is necessary for useful research, but knows well, and says, that this 'malady' is not restricted to developing countries, but infects our own laboratories too. In applied sciences especially, the visitor can find good research being done both by individuals and by organisations, and can often see his own function as little else but to encourage forward movements whenever and wherever he finds them.

STUDY IN BRITAIN

How far do these difficulties of cultural intrusion into the transmission of knowledge repeat themselves in the reverse situation, in which students work in developing countries to acquire techniques of economic and educational development for use at home? Does cultural difference interfere in the efficient acquisition of Western techniques? According to Dr Amya Sen, in her study of overseas students and nurses in Britain, there is a high rate of failure; but she is reckoning on all students, and not just on those chosen for support by universities, governments, and agencies. Among these there is a very high success rate, sometimes 100 per cent per annum, and it often approaches that mark. Many overseas students, in spite of discouragement and various emotional problems, as well as linguistic ones, overtake the achievement of their Western fellow students. Yet it would be wrong to pretend that all is made well by the fact that so many thousands of fully qualified students return home from Europe and North America.[11]

It has long been agreed that it is best if students do not come to study in the West at the undergraduate stage, and it has been agreed by all concerned—by the international agencies and the bilateral donors on the one side, and by the recipient countries on the other. The British Government, for example, does not give help to study in Britain if the teaching needed is available (and available at the right level) locally. This is eminently sensible; it is not only economy of money and effort, but it is educationally much better. It often harms a man to leave his environment, and most often when he is immature. Moreover, he loses a common experience with his compatriots, and risks becoming alienated from the ideals and ideas of his own culture. At best it imposes an emotional strain on him too young. Numbers of younger students come to Britain because their own countries' educational systems are even more over-burdened than our own. Some of the failures who cannot get places in their own countries come to our technical colleges, and the more determined of them ultimately earn the university places that determination deserves. In such cases we simply let them into places because we have more, not (in this hypothesis) because we have better.

No serious overseas student wants an easy qualification—and I am not now saying that he never comes down to asking for it, or that he never gets it. A great majority come to Britain to get exactly the qualifications that Britons get. A lower qualification, one specially designed for foreigners, is insulting, and is without international currency; no one wants it. Of course, a realist may finally accept what he can get; and someone from one of the few countries left where there still is not a full, however inadequate, educational system, may also realistically expect to attain only a very moderate standard, or else to take a very long time acquiring a higher one. What everyone wants out of an education system is a qualification; even those who seek pure knowledge expect a recognition which will enable them to secure, not only the respect, but, even more important, the attention, of their colleagues. The qualification must be the best, or it will have very little value. Within any country, the students in one group can press for higher recognition of their own course of studies than has been customarily given. For example, right across both the 'developed' and the 'developing' world there is a tendency for technicians to press for recognition, in one way or another, at university equivalence. The various remedies that can be tried within a country, political pressure, strikes, and so on, are not available in the assessment of foreign qualifications. International value, however much it may fluctuate, and however inaccurate and inconsistent, is earned by the qualification itself, and in the end the counterfeit will always be rejected. If, for example, the quality of the Ph. D is lowered too far, the best students will demand a new degree of a higher quality.

The position of the Ph. D student is a concentration of difficulties. In some countries a foreign Ph. D has acquired a higher status value, presumably because it is harder to come by for a number of reasons, including the obvious reason that it is necessary to travel and to live abroad at considerable expense. The inherent value of the foreign degree may in fact have been greatly exaggerated; anyone familiar with the ways universities work knows that while a degree has one face value, the real value varies according to the supervisor, examiner, department, faculty or university. In the last resort, the only accurate evaluation is the actual work that the student has produced, but the only available, and the only official, assessment of this is the degree awarded. The only evidence, therefore, that can normally be consulted, is unreliable, and the alternative evidence, the thesis presented, is normally published only technically, and is accessible only in the library of the examining university, and by photograph. It is a thoroughly unsatisfactory system, and it lends itself to exploitation by any assiduous climber of the ladder of academic promotion. One of the greatest inconveniences results from the kindness of academics. If a student has managed to get himself a great distance, it seems unkind not to admit him to work for the degree. If he then proves inadequate, he is condemned to perpetual candidature. He cannot get his degree, but he cannot return home a failure, and will have no reasonable career if he does. Compassion causes real hardship when it causes such a candidate to be admitted to study at all. Alternatively, compassion causes damage if the degree is awarded in conditions where it would not be awarded to a native student. The immediate problems of the individual candidate are solved, but new and much worse problems are created for everyone else. The native candidates may not very much mind the inflationary treatment of the degree for foreigners, because they can argue that degrees given to foreigners are compassionate and do not count. For other foreigners, the currency has been devalued. Nothing could be more harmful for fruitful exchange between the cultures concerned. A degree of suspicion of all Ph.D study has now been engendered in the minds of those who handle the funds that enable foreign students to come to British universities. People begin to say that their money will be given in future to practical courses; foreign students will in all circumstances be discouraged from taking Ph.Ds. Meanwhile, many universities have taken the practical precaution of registering students first for a higher degree of lower status which will be convertible into a doctoral registration if the candidate does well enough in the initial year. From the university end this ought to solve the problem, although there will always be some students who will be able to invoke the compassion, or sometimes the ambition, of supervisors, to get their registration turned undeservedly to the higher status course. From the point of view of an administering authority, any unplanned change of course, whether academically right or wrong, is a breach of an agreement between donor and recipient authorities. Indeed, in the eyes of the administrators the lower sounding course has begun to look more practical simply by virtue of not being doctoral.

Yet what in fact is desirable for the fruitful exchange between two cultures? The country that sends the student (irrespective of whether the student's government, or an aid donor, or the student himself privately pays) needs a man highly trained. The country where the training is done may be motivated by its wish to help the sending country's development. It may be motivated politically. I believe the best motivation is the wish to maintain communication with the foreign culture. Whatever will enable the student to work usefully on his return, to put his new expertise into practice and to fulfil a self-satisfying function (and incidentally promote his career) is what is most likely to create the best conditions for communication. The interests of the nation to which the student belongs, the interests of the nation in which he trains, and his own personal interests ought very largely to coincide. From all three points of view, the student's primary aim is to acquire a technique. Certain techniques do not lead to Ph.Ds – not yet at any rate. The student must be coming either to do a special course, or to do an ordinary course available to everyone in the country of training. Unless his country is exceptionally badly provided with teaching institutions at a certain minimum level of higher education, the reason for his coming abroad is to get a higher degree. In that case, we may argue, the higher the degree he takes, the better; and for that matter, better than taking a higher degree at all would be to come for post-doctoral discussion and research. This would be to approach the ultimate aim, perfect equality of exchange. In the meantime, what ought to be our attitude to the many who still want P h. Ds?

If that is the stage at which at this juncture we can get most mature visitors to our country, then it is good and appropriate. If, instead of considering the case of the unsuited P h. D candidate, we consider the case of the man or woman who is well suited, the value of the course becomes obvious. Because in many countries training cannot keep pace with development, the number of people available to conduct research, both in universities and in government applied science research centres, is still not enough. This is more easily remediable than the gap between rich countries and poor. Because the educational gap narrows faster than the economic gap, and even narrows when the economic gap is widening, the time will come sooner than in other matters, when we can deal on equal terms in the field of education. In the meantime we need to deal as nearly equally as possible, and one of the best steps we can take is to provide countries with adequate self-generating research centres. Instead of being suspicious of the P h. D candidate, we should encourage him in every situation where his earning the degree is impossible at home, and where his having the degree will help to build up a research centre in which his successors will be able to do the work he had to go abroad to do. The P h. D may vary enormously in actual value, and its quality may be deteriorating, but it is still given only after a period long enough to ensure that the candidate knows how to conduct research. There is nothing more important to any country; and nothing would look more 'neo-colonialist' than to give only training that falls short of this level. The P h. D is an imperfect instrument, but it is the most easily available way of getting over the hurdle that separates the ability to train fully abroad from facilities to train fully at home.

One thing is essential, and unfortunately it is hardly susceptible to treatment. As long as there is a prestige value in coming to Britain or elsewhere in the West for higher degrees in subjects where the teaching is adequate at home, the end at which all sides are aiming in their own interests will be deferred. If the quality of our degrees deteriorates sufficiently, the problem will solve itself, but we can hardly wish for this solution. It has also been pointed out, I think rightly, that a P h. D is not enough. Research cannot be confined to the only subject of which the doctor concerned has experience, if it is to live organically in a new setting. It has been suggested that the overseas student should not only do his P h. D but also at least an additional year. This is right, whenever the overseas situation is one where the research experience in the field concerned is still limited. An increase in post-doctoral visits would not only be likely to be fruitful, but might give prestige to work to which no degree is attached. Against this it must be said that there is no guarantee from a government's or a university's point of view, if no degree is given, that any work at all has been done. However, we have to act as though human beings at both ends of the operation were likely to be reasonable.

Some competent critics are opposed to the policy of aiming at self-sufficiency in research, because it is a slow process, and there are pressing reasons, if only momentary reasons, to prefer practical and applied research with immediately beneficial results, to basic or 'pure' research. This policy obviously can never produce self-sufficiency. Yet, if every party is to profit, can our aim be anything else? The result of too practical a bent may be seen sometimes in overseas universities that are in an advanced state of development, in the sense that they are staffed entirely by their own nationals; but where the work done is described as 'pedestrian' or 'non-creative' in quality. It must be—and often is—recognised that this is itself some achievement in conditions of low economic development.[12] A greater difficulty than poverty is probably inherent in trying to acculturate any technique, and its adaptation and re-orientation may need to be worked out gradually. For this basic research is likely to be the necessary foundation, for the poor as for the rich. Those who are competent to judge are the people of the countries concerned, and they, rather than our administrators, or even our academics, can tell what courses their students ought to be following in Britain, or what kinds of research their country most needs. As in the case of sending British staff to teach overseas, so in the case of determining the courses that overseas students shall follow in Britain, we, or any donor country can only offer what we are asked for, and should refrain from giving advice that is not asked for, or from feeling annoyed when our advice given is not followed.

This applies even more clearly when we consider the special course, or 'generalist specialist' course, or 'specially tailored' course, designed for overseas students only. Tailored, indeed, for whom? We cannot tailor for 'overseas', as though there were only one culture overseas; what is tailored for everyone is in fact off the peg. In this connection the Cambridge University course on development is interesting. This was fairly drastically revised for 1970–71, and the up-dating process illustrates the way in which one British university has come to look at the kind of course that we have here in mind. This course was originally designed for British Administrative Cadets before taking up their appointments in the Colonial Service. The course simply continued when there were no more cadets, by substituting their overseas successors, now no longer looking for basic training, but for in-service training. An outside observer looking at the original booklet describing the course before its reform might wonder how much it was calculated even for the needs of the original cadets, and how much they had to fit into the teaching available in the University. It was in any case unsuited to the needs of administrators from the civil services of developing countries. The most obvious change is in creating a flexible course with alternatives both in subjects and in types of work and of examination, intended to accommodate a wide variety of officer. This is evidently calculated to meet the criticism sometimes made of this type of course, that it cannot satisfy simultaneously the needs of a variety of individuals holding a variety of posts of varying seniority in a variety of countries of varying degrees of development. The old course was firmly entrenched in culture-bound subjects, even colonial history. We find, as we expect, that seminars and book-lists concerned with applied science such as agriculture and economic development are much less culture bound than those concerned with history, anthropology or international relations. The chief change is in the practical orientation towards the processes of economic development with which the students, mainly, by hypothesis, senior officials, actually have to deal. Here the emphasis has shifted towards the techniques, although there is in fact some survival of largely cultural elements (and it will be interesting to know how successful the course is in presenting these in a culture-transferable form) in the 'governmental aspects of development': 'the significance of politics in general — and to politicians, their party organisations and their ideologies in particular — as a factor in their own right in creating a climate favourable for economic and social development'. So many British political scientists and sociologists are immersed, as much intellectually as emotionally, in the political controversies of their own culture, that it will be interesting to see how far they can satisfy a public from outside cultures.[13]

The Director of one Course in Development Administration justifies 'generalist' courses primarily as an effective means for getting administrators out of their own environment and into one where they and others from different countries and from ours can argue things out, and as a means of giving them time to reflect and read and expand intellectually.[14] By the early seventies there were several courses with practical bias, based on projects, usually actual or imaginary case-studies. This is wholly admirable, if it is not biased in favour of our own culture. In one country in Asia overseas courses were considered 'as means of gaining information'; specialist rather than generalist courses were wanted, implying the acquisition of techniques without the advantages of cultural exchange and equally without the disadvantages of cultural imposition or intrusion. This whole field is singularly open to the sentiments appropriate to colonialism—paternalism, kindness, taking the victim by the hand and leading him into the light. It has been said that where most foreign (that is, Western) reform proposals founder is in that they are so far ahead of local opinions and practices that they never have a chance. This is an acute remark; if we substitute 'from' for the one culture-loaded phrase 'ahead of', it is faultless. 'Ahead' assumes that the cultural difference is one of being behind on the same road, and this may look inevitable if the techniques of management are too much embedded in their culture of origin. In fact, other societies may follow different roads, and this we shall discuss in another chapter; but if we suppose that they will indeed catch up with—or, let us say, intersect— Western attitudes at some point, that might well be in a future which we might find hard to recognise. We are dealing here with incalculable, cultural differences in time and place, not only across the world and across the past, but across the world and in the future. A technique of management which is indigestible because of differences in culture ought not really to feed our own cultural ego; there is too much that is wrong with our own affairs, and too little reason to assume that others must go along our road, on which at the moment they seem to lag behind. Not the least of the problems of courses that are created solely for foreign students is that those which are meant to cross the cultural barrier are perhaps those which are most in danger of falling at the jump. The foreign student normally expects to disentangle for himself the technique he wants to borrow from the cultural wrappings in which it is presented to native British students. This has the advantage that he is getting the genuine indigenous article, intended for home consumption, unaffected by his foreign status. If what he gets has in fact been moulded to suit his foreignness, the upwrapping has been attempted by those who only know how to wrap. The 'special' course does not pretend to be universally valid; it is meant for a few foreigners, and ideally any course on development ought equally to serve British members concerned with development in their own careers. A special course that was not cut down to fit an imaginary public from developing countries, but was shaped to make room for developers of all cultural origins, and from either side of the development divide, might be largely culture-free, and of inestimable value. This is the direction in which the Cambridge course is tending.

TEACHING AND LEARNING

The actual teaching is obviously also a source of possible cultural division. For example, it is possible to find a teacher of history who will deliberately ignore the doctrines that obtain throughout the developing world about imperialism, and who, half intending to tease, will teach instead the benefits of British imperial rule. We cannot expect that our own academics should subscribe to, perhaps not even that they should tolerate, the attitudes that are shared by the Marxist and the ex-colonial countries on this subject, but we are still, in a half-shamed way, over-sensitive to criticism of imperial rule. We welcome every sign of an intellectual reaction. Sometimes the defence of colonialism to ex-colonial students claims to be justified on the principle by which a teacher says outrageous things to a dull student from an English school, in order to provoke him into thinking for himself. In this case, however, the teacher tries the method because he thinks that the argument is right. There is no true parallel. It is not that the overseas student has always accepted uncritically an unscrupulous political attack on imperialism, the case for which now for the first time he hears truly represented. The overseas student may indeed not have heard an imperialist defend im-perialism before, but the difference is not a personal one between the thoughts of individuals, but one between the cultures. The anti-imperialist thesis can easily be held for ever, just as can the pro-imperia-list one, and it is pointless to adopt a 'teaching' attitude to what is really an attitude of our culture. I remember an English teacher in an African school: when the Americans dropped parachute troops into the Congo to save Belgian civilians, his students attacked this as imperialist aggres-sion in their wall magazine. He was so upset that he contributed to the wall magazine a picture from *The Times* of a little Belgian child stand-ing forlornly waiting on the airport for his airlift. Both sides were governed by emotion, the English teacher on behalf of the civilians and children, his students on behalf of their threatened fellow Africans; each indeed felt vicariously threatened. It was wholly pointless for either side to utter to the other; emotion prevented communication. Explo-sions of steam cannot listen to each other. This illustrates the teaching situation in England: the same cultural impediment is repeated in the case of the teacher who defends imperialism to those who are brought up to hate it, in just the same way as we are brought up to be attached to doctrines like the freedom of the press and democracy. These are the assumptions within which any discussion takes place, and outside which very little can. Teacher-pupil relations can very subtly affect or be affected by a cultural relation. There was a case of a Commun-ist from an Afro-Asian country who came to England to study; he had a Communist tutor, but later ceased to be a Communist; the bonds of a common theology may prove weaker than the differences of cultures.

I have spoken only of the cultural obtuseness of the teachers, whether at home or abroad, and this is right, because the whole question of educational aid is a question of teacher and student, the imparting of knowledge by one culture to another; and the obstacles are my subject. There may equally be obtuseness on the side of the student. The lack of sensitivity in some teachers can be paralleled by a lack of receptivity in some students. Many teachers, themselves very familiar with the cultural barrier and of long experience in overcoming it successfully, both here and overseas, know that some situations can never lead to profit to either side. A few students will never learn the Western technique of study, because they are prevented from getting at the technique by ineradicable cultural notions. To acquire a technique of historical thought, a rigid approach to documentary evidence is necessary. It is no good preserving personal or cultural prejudices against the criticism of sources. An overseas student may suspect cultural aggression on our side, if the technique is applied to some occasion of national glory in his country's history. We have too often allowed cultural intrusions not to be reasonably suspected; but this situation is an impasse. There can be no compromise about the technique, however complex the cultural influences. Let us take a very uncontroversial point. If we were to read that an Irish saint crossed the sea to Cornwall on a mill-stone, we would not believe it. The reason is a cultural one, the philosophical assumption by our culture that this is, *a priori*, impossible (or, for those who theoretically believe in miracles, negligibly possible). Yet even when we recognise that this is not the application of historical technique, we realise that historical criticism of the specific evidence will have the same result. It would not allow us to accept the alleged fact as stated by the source. The student must accept this historical technique, and recognise its validity, whether conformable to his cultural prejudice or not; he must apply the technique to the equivalent of the Irish saint in his own culture, or renounce the technique. Some cultural adaptation is required by every technique, however much this may differ from the practice of the donor culture. A total rejection of change makes it useless to try to impart or receive the technique.

The infinite possibilities of misunderstanding, either here or overseas, are only too clear. We are far from the aim of 'equal exchange'. Exchange agreements which in theory are ideal cannot be so unless they are based on actual equality. No one will doubt that he should always expect to find man-for-man equality, but if this is combined with technical inequality, it will only be a source of greater friction. A little thought shows us that this is inevitable. Straight exchanges are rare or unknown in teaching, but there are active attempts to have joint research projects theoretically based on equality. If there proves no equality in practice, the result will be most unhappy. The Briton overseas, miserable in a tropical climate, will find himself in a culture less used than his own to mechanical devices, with the consequent misunderstandings, failure to maintain equipment, uncritical reading of equipment, and so on.[15] The people on the non-British side of the exchange may find that everything, ideas and plans, originate at the other end, so that eventually they are even deprived of the use of their own equipment. The oysters should not walk with the walrus and the carpenter. In conditions of unequal exchange, there is an infinite number of things that can go wrong. They can also go right. Excessive pessimism is deterrent; but so is optimism that is disappointed.

My reason for talking about barriers, and not about the great leap across them, is to facilitate their being really crossed, and soon. The first step is to recognise them when they are there. The second is to plan their crossing. In these matters we have been too often at the mercy of tomorrow's job to have time to think about where we are going the day after. For this reason it is wise to see two-way traffic as one; the cultural difficulties are the same at either end, and very largely they derive from the inability to accept the differences of cultures. To do so is always the first lesson for anyone who lives abroad, and most human beings seem to find it a very difficult lesson. For the European teaching overseas the problem is simply one of adaptation. For the student living in Europe it is a little more complex. The problem is always this: it is easy and simple to take over a technique. The cultural adaptation, both to the process of learning from people deeply imbedded in their own culture, and of adapting one's own culture to whatever the requirements of the new techniques may be, is complex and difficult.

The problem of the Briton abroad is only a temporary one; sooner or later, he leaves. What he leaves behind him, and whether he leaves anything behind him at all, does depend on the success he has had in communicating across the barrier. Those who leave at least the technique they came to teach have done something useful; and a few have managed to effect a real cultural exchange: learning and imparting the interpretations of techniques. Cultural exchange, unlike technological exchange, is a continuous flow; what we impart will never stay the same; and what we acquire we must digest into a form suitable to take home with us. The problem of the student in Britain is permanent; what he acquires will be with him for life, and what he fails to acquire is a loss he may never repair. His is the vulnerable culture, and the one most apparently in need. This is not the whole truth. If Western society could be influenced by developing societies, it would gain much; but in practice we do not learn from the needy and vulnerable; on the contrary, they must defend themselves, so that they can preserve their identity while satisfying their need.

The situation of the individual in these cultural interchanges is the subject of the next chapter. The state of mind of people actually caught up into the process helps to answer questions like 'Do we understand what happens when different cultures act on each other?' 'Do we know what we are about, when we try to communicate across the barrier?'

Cultural Shock and Adaptation

BY CULTURAL SHOCK we mean the initial condition of disorientation in which most people find themselves when they first live in a strange culture. It can be extended to include the period of cultural adaptation which normally follows, or the alternative of settling into a stable condition of hostility. Where it results in total breakdown, the word is of course quite appropriate. All these different conditions can be summed up as effects of cultural differences on individuals. This chapter must try to distinguish clearly the cultural element within the mind of a person.

A young boy who is sent to boarding-school suffers sometimes very much because he has suddenly been thrown into an entirely strange culture. At least in the past, it was often a cruel society, especially and deliberately to the newcomer; but whether this was so or not, the boy found the new culture, all its ways, habits of thought and action, its esoteric language, its basic attitudes to life and to the individual all quite different from those to which he was used at home. A short period of intense misery normally issued in a completely successful adaptation; the boy adapted with such facility that it was genuinely easy for him to change his cultural attitudes backwards or forwards in the short journey between school and home. His only moments of difficulty usually were at the point of overlap, the departure of the school train, the visit of parents to the school, and so on.

The foreigner living in a strange society, whether the European 'expert' abroad or the overseas student in Europe, has essentially the same problem, and much the same history. He is more or less adult, and therefore less dependent on his social links, and better able to understand and analyse what is happening; but also, and for the same reason, he is less adaptable and flexible, slower to respond to something new, less intuitive. His resources are different, but his experience similar. As he adapts, like the schoolboy he will behave somewhat differently when he goes to live in the new culture; the difference between his home behaviour and abroad behaviour may be the measure of his adaptation to life abroad. In a well-balanced personality, this needs no deep change of *persona*. Anyone who is accustomed to adapt himself to the different people whom he meets or has dealings with in the ordinary way should have little difficulty. A less outgoing personality may find more difficulty in cultural adaptation, although, if he is ill-adapted to his own culture, he may be no worse adapted to a strange one. The characteristic of cultural difficulty is to be unable to behave as usual in a new cultural environment. Emotional instability must make it harder to manage without the support of a familiar background of life; perfect emotional stability, if it exists, will make it possible wholly to ignore changes of background. If it be combined with intellectual curiosity, a fair degree of emotional stability must make for positive enjoyment of cultural change. I am not concerned with the psychological analysis of individuals caught up in cultural problems, but with those problems themselves, which the state of mind may diminish or increase.

A doctor making a medical examination often decides in cases of, say, depression, that the candidate is fit for service at home but not overseas, because of the 'stress' of living abroad. This exemplifies a widespread assumption, doubtless justified by the majority of cases, although there are also those for whom, if they are accustomed to live abroad, there is greater stress in being at home. There membership of the culture makes demands that cannot, by definition of the situation, be made upon a foreigner; social neuroses are communicable in inverse proportion to other diseases, and immunity is conferred by not belonging. For the temperament of the observer, living abroad is a happy state; for the temperament of a keen participant, it is not. In any case we should expect that someone who is living abroad will retain his own cultural characteristics. (I am assuming an individual who approaches a hypothetical norm.) He will always look at what he sees in a new country from the critical angle of one accustomed to different ways and attitudes. He may acquire a considerable tolerance of the ways and opinions prevailing among his hosts; if he is personally confident and secure he can judge this thing to be good in its context, that thing to be bad in any context, a third thing to be worth adapting and borrowing. He begins to acquire an amiable tolerance for his hosts in general, and relations of mutual confidence and respect with individuals among them, from whom cultural differences now divide him only minimally. I am describing, of course, overseas residents, whether British overseas or overseas students in Britain (and the same would apply to other European countries and America).

Still speaking of traffic in either direction, it is possible to find an extreme reaction which shows itself in cultural terms, although in these cases there is a strong subjective factor, emotionally unbalanced. Extremes by definition are at alternative poles. One extreme is to see everything as hostile, alien, and to be rejected; the other is to see everything as better than anything there is at home. Both these represent a failure to adapt culturally. It can do no good to the sending or the receiving country when visits from abroad end in hatred and contempt, and no culture deserves unrelieved condemnation, still less contempt; this result must mean both a personal failure and a missed opportunity for intercultural communication. Xenophilia is almost equally disastrous; its victim can only be happy in a foreign situation, and so he, too, contributes nothing to communication. There is only communication when men or women who are strong and contented in their culture of origin can also appreciate the good they see in the communities they visit. They do not have to think anything they see worth copying; it is enough to understand. Enough, but unhappily rare. It is also true that some rectification even of the most extreme cases takes place, apparently without conscious decision. It often happens that someone who has failed to adapt, and has assumed an attitude of suspicion in the host country will react on return home, feel less hostile in retrospect, and be able, recollecting in tranquillity, to derive advantage from his experience, and so benefit communication. Unhappily the reverse also happens, and a case of xenophilia, or of apparent excessive appreciation of the host country, may turn sour in recollection.

The personal confidence of those who adapt most successfully is made up at least partly of well-integrated cultural characteristics. A rootless human being is bound to be a little unbalanced. A balanced person is the product of interlocking societies, the family, locality, past schools, service or occupation group, even national ways; familiar artefacts and customs make up the background of the mind. Someone who is able to travel, in the sense of living abroad among the members of another culture, with other ways at every level, family, school, occupation, is someone who can carry his or her culture of origin with him without fear of losing it, or of disloyalty to his background community. People like this, if they take their culture with them, need never obtrude it, can always welcome the new culture in which they are living into their hearts.

The people who come to grief are those who are fearful, and are not confident in what they carry within themselves. The *persona* that the home society has shaped is unfulfilled. When familiar sights and sounds are absent, these people are lost and afraid. There is such a thing as a case of incurable cultural shock, a case that can only be cured by repatriation. The symptoms are a combination of personal neurosis and cultural conflict. There seems to be a panic urge to go home, no different from that of a boy in his first day at boarding school, or a young child frightened and looking for the protection of a mother. Once gripped by panic, a visitor is beyond useful help. The psychologist might attempt a cure, but the obvious cure is to go home. It may happen that someone will apparently without warning suddenly insist on taking the next plane home. There are suggestions of paranoia in people who showed no such sign when they were at home, and who show none when they go home again. We can say that the ability to adapt depends on personal qualities of character and state of mind, but that the difficulty in adapting comes from the cultural differences. The desperate case fails because of an internal weakness, but what goes on in his mind, or in her mind, is a sense of fear and hatred of unfamiliar surroundings, a craving for the support of familiar people and things.

All the situations that we have been talking about are situations unaffected by whether it is the European abroad or the student from abroad that we are thinking of. So far we have talked about a universal human situation. Now we must think about the different situations that arise in cases of different kinds of traffic. The universal situation has many local variants. People who go abroad in order to teach may go expecting to be treated as important, to be deferred to as teachers, and still more as bearing the cultural superiority that they suppose whoever asks for foreign teachers must concede. People who come to Europe may come expecting to be 'got at', may come expecting that society will not be easy to understand, realising that not their teachers, but they, will have to adapt, that they will be able to do little to change their surroundings, and must watch lest their surroundings change them. Again, less likely, the teacher may go ahead in fear and trembling; the student may come in a state of confidence, expecting the ducks to be kind to the cygnet. The general observations I made earlier must be modified by differences of situation. Each person who goes abroad is at a potential disadvantage, but how much so will depend on the status that the visitor will occupy.

Much more attention seems naturally to have been given to the overseas guest who has come to study in Britain than to the Briton who has gone abroad to teach. Both are to some extent the products of the decolonisation process. The Briton is often teaching in a post which in a normal situation would be occupied by the people of the country. Because of the relative rapidity of decolonisation in the fifties of this century, or, if we prefer, because of the earlier delay in foreseeing and consenting to independence, which had to be achieved relatively unprepared, the education systems of many countries, especially in Africa, were left undeveloped. The creation of a cadre of secondary teachers, let alone of University teachers, has been, or even still is, part of the process of decolonisation that follows independence. Britons are teaching where they should be replaced as soon as possible. On the other hand the enormous numbers of foreign students that still come to Britain and to other countries in Europe, witness equally to the length of the process. Partly these people are preparing as counterparts to take the places temporarily occupied by my earlier category of overseas Britons.

Partly they are simply training overseas because there are not enough places, or no places at all, to train at home, in the various skills required. Sometimes there have not even been universities. Although the tendency is to push the age and stage at which overseas students study further and further into maturity, as suitable training at the earlier stages becomes available at home, there are still far more students overseas than there would be if their own educational systems were fully developed. Thus both the numbers of teachers in foreign posts and the numbers of students unable to find places at home are abnormally high. When this ceases to be true, we can say that the decolonisation process has ended.

It may be useful to consider first the Briton overseas. There is one set of circumstances that may in fact be called the typical decolonisation syndrome; in a more or less attenuated form it may recur as long as there is any survival of Western educational domination. Where a university is built on a British model almost every organic change will by definition move away from its exemplar. 'The African University is a child born of a European mother and adopted by African parents. . . . If suddenly denied its native requirements it becomes a weakling, if not gradually adapted it is eventually disowned by the new parent.'[1] The Briton on the staff of an African University — or of any university anywhere that is shaped after the English model — is in the difficulty that his idea of a university is just the one that is being left behind. If he stops to reflect he will see that this is not only inevitable, but actually desirable. There is no British model from which British universities similarly do not move away. Yet when organic growth coincides, as it inevitably will, with the replacement of Britons by people of the country concerned, the changes will seem to the Britons who are left as a move against them personally, probably rationalised as 'anti-British'. It is natural, although it has no logical justification, to confuse any group of Britons to whom one belongs with the British culture and the British interest and the British people, because all of them are associations of one's own identity. On reflection, we should all agree that the organisation of a university or any other institution should be in the hands of the people of the country in which it exists and to which it belongs, to the extent at least that any university anywhere is predominantly manned by its own nationals, and that the people who make it up must give it whatever shape they like. In practice, this is not all that we believe; we also believe that they ought freely to choose what we think is best for them, and this just does not happen.

Where there have been expatriates in the administration of a foreign university they will often believe that they can be more just and fair than people who are touched by local factional loyalties; but in fact their authority is resented, not only because their holding office inter-feres with the administrative career structure, but still more because no foreigner is ever more than a second-best in administration. Those foreigners who have been most successful in such positions, and who have been most sensitive to the realities of local sentiment, will be the first to agree that the outsider, however long he has lived in a country, remains to some extent an outsider, marginally insensitive to some of the shades of changing local opinion, and unable to judge the tactful and the tactical thing to do, with as sure a touch as a man who belongs by birth. This applies in obviously greater degree where a man has relatively short experience in the country. Such people are practising a craft usefully just so long as there remain no nationals to do the job. As soon as there are, they are redundant; and even while they remain irreplaceable, they are practising a skill or method for others to observe; they are not there to impose an idea. Yet when the time to replace them does come, they sometimes feel that there is public loss to the extent that their ideas are no longer followed. This is only natural human weakness; it has no substance in actual loss to the community. There is a group reaction as well as a personal one. The revolutionary head of a military Arab government referred to foreign members of staff in the university of the country in these terms: '. . . members of the inter-national community — I do not call them foreigners, because he who disseminates learning and imparts knowledge belongs to the whole of humanity'.[2] We ought to be able to say that this pious, and I think representative, sentiment, offends only if it be thought an empty phrase-ology; but in fact, even if it be taken literally, it will not satisfy many expatriate communities. It is not as members of the human race that they want to be recognised. The first reaction of such a group of any size to the independence of their host country will be to think, as gradu-ally they are replaced, still that all will be well: the ways they instituted are being carried on. Then this begins to change, and they find that after all they resent the transfer of administration. As this progresses, their numbers diminish, and as their numbers diminish, relations deteriorate. Often they deteriorate faster for the arrival of new expat-riates who quickly pick up the idea that they belong to a privileged or even dominant group, or who have actually expected to find themselves so in advance. In the expatriate community a few will bitterly resent the position; more will grumble away until the mutual confidence between them and their colleagues of the country is eroded.

It seems that this situation can recur. The expatriate community is sensitive to changes of government in a way that is different from the sensitivity of the nation that is their host, but that is definitely a group reaction. Expatriate teachers may be satisfied with the security offered by the existing government of the country. More exactly, they may be living in a sense of security; they may simply be satisfied with the security they suppose the government to offer. Then there may come a change of government, perhaps by irregular means — irregular from the point of view of Parliamentary democracy. Foreigners ordinarily find it very difficult to assess the degree of danger in a revolution; difficult even to assess the intentions or the mood of a crowd. The actual experience of living in a revolution may be disturbing, for some, traumatic, because the shock of surviving an imaginary danger can be at least as great as the shock of surviving a real danger imperfectly perceived. Having passed into a new regime with a degree of shock, the expatriate community reacts with greater suspicion than formerly. It is nearly always feasible to identify symptoms of hostility in another group of people, and, once suspicion has been aroused, this almost inevitably happens. In the case that I am imagining, this group of teachers will begin to look for new jobs in other places. Other people, perhaps having vacated the jobs the old teachers are going to, will come into the new situation and, being new to the country, and having nothing in that country with which to compare it, will be perfectly satisfied. It is quite conceivable that two groups, dissatisfied by the sense of insecurity deriving from a new regime, may change places, and both in the new situation be satisfied. When there is another revolution, the cycle may start again. Always the new arrivals in a post-revolutionary situation will feel secure, and lose the feeling in a new revolution.

The characteristic of all these situations is that they are group situations. Very much will depend on the usual 'herd' factors. If the senior people are calm, experienced and reasonable, there is less likely to be panic, but, once a panic move starts, it is likely to affect a considerable proportion of the group involved. The tendency to act and react as a community does not apply only to the basic sense of security. Satisfaction with the terms of living in a foreign situation is composed to some degree of trivia. It will often happen that all or some of a group of foreign teachers will expect administrative services that no British university will offer. At home they will expect to fetch the plumber themselves. Overseas it often happens that because of language difficulties, or because of unfamiliarity with the local way of doing things, foreigners are reluctant to undertake quite ordinary chores. Here their sense of not belonging is operative. People also resent slow or uncooperative treatment, or occasional discourtesy from clerks or minor officials. It is not clear that they have been treated differently from any national of the country; often they have in fact not been treated differently from the way they would be (and are used to being) treated in their own country, where discourtesy can also occur. This situation arises in the sense of cultural difference, of belonging to a separate and, of course, superior community. It commonly spreads by infection. It may involve spontaneous 'action groups' of two or three, possibly because each man wants to show the next that he is tough, or will not be 'put upon'. It is more often true of a group, than of individuals, that they fail to realise how they look to others, or, indeed, how closely they are observed. Foreign 'experts' are notorious, sometimes, and in some countries, for their importation of 'rat-race' attitudes, for their total lack of any sense of solidarity with their colleagues in the host country, and for changing their expert advice to suit the supposed predilections, only vaguely apprehended, of the highest local authority to whom they have access. This applies most often in the case of experts in Ministries, but can do so also in universities.[3]

Another kind of cultural conflict altogether derives from the different phases of development of different cultures. The particular phase of our own culture currently prevailing is not acceptable in many other societies, and, equally important, we have so strong a missionary sense that we are often quite unwilling to subordinate our own cultural notions, even when we are in the position of guests, to the host culture. We are so pleased with ourselves for what we call our permissiveness that we are unwilling to be permissive about the impermissiveness of others. It is surprising how easy it is to be fanatical about being unfanatical. A key factor, and relevant here, is our opposition to what we call 'hypocrisy'. If a society forbids some kind of behaviour, anyone who defends the society but offends its code is a 'hyprocrite'; indeed, if a society forbids behaviour in public which it permits in private, all its members by this view become 'hypocrites'. Can we permit this hypocrisy? Are we content, if the host society will leave us to our own devices, to allow it in turn to continue in its hypocritical ways? No more than our missionary predecessors, but in a different cause, can we leave others to go their wicked ways in peace. All these questions are important, in matters which can cause acute feeling and controversy: dress, manners, entertainment, convention and, what we seem most to care about, sexual morality. We are not here concerned with politics. Members of foreign communities do sometimes have political attachments, and do sometimes exploit their position to play at politics. This is only marginally a cultural question, and most states, politically left, right or centre, can look after their own security problems, at least as concerns the movements of foreigners. These are more carefully plotted than the foreigners always realise. We are concerned with conventional actions, which are watched less officially, but doubtless just as closely. If our culture throws up new conventions of dress, appearance, even behaviour, it does so within its own scheme of affairs, and is rather less revolutionary than it looks. Cross-culturally this is not so obvious. There is a real arrogance in saying that we are so sure of our new ways that we have the right to intrude them on other people, whose own cultural development is slower in the same direction, or even going in a totally different direction. To intrude them may produce a serious and painful conflict; we must be very sure of ourselves and the rightness of our cause to justify this; and it is impossible to call such certainty anything less than missionary zeal. If we are sure that the cause is right, almost certainly there is a duty to impart it. If it is our duty to intrude, why not to impose it? But, intrusion or imposition, this is 'colonialism'.

There can be no difference between the Victorian missionary preaching Christianity, which was what he believed, and the young man of our day preaching the pop life, at least in respect of cultural imperialism. It is no good saying that the new ways are better, and more progressive, and for the good of all, because that is exactly what the Victorian missionary said and believed. The fact is that any cultural intrusion, even if we concede that it is good, is doing good to other people, not leaving them to find their own good. Any unguest-like cultural behaviour can quite reasonably be called neo-colonialist, and the next chapter considers this question in more detail. For the moment we are concerned with the behaviour of people living abroad, and the ability to conform to the local culture to some degree in at least some situations, and in any case enough to avoid conflict and intrusion, is part of a successful adaptation of living abroad. To maintain a separate community is in some sort of a failure, and even the national clubs that are so common abroad — American, Russian, British, French, German, Italian, Greek, Syrian and the rest — are all confessions of not wanting to live abroad while forced to reside there. The failure is incomparably worse if it creates an actual conflict, instead of just going on behind closed doors, whence denigration of the country is carried only by the servants to the security officers of the country.

Conflict between the guest culture of an expatriate community and the host culture of the country may be more or less dramatic. Conflicts arising from bad manners are the least dramatic, especially when the bad manners, as so often happens, are confined to the guest. It is astonishing how often a foreigner will expect that manners should conform to his own home norm. This may be caused by the failure to recognise what changes from one culture to another. There are people so parochial as really to believe that only one code of manners (let alone one code of behaviour) exists. Even those possessed of some imagination, or capable of admitting the knowledge acquired by experience, often have more difficulty than might be expected. I shall analyse one instance. A British 'expert' is preparing a report on an institution of higher education in an Afro-Asian country. He is invited to a dinner in his honour by a senior official concerned. The dinner is late, is served as a buffet in stages; the visitor has to work late. He leaves before the last stage of dinner is finished serving. This causes deep offence, much deeper than he realises. He has destroyed his own purpose. One result will be that his report will be taken less seriously to the extent that his personal esteem has dropped; and that has dropped because he has offended against the code of behaviour accepted. Cultural differences here include these points: the visitor underestimates the value of giving and receiving as a means of communication, probably he underestimates the value of communication, or the ease with which it may be interrupted and the harmful consequences that may follow; he is impatient of whatever impedes efficiency, and he estimates efficiency in crude terms of the product in written words. He could make an excuse about feeling ill, if he is not prepared to work later than he would otherwise have had to do; his impatience with courtesies suggests a cultural intolerance.[4]

Conventions of dress come on the borderline of morality, because they are supposed to imply kinds of sexual morality, for example, women's short skirts, men's long hair. This is not a point worth labouring; its implications are obvious. The effect of an action, and therefore its cultural position, is different from culture to culture. The exposure of female flesh will be anaphrodisiac where people are used to it; where the contrary applies it will be resented as immoral. This relates to the cultural rather than the moral field, because the moral implications vary with the culture. It varies too from time to time; the exposure of the female ankle, at a time when it was not customary, would have the same effect as the exposure of the breasts at the time of writing. In countries or societies where females are not free to mix with society, it may be assumed from the side of the host that every European female is promiscuous, and this was even a tendency at a time when it certainly did not correspond with the facts. On the other hand, this is a level of cultural difference where new conventions are fairly readily learned, and most females that are not promiscuous are able to establish the fact, if it is a fact, without too much difficulty. It is also a level at which a determination to defy the local conventions is likely to lead to trouble, and one where a degree of compromise is likely to be successful; those to whom any sort of compromise is wrong will have to bear the consequences. This is a purely cultural situation.

The area of sexual morality is also one where the group loyalties of expatriates often come quite powerfully into play. A factor here is probably the conviction that English society is superior because progressive, so that any criticism of its progressive attitudes seems to diminish its

superiority. I will take one example. A man from a third country, himself Afro-Asian, is teaching in another Afro-Asian country. He is psychologically compelled to disown 'oriental' ways; he is totally alienated
from anything resembling his home culture, and the culture where he
is teaching does resemble it. (He has in fact 'gone native' in Western
Europe.) He enters into a sentimental attachment to a female pupil,
also not a national of the country. In a spirit of defiance of the 'oriental'
and of local convention, he meets his girl in his public office, and this
attracts attention from students. They regard this behaviour as an
affront to their religion, which forbids anything that resembles a public
display of love-making (by human beings). There is an outcry, and the
authorities express disapproval, and the question of dismissal or resignation arises. At this point the European expatriates, who regard love-
making in quasi-public conditions as normal, and certainly not as particularly objectionable, start indignantly to organise a petition. This is
taken by the people of the country as being, what indeed it is, a defiance
of their local attitudes to proper behaviour. The easily foreseeable
result is to secure maximum penalties for the delinquent. In the light
of this publicity no compromise or mitigation can now be 'arranged';
both sides have reached a state of intense mutual irritation. Yet it was
unnecessary; each side based its self-righteous conviction on opinions
that were purely cultural (the expatriates would have taken a very
different view only one generation ago). It is a conscious resistance of
cultures which has provoked intransigence. The foreigners are the
more intransigent, because they are importing their attitudes; however
much they may dislike the contrary opinion, it is the opinion prevailing
in the place.

To sum up this side of overseas living, a body of foreigners tends to be
united by criticism of one of its members, whether for casual bad
manners or for something more serious; bad manners in any case tend
to cut the foreigners off, by impeding true communication. Accusations
of illiberalism, hypocrisy or unwarranted intrusion into private matters
are made against the host society, of which the European community
is intolerant by reason of its very liberalism. Any such communal reaction provokes in its turn the resentment of the host community. A
community does not like to have to deal with a separate community
within it; it is like a body with a growth that may become malignant;
its instinct is to reject the strange entity. The host society wants to deal
with foreigners as individuals; to the dependent individual the greatest
generosity may be shown. The foreign individuals do not want to
depend on generosity; they look for support to those who share their
cultural preconceptions. Like the Black Power people in America, they
do not want to depend on the generosity of a majority. Yet probably

this is not the basic source of conflict. The guest, by definition, is not in the position of Black Power supporters, a citizen deprived of a citizen's rights. He is a guest, he proposes to stay for a short time, and has no permanent stake in the country. A condition of dependence is in the nature of the status he had deliberately chosen or accepted. The underlying fault in this situation is therefore probably the belief of any European community that ultimately all other cultures must come in time to conform to our Western or Northern pattern.

Some of the other characteristics of foreign communities in the kind of situation we are envisaging we must take in less detail; and the background to some we have already dealt with in the previous chapter. These are less communal in type. It is curious that there is no detectable correlation between theoretical liberalism about race, and the natural absence of a sense of racial superiority. We earlier noted this false and vulgar sense, which may be aggravated by individual weaknesses of character, as when one (European) scholar publicly reproves another (non-European) for unscholarliness, for example, for anticipating the results of research, and then falls into the same error himself. By what right was the reproof delivered? We cannot avoid the impression that this is an example of double judgement; the personal rivalry would seem too obvious to allow it to occur, if there were not some idea that the speaker inherits first rights in the principles of modern scholarship. Certainly there are examples of academics, especially young academics, who do not treat their superiors, Afro-Asian in nationality, as better than themselves in their own subjects, although they have the same, or better, and in any case British, qualifications, and much longer experience. I do not think that most of those to whom this applies are aware of their own attitudes; but they act as though they enjoyed an inbred advantage in an academic technique. This, of course, if it were true, would mean that a technique could not be totally acquired; it would mean that it was attached to the culture, and every man, of course, has a superiority over anyone of another culture, in his knowledge of his own. I do not believe that techniques are undetachable in this way. Occasionally we encounter an explicit cultural hostility. In theory, any case of junior lack of respect might be the product of generation gap; often in practice we know that this is not so, and when it is couched in terms of traditional European hostility to Islam, if that is the religion of the country, or of contempt for a pagan religion (animist, henotheist, and so on), its cultural quality becomes explicit. Finally, the phenomenon that I have earlier described, where a Western scholar believes that he has achieved a high standard in his study of a subject unknown in the West, although well known in the country where he is living, may be just another example of the failure to adapt. So is it when a group of expatriate scholars find it natural to undertake a combined-discipline research project without bringing a local expert into it on an equal basis.

A few individual case-histories would lighten the stodge of this stage of our subject, but it is practicable only to hint at the kinds of behaviour that may be observed. One is to dramatise; there is a type of fantasy which seems to be acted out from memories of classical travellers' tales. If distant parts are quaint and amusing because they are different, nothing is so funny, nothing so self-flattering as familiarity with the exotic. Drama can be extracted from something as ordinary as a drum beating, if it beats in Africa. Suppose it to be accompanied by clapping: some sort of dance is in progress; sounds travel far in the open, and the weather is warm; culturally nothing stranger is happening than goes on at any party or in any English dance-hall, but childhood memories of adventure stories in Africa, or of African films, give a fantasy value to the African setting. This sort of dramatisation is occasionally revealed in a careless report or an unguarded letter home; but if it becomes a deliberate posture, the fantasy has gained the upper hand. Of course, this sort of thing has no value for intercultural understanding; rather the contrary. Dramatisation of the unfamiliar may well go with suspicion and resentment, especially when the people of the country take over positions of authority in the teaching world; they are resented because they are not being, and have not been, taken seriously as people at all. The opposite extreme, exemplified when a teacher marries into the country, may result in a happy adaptation. Despite the problems that any kind of mixed background may cause to a marriage, it is hard to imagine a more effective way of crossing the barrier, or at any rate of getting into position to do so.

Cases of percipient panic among teachers overseas are relatively rare, probably because these teachers enjoy a privileged position, but cases do occur, with symptoms that a layman thinks of as paranoid, and that are certainly not less than hysterical. Such cases lead quickly to a medical clinic. When a teacher goes overseas, there is usually an initial period of irritation with administrative arrangements; often an expectation that British officials responsible for the care of teachers abroad will be able to give more support than is in fact possible (or necessary) leads to disappointment. The less easily a teacher can adapt to the strange environment and mix happily with his local colleagues, the more service he will feel he is owed by British officials. Sometimes the teacher feels surrounded by enemies, and believes that the British official ought to intervene to enforce the teacher's authority, as though there were a simple colonial situation. In such cases, there is a strong cultural constituent to the instability of the individual; curiously enough this 'paleo-colonial' attitude does not necessarily occur in members of the class from which the former colonial rulers were drawn. Termination of contract is the only cure. Yet such cases may quite naturally end with all the excitement forgotten, in a nostalgic retrospect of the whole inglorious story, remembered as a splendid and courageous adventure, even as a happy time. Most well-adjusted teachers with overseas experience can remember a few cases of this sort. Chronic cases of teachers who only partly settle down may occur more often. Again, personal failure is often attributed to an objective situation. The teacher is horrified to meet a latent or even open xenophobia, which he thinks of as assuming many intricate and subtle forms; perhaps a little sensible briefing to explain that all countries — all human beings — tend to xenophobia might reduce the number of people made miserable in this way, but there are many who can recognise xenophobia in themselves only with difficulty; it is in the nature of the disease that it is the victim who is sensitive to it. It is possible also to meet the other extreme, the teacher over-responsive to the host society. In every occupation there are always some who feel that they alone understand a foreign country that they live in, and fear that their knowledge is not utilised or appreciated. They seem to be looking for the official recognition that would amount to making them what all the anti-imperialist world never hesitates to designate as spies. Sometimes this may be the truth; we may assume that no intelligence system will refuse gratuitous information; yet, if the espionage syndrome penetrates the educational world, the harm that results outweighs immediate political advantage, if any there be. Such a situation, like the others we have been considering, arises chiefly out of individual maladjustment to an alien culture. Many different ways of dissociation from local society exist.

In general, what applies to outwards traffic applies also to traffic inwards. Certain questions involved here I must exclude. The question of 'colour' I have already excluded; but it is worth noting that Dr Sen observes a tendency to attribute a normal rate of failures and social misfortunes to colour prejudice, to do so, that is, on inadequate objective evidence.[5] Most people with experience would agree with this. Is this, however, in any way a different situation from that of the European teacher overseas? If there is a difference, it seems only to be a difference of function. Teaching and learning have very different implications. This determines the answer to another question: Why should the foreign student integrate with the host community?

In teaching a technique, it ought (in theory) to be possible only to transmit it; the receiving side (as we shall see in more detail in the next chapter) will filter any cultural accretions that may be attached to the techniques. In practice it is not possible to transmit anything without some further communication, without a tincture of natural sympathy, so that if the recipients do not want the donor's culture, it is the donor — the teacher — who has to make the effort to bridge the cultural gap. If the teacher is overseas, he is the minority figure; he must learn to transmit in terms acceptable to the culture whose guest he is. The postion of the overseas student in Britain is largely the reverse of this. It is he who is in the minority; if he wanted to, he could not change the masses round him in any important way, and his only motive for wanting to change them in a minor way would be in order to make his own country and culture better understood. He needs to understand his teachers, but he does not really need them to understand him. He is not in England to exchange knowledge, to give as well as to receive. Unless he has the peculiar vocation to travel, which in fact few people seem to be born with, he can achieve his purpose without integrating into the host community at all. He is in the same relation to his hosts as are, for example, English commercial men trading in his own country. They will live apart, play English games, eat English food, drink English drinks and see no one but the English, in a British club; so may the overseas student do with his compatriots in Britain. The traders will leave his country with their profits, or at any rate their salaries, and he will leave their country with a new skill and new knowledge which he can put to use at home. Both have done well for themselves. Neither has done much to improve communications between their two societies.

Most British university towns contain a large enough group of overseas students for it to be possible for many of them to live largely with their compatriots. If it is possible for them to do so, especially if they share a language as well as a nationality, they will see a great deal of each other, and not very much of their hosts. To speak without a barrier, without the need to look for the words to express the thoughts; to speak without fumbling for the polite thing to say, and without worrying about what will interest the person you are talking to; to be able to speak about things of familiar interest to yourself; to be able to eat familiar food at familiar times, in fact just to be able to relax; this is what the British overseas seek, and this is what many overseas students here seek too. Some people find a genuine pleasure in exploring new conventions of thought, in finding out the character of a strange culture, and, if so, they enjoy living abroad. They do in fact live abroad, rather than live at home when physically abroad. These people are lucky, but they are not the majority in any nation. Unless those abroad are only those who like being abroad for its own sake, there will have to be some sort of compromise; and there are far more people abroad than want to be.

A glance at some of the cases of students who break down does not suggest that there is a relation between cultural shock and the type of culture of origin. All cases do suggest the interplay of personal mental or emotional weakness with the cultural situation in which the students find themselves in Britain. When a British academic comments on an East European's elementary critical sense, or naïve understanding of an academic discipline, we easily perceive that the student in question has had a serious cultural gap to bridge. When a student's intellectual foundations are judged to be shallow by a British host department, it can never be quite clear whose capacity to cross from culture to culture is defective, the student's, his hosts', or both. A British university expresses surprise when a Latin American student, accustomed and habituated to life in the USA, becomes depressive in Britain. In this country we may be resigned to following in American footsteps, but we usually believe that at the present moment our neuroses are less infectious and even less severe. In fact it is not at all easy to pick a consistent pattern out of the troubled minds of students' failures. We find a cheerful extrovert from a neighbouring country in Western Europe, robust, possessing intellectual powers above the average and a stimulating personality : he suffers from severe mental strain and breaks down for lack of self-confidence. Another West European feels that he is an isolate, and that his hosts are alien and hostile, really only because he misses the finer points of conversation; missing that little, he feels out of it, he cannot feel that he is 'one of the boys'. He too breaks down. A North African feels 'quite desperate' and 'absolutely unproductive'. Yet another West European (from a third country) seems entirely changed from the self-possessed young man who 'set out confidently' four months earlier. The number of those that break down is not great, and certainly not enough to provide an adequate statistical sample ; but my examples, chosen at random,[6] show no sign of there being a difference between students according to the regions of the world from which they come. There is no indication that Europeans are less liable to suffer cultural shock, although they come from cultures closely resembling our own, and it might be expected that there would be a higher incidence of shock among those who come from more different cultures. The element common to all cases seems to be the sense of isolation, of not being able to manage in the absence of familiar supports—or to tolerate a scene in which no familiar landmark is in sight—and particularly every failure to communicate is a source of misery. Language plays an obvious part in this, even in the case of someone whose English is excellent, if he expects more than his command of the language can give.[7] It is indeed the expectation that is crucial. If, as a result of all that is said nowadays in many parts of the world about colour prejudice in

Britain, a man coming from Asia or Africa expects to be treated worse than he is in fact treated, the cultural shock will be less than that of a West European who expects to be accepted as one of the boys and finds that this just does not happen. The Afro-Asian has steeled himself to face the worst, and has not expected to find friends, just a technology. He can stay buttoned up for the year or two, or even five years, that he may be in Europe, especially if compatriot company is to be had. He has no shock, and he need not try to adapt.

One problem is always with us, anywhere in the world, in any human being, and that is loneliness. 'The YMCA,' a Latin American once said, 'has been a very nice place full of kindness and homeless love'. *Homeless love* sounds culturally quaint to us but it is what people want, and, often through both their fault and their hosts' fault, rarely what they find. Some African critics have said that the African students in particular (but it doubtless applies to all who are used to warmth of friendship and to family affection) feel the lack of their families. This is one reason why such students marry while they are here; it is also a reason why some bring their wives with them, or even marry in order to come. If it is true that Africans feel this more than others, the reason can only be that more than others they are accustomed to the personal warmth of a family; it is true that there is not necessarily personal warmth just because there is a large family structure; and so some may feel this less than others, but all must feel it somewhat. A temporary liaison is quite likely to lead to unhappiness; it may or it may not imply integration. Every human relation that the student forms — close or distant — will depend on the quality of the individuals concerned. There is no way to 'integrate' a foreign student; if he is integrated, he is no longer foreign. The foreigner who remains foreign — and there can be no interchange unless he does so — can take part, a guest's part, in the communal life around him. We can hope that he will be reasonably detached, neither hostile nor over-friendly, with friends of his own nationality and friends from among his hosts, living a life that is spent partly in the home atmosphere and partly in the local one. It is abundantly clear that no student wants forced or dutiful kindness. His contact with his hosts must spring naturally out of some occasion or common interest. It is in fact the occasion or the common interest that alone makes any cross-cultural meeting of any sort whatever possible.

The great difference is of course the feeling that there is a difference. The person abroad is aware of what is around him and aware by memory of the culture which he has left and to which he will return; lastly he is aware of the compromise, more or less biased towards the one culture or the other, by which he is actually living. Every foreigner, every human being abroad, has an in-between culture of his own, sometimes successfully adapted and sometimes not. The best that we can expect is a background of family life in a house or flat, from which both husband and wife can come out, and to which the people of the country can be invited. Mutual entertainment is a vastly happier thing than one-sided entertainment. It is better for the foreigner to live in his small family enclave which gives the security of familiarity; it will be easier for him to come out to meet people. This is the pattern of successful adaptation for either the overseas teacher from Britain or the overseas student in Britain. I mentioned earlier, speaking of temporary cultural adaptation, that the over-friendly visitor sometimes becomes over-critical when he returns home, perhaps because he feels his period of apparent adaptation as one of disloyalty to his own culture. When the reverse occurs, it may be because there was a sense of uncertainty or apprehension in the foreign setting, a fear of alienation from the true parental culture, and when the traveller returns home, he realises that he need not have feared, and can recollect his former hosts with greater justice. A man who can see nothing of value, of course can pass nothing of value back, but he will equally be prevented from doing so, if he has surrendered any important part of his own culture, and ceased to be able to communicate with his own kind. The value in learning to appreciate a strange culture is in exact proportion as we retain a firm hold on our own.

Techniques and Cultures

WHEN OVERSEAS NATIONS send their students to Britain (or to other countries in Europe, or to America), or when they invite Britons (or other Europeans or Americans) to teach overseas, they want our techniques, certainly; our culture, only if it is the price that must be paid. *Prima facie*, they can take the techniques alone, and the burden of proof is on those who say otherwise; but investigation is useful, even when we do not expect to reach certainty. Is the current culture of our own area, which is scientifically the most advanced, the product of the sum of its history, or only of its present technology? In the latter case, must we expect the same technology to create the same culture universally? Or is it open to other cultures to make a different use of it? Does the character of Western culture tend naturally to produce the most advanced technology and the most efficient techniques? Or is there an interaction of all the factors? The most useful way to try to answer these questions, to which there may well be no clear and unequivocal answer, is, first to speculate about the supposed effects of modernisation on other cultures, if only to see whether any assumption at all can be justified; and, secondly, to ask whether our own Western culture can be seen to have any necessary relation to our techniques.

Why do we expect the adoption of our techniques to change other cultures in the same direction as our own? Our techniques are not really radical. They do not enable us to do something entirely new. They enable us to do what we can do already, but to do it better, or faster, or more easily—travel, talk, listen, eat and so on; we use aeroplanes, telephones, wireless and deep-frozen foods, but the same purpose was achieved by horse, or word of mouth, or the gossip of the market-place, or a slice of dried meat. When we substitute the tractor for the horse-collar we improve our technology, but we do not have to re-orient our minds. Just considered as techniques, these changes are not really as revolutionary as was the invention of writing; they are not more revolutionary than the substitution of the alphabet for cuneiform. It is not so difficult to cross the cultural barrier that is created by doing the same thing in a new way. We cross such a barrier whenever the tempo of our own lives fluctuates, if only to take a holiday.

The real change is not in the thing done but in the numbers of people doing them; old things done in new ways by many more people. The richest people and the most powerful always, in any political system, remain apart, but more and more of the poor are becoming, if not rich, at least able to consume more richly than once the richest could hope to do. This is what 'development' is about. Consumer welfare has extended to so many in Western society; how much further will it go? According to the economists the more we have the more there will be, and the planners and developers know just how to set about it. The public wonder how there can be anything but a thinner spread of the same total; and this includes many in the underdeveloped countries, who accordingly assume the truth of the anti-colonialist theory. Certainly the benefits of modernisation do not extend everywhere or reach everyone; but culturally it is true that those who do not yet enjoy the benefits have already consented to them. We should expect this, because it is for the masses that the improvements of the present day are calculated. Of course, the cultural effects of extending benefits to the masses are incalculable, anywhere in the world; we do not even know how far the apparent changes within our own culture are the result of the growing equality of our society and the self-expression of formerly oppressed classes. We can only assume that the process is unlikely to be without results. On the other hand, none of this is a reason to assume that the same process in different circumstances will not produce different effects, or that it must obliterate diversified cultures. The masses may produce something new but not everywhere the same new thing.

It is sometimes argued that any culture of affluent masses must be the same, and that we merely see its most advanced stage in our own society, more specifically in its American form. This must mean that the determining factor is either numbers, or the combination of numbers with affluence: put crudely, either the overcrowding of the rich, or just overcrowding. As a result of increased medical services and a somewhat better organisation of food supplies, there is already gross overcrowding in many areas, without compensating economic development, or extension of privilege. Even in Western Europe, overcrowding came first, and afterwards advantages were distributed to the unprivileged. In fact, we already know that overcrowding affects the behaviour of either rich or poor, because it is not a new experience; all that is sure is that the town swallows up more and more of the country, and it is not at all clear that the consequences need or are likely to be everywhere the same. Our conurbations and the greater conurbations projected for the future are only an extension of the concentrations of population already known to humanity; and though we see that cities change cultural characteristics, we also see that different cities do so in different ways in spite of certain common factors. So far, the life of the people in different urban cultures is different, even when the architecture seems interculturally standardised. Very probably over-population causes, in various ways, a general loss of moral fibre, but we have no reason at all to think that different communities must recover only by means of some single formula, or to suppose that they cannot develop differently under the same stress of overcrowding.

We are also told that conditions of manufacture always destroy existing cultures, for example, by substituting monotonous factory chores for individual skills, or replacing stable social structures by mobile labour. These are guesses, uncontrolled by statistical comparisons difficult or impossible to obtain. New skills are constantly created, and the proportion of monotonous to interesting work in industry and in unmechanised farming is incalculable. There may indeed be a marginal advantage in unskilled rural occupations; there is an element of decision in using a hoe which is a little better than the concentration of attention in monotonous conditions which industry may require, but monotony is not a revolutionary experience for the human race. Galleyslaves would recognise it. Indian sweepers might even envy monotony that is not excremental. There is no real assessment of the change in cultural content imposed by new techniques on a pre-existing culture. So too with mobility of labour. Many rural societies are familiar with mobility already, either semi-nomadic family groups (and semi-nomadic groups are all that industry requires) or with wholly itinerant labour where a cash crop prevails over subsistence farming. Its mobility is not new, it is hard to believe that it is the cause of cultural breakdown.

It is not so obvious that modernisation must create one single culture. Let us glance, however superficially, at some of the arguments which claim to show that the outside world cannot retain its old ways, if it wants to absorb Western techniques of development. For example, it is said that industrialisation must destroy family life. It is said that developing countries over-educate people in the arts and the law, but cannot train technicians. It is said that the 'third' world is unrealistic in politics, too romantic to compete with the politics of our hard-faced business men. Of Muslims it is said that they can never become administratively efficient, let alone industrially productive, while they observe Ramadan. I think that all these are based on false antitheses; but let us take them in turn, in reverse order.

The argument about Ramadan runs like this: if Muslims keep Ramadan, they cannot compete, because it means a month when no work is done; and if they do not fast, they are no longer Muslims. This is not altogether ridiculous. Ramadan has often been made an excuse for idleness, and it can genuinely disturb people's capacity for work. An office worker who is determined need not let observing Ramadan affect his output, as has been proved time and again; but a manual worker has more excuse, and he has most excuse in respect of not being able to replace the water he loses while he sweats. So there is a difficulty. I once argued frivolously that, if Arab workers did not strike, they could use the time saved to observe Ramadan, but as they need to strike as much as anyone else, another answer is better. Industry can organise a great deal of leisure for the workers, and should be able to do so increasingly. I do not believe that it would be impossible to work out an accommodation for Ramadan. If, on the other hand, we suppose that the Muslim world will give up its faith as Europe has given up Christianity, the problem solves itself; but it does not necessarily do so at the expense of Islamic culture, because a hypothetical post-Islamic world would not be at all the same as the actual post-Christian world. The Islamic stress on the *umma*, for example, would be likely to survive in a much stronger sense of community.

It is sometimes said that the peoples of the less developed parts of the world are willing to cut off their noses to spite their faces. It is meant by this that they want to take political action that seems right to them, although it must tend to their disadvantage. This extreme romanticism may have only a low survival value in the international rat-race; but it is interesting that, in one respect at any rate, Europe has trodden the same path as some developing countries trod nearly forty years earlier. I well remember the amused contempt with which we used to treat the students of the Arab world, when demonstrating or striking; but they argued that while they were without family responsibilities was the time to run political risks, and to speak for others who were not so free. 'All students should be in the front line of the revolutionary forces by virtue of their education.'[1] This is a recent restatement of an old doctrine. Many years later, European students started to share something of this attitude, and it was treated as if it were quite new and hitherto unheard of. The heroic campuses of America and barricades of Paris were not the models, but the copies. It is always possible that Europe will come to adopt other attitudes already familiar in the developing world. At least it is no longer possible for Europeans to be sure that practices that are new to them are new to the world. Many tendencies appear unexpectedly and unmistakably in all parts of the world, but in different cultural forms, and with no obvious causal relation. It is impossible to think of all those phenomena that occur everywhere as having originated in Europe. The more probable hypothesis is that common situations do not have their source exclusively or primarily in Europe and America, and so are not the necessary product of industrial or technological society.

The question of education is itself a case in point. The overproduction of arts or law graduates, to whom we should surely add those in social sciences, may be uneconomic, but it is common to 'developed' and to

'developing' countries. So is a tendency to satisfy the demand by technicians for degree-level qualifications. Despite economic factors, it
may be right to give people the education they want, rather than the
education society needs them to have, but it cannot be a good thing in
Europe and a bad thing at the same time in Africa. It may be because
the developing countries cannot, as Britain can, live on a technological
past, that economists recommend that manpower assessments should
determine their education systems. When we are asked how education
developed in our own countries, we have to say that it developed just
as it is doing in the newer and poorer countries—in response to demand
from ordinary people who thought it would raise their standard of
living. We are told that the economic gap is widening, between the
more highly and the less developed countries, but the educational gap
is narrowing. It is narrowing in the first place because there is less
illiteracy in developing countries. There is no educational gap as great
as that between the literate and the illiterate. In the second place it is
narrowing because most countries can afford to have University level
(and still more primary and secondary school) teachers of their own
nationalities, whereas formerly they depended on foreign teachers, as
some must do for a time yet. A country can afford to have an unambi-
tious but effective educational system in the sense that it can find and
pay the teachers. It may not pay them very much, but whatever it
costs, it is likely to prove more costly to reject the popular demand for
a chance to learn. In any case, the trend is everywhere the same, and
ignores levels of economic development.

Economists as such must confine themselves to economic factors,
omitting outside considerations. None of the social sciences claims
mathematical certitude. Many academics concerned with different
aspects of development would agree that there are great uncertainties,
and a large area of speculation. P. C. Lloyd, in his *Social Change in
Africa*, does not accept the claim that the extended family militates
against economic development (supposedly, capital dissipated in gifts
is unproductive).[2] Without justifying real waste, we may in all rever-
ence (and aptly) paraphrase the Gospel, and ask what advantage it is to
society to develop economically, and lose its humanity. Must social
welfare be impersonal? So much is speculative. We hear it said that
family life is bound to be destroyed by an industrial society which separates the members of a family, often by considerable distances. We do
not really know what factors determine the break-up of the family; it is
only a guess that the mobility of labour was the cause in the Western
world. It is an equally good guess that it need not have broken up;
families have held together in spite of distance. Equally to the point,
families in the West have broken up without being affected by mobility

of labour; it is the extended family that this is supposed to weaken, and it can hardly affect the divorce rate, which we must surely attribute to other factors. The 'nuclear' as much as the 'extended' family is affected. Although public opinion in the West no longer ostracises those who show no generosity or affection, a great deal of family attachment survives; and, at the other extreme, it is as likely to survive the threat of the 'drop-out' communes as in the twelfth century it did the competition of cenobitical enthusiasm. The present situation is easy to misjudge. Certainly developing countries may do well not to allow themselves to be bluffed into losing flourishing institutions unnecessarily. Europeans living in those countries used to deplore the free and easy admission of the friends and relations of patients to hospitals; this destroyed not only hygiene, but also the discipline and order without which it was difficult to create the desired atmosphere of frigid inhumanity. This situation recurred in all sorts of 'developing' areas. Now our doctors, and especially the paediatricians, are saying that admitting the patients' friends and raising their morale is exactly what we ought to be doing. New hospital designs favour this new thought. My point is just that no one should think that it is necessary to adopt all the Western concomitants of a technique; and that terrible destruction can be done to a culture for no good reason at all. It has yet to be proved that a society cannot adjust, more successfully and more coherently than we have done, to a high degree of urbanisation. Neither can I prove the contrary, The question is open.

In ordinary conversation, which is the usual channel of cultural intolerance, we hear a number of antitheses which are familiar but false. For example, it is often assumed that there is a necessary correlation between mechanical ability and a less warm or casual or human way of life. If Europeans are cold or inhuman, is this because of their technology, or of their inherited culture, or of the way they have allowed the two to interact; if the last, was it necessary? Europeans tend to excuse themselves by saying that the kindness and hospitality which survive in Arab, African, and Asian society are incompatible with an attitude that maintains machinery properly and runs business concerns with computerised efficiency. If so, for the sake of efficiency, all mankind must become cold. I should suggest that there may indeed be a correlation between the failure to maintain machinery and the social situation in which the necessity for doing so is not perceived (and least perceived by the individuals immediately responsible); but this is not the same thing, and no one has yet shown that it can only be remedied by a change in social values. Pockets of kindness and hospitality survive in the Celtic parts of Britain, and a Highlander or islander who has been twenty-five years at sea as a ship's engineer, as many have been, returns to his home and fits in as well as if he had never kept a ship's engines turning. This may seem a trivial example, and admittedly it does not prove very much; but it does prove that there is no inherent mental incompatibility between the two attitudes. I shall assume that it is a popular myth confined to our own culture that the attitudes appropriate to mechanical efficiency and to human warmth are psychologically incompatible.

We should approach the problem with a number of possibilities in mind. One is the thought that we may have dehumanised ourselves more than we need have done in order to modernise. Serious and responsible leaders from countries on the verge of industrialisation recoil from the effects of industrialisation in America and Europe. They are surely right to hesitate, because there must be some danger that their peoples will follow the same path as ours; but it does not follow that there is no alternative road. Even within our own culture, immigrants from its fringes, Irish, Greeks, Cypriots, Sicilians, Lebanese, retain, with astonishing and wholly admirable obstinacy, important cultural characteristics which we have lost, in particular the close family attachments allegedly destroyed by industry, a claim that I have already questioned. In the Arab world, and I have no doubt in most parts of the world less exposed to certain kinds of social deterioration, the great personal occasions, especially marriage and death, lay a considerable social burden on the individual, both in time and money, sometimes an exaggerated and excessive burden. I recall a group of Arabs arguing that efficiency of industrialisation would require the customary three days of condolence to be discontinued; but a political progressive present denied this, arguing that time could always be found for the humane purposes that the traditions of the whole people required. In an English newspaper I saw it recommended that happy children should be preserved from contact with children who are grieving in bereavement. This was put in terms of popular psychology, in order to mask its true character. It can in fact be interpreted only as a reversion to the instinct of the animal herd to isolate the unfortunate, and leave them to destruction. We rightly enjoy reading about the animal instincts which explain so much of our behaviour; it is incredible that there are people who would like humanity to add nothing and control nothing. This has travelled equally far from Christianity and from humanity; it marks the degeneracy of some of our cultural developments. The fact is that society will organise whatever activities it judges to be worth organising. There remains some danger that people outside the area of real development will be mesmerised into thinking that they can create conditions that favour development by adopting Western culture. As we saw earlier, many people are protected from this by the conviction that greater humanity is required in the way techniques are used, and also, of course, by their suspicion of the motives and actions of the 'colonialists'. There are unknown factors. If our Civil Servants spent more time being kind to the public, would the gain in public contentment be worth the loss in the time of the government officials? I do not know if this has been or can be tested. Suspicion of the colonialists is only too often suspicion that the colonialists are depriving the public in the underdeveloped areas of precisely that cultural deterioration which has damaged our culture and may damage theirs. This attitude of suspicion will provide a filter of Western ideas, but it will not necessarily provide the discrimination which is essential to enable the culture that borrows the techniques to borrow nothing more.

This appears very clearly in the field of education. There is a widespread conviction that a Western type education is an all but magical source of Western power, and it is at least true that technical education and scientific education are essential to modernisation of any kind. The prestige of the Western, alien and secular is enormous, but the continuing surge of African and Asian students to Europe can also be regarded as an attempt to wrest the secret of technological superiority from its present guardians. It is often less a logical attempt to master technical education than a general notion that the educational method and popular education that have been successful within the West must be the source of Western success in the world at large. To an older generation in former colonial territories, who knew the old colonial rulers personally, it seems that the education that produced a successful generation of colonialists must be more effective than the present day reforms that produce less successful and effective people on the world scene. Be that as it may, the question is still open, does this imply an acceptance of Western values? It may only be an idea that Western methods can be taken over like any other technique and that they can be disinfested of cultural parasites of the limitations and the errors of the West, as seen from outside.

A large part of our academic disciplines are indeed only a question of techniques. I do not think that it was accidental that one of the subjects adopted by Al-Azhar Islamic religious university when it was modernised was business administration. This subject will have looked eminently culture-transferable. It is so new a technique in the West, at least in the form of academic discipline, that it must have seemed that it could not have become culturally loaded in so short a time; as a business technique it may be older in the West, but business is equally ancient and perhaps more prestigious in Islam: the Quraysh were merchants. Even to the Arab socialist, of course, management techniques are necessary, or more necessary. Yet there is a very heavy cultural load in buying and selling. This is a good case of a technique that carries with it a strong cultural accretion in the West, and that may yet be acquired as a technique and disembarrassed of its accretions. I see no evidence to prove, although there may be some to suggest, that we need to change the human character of society or of individuals, just so as to be able to manipulate techniques. Management, then, appeals more as a 'modern' than as a 'Western' subject; if (in this instance) it has its effects upon the development of Egyptian culture, they must be seen as a natural and indigenous modernisation, not as acculturation to the West. This applies generally to new subjects which are as much techniques as subjects, such as social anthropology; of course it applies to the obvious methods, like engineering and medicine. Subjects like history and law are easily transferred by an adjustment of the field studied, the Abbasids or the Sassanids or the Mings substituted for the Hapsburgs, and one legal code for another. Comparative law is a field in which Muslims at least feel at home, because they find that Islamic jurisprudence stands up well to comparison. In most outside cultures, European history is considered to begin at the French Revolution, which (in the Arab world especially) is seen to mark a break in the European tradition. Revolutionary ideas are often seen as belonging to all the cultures of the world, although they originated in Europe: revolution itself is a technique that can be transmitted. Modern critical methods are a sharp and accurate instrument, at least in comparison with earlier methods and blunter practice; if a scholar from another culture uses the older techniques there is little possibility of mutual understanding. Critical methods are an example of improved techniques which it would be folly for any culture to ignore; but we must not be misled by our own familiarity with them, or by associating some foreigners with the lack of them, into forgetting that they are only an instrument, devoid of inherent cultural content.

The adaptation of Western educational methods to local conditions has often not followed the recommendations of experts from outside. There is a healthy suspicion that the outsider is incompetent to adapt to his own ideas. It is sometimes thought that Europeans or Americans will try to trick the recipients of Western education out of the benefits of it. In a later chapter I discuss past examples of the successful application of a cultural filter in acquiring knowledge from an alien source considered to be tainted. At present there are special difficulties. Dependence on foreign teachers is one, though it is being progressively eliminated. Dependence on foreign language is another. While Europe retains its technological skills, other cultures must maintain a special expertise in European languages, at a higher level of language learning than under present conditions is necessary in Europe, in order to keep in touch with scientific and other professional advances. This makes harder the application of a cultural filter to exclude Western cultural accretion. The conscious and deliberate barrier of suspicion and hostility today functions usefully as a filter, but it is erratic in its working and not sensitively selective. It is quite understandable, but that does not make it desirable; nevertheless, if it were not there, we wonder whether Western culture as well as techniques might not be unselectively and indiscriminately adopted.

At any rate we can say that the case put forward by those who expect to see one technological world culture is unproven. Their arguments are entirely negative, and are simply based on the observation that our Western culture continues to develop economically with considerable success, while the other cultures do not even seem to be narrowing the gap. This brings us to our second great question: how are the techniques and the culture connected in any society, and especially in our Western world?

The interaction of these two is not easy to assess, even though we have it under our eyes. Most people outside the West will naturally argue that the accidents of geography alone caused the industrial revolution to occur in Europe, rather than anywhere else. The old, traditional explanations of industrial development in terms of the proximity of natural resources—the iron and coal we learned about in school—favoured this line of thought. From this point of view, imperialism is a natural result of precocious economic development, and it might all have happened just as probably in other cultures, had they been endowed with the same natural resources. This opinion is natural to many non-Europeans. The opposite view is that there is a very ancient tendency in the West, if not always to actual inventiveness, at least to the full exploitation of what has been invented. The ancient world is seen to have failed to industrialise because of its reliance on slave-labour, an argument which, if valid, would apply to many areas at many periods; but historians can look back to the use to which the West put the discovery of the stirrup, and then of the horse-collar and the heavy plough, to ensure an increasingly efficient economic and military development, at least of North European resources, from the beginning of the present millenium and earlier. According to this theory, efficient development spread out to the South and East of Europe and to North America; and a solution of the development problems of the rest of the world would represent a further outward radiation. This success is attributed to the genius of the 'race', that is, of the culture; but this genius can be seen as good or bad, and logically either theory can be held by either 'imperialists' or anti-imperialists.

Certainly Europe put its inventions to a more successfully expansionist purpose than ancient China did its own indigenous inventiveness. The use Europe made of whatever inventions came its way created opportunities for more inventions, and so success led on to more success, and China was outstripped. The more we muse about it, the less is it obvious whether the people make the processes or the process the people; all that we can be sure is that there is an interaction. There must be at least a big element of luck in all economic development. There was luck in the early development of civilizations in Mesopotamia and the Nile and Indus valleys and elsewhere. Development came in favourable conditions, but the line of development was different in each case. Once a culture begins to develop in a certain direction, it advances under its own creative momentum, whatever geographical conditions continue to play their part. All are agreed that available resources and internal momentum contributed to the growth of Western society, but its characteristics are defined differently according to the emotions of the definer; the anti-colonialist criticism of Western savagery, cruelty, and aggression (in so far as it is not just tit-for-tat for Victorian allegations about those same qualities in Africa and Asia) is the obverse of our own assessment of our efficiency, energy, and enterprise.

Every culture is its own mental prison, from which few can escape for long and none escape altogether. As a matter of fact, we know very little about how ideas are formed in a community. We do not know why something that has often been said before will suddenly catch on, or why both events and opinions seem to remain static for a long time, and suddenly begin to move, and keep on moving. Most mysterious of all is how a consensus of opinion forms, and why it takes the shape it does. We observe the process, but its aetiology escapes us, and prediction is wholly beyond our powers. We can often sense that a given political, social or economic situation must change, either because a loosening of received opinion creates a vacuum and invites something strange to enter, or because there is a tension which demands to be resolved; but this is not a prediction, it is a judgement on an existing situation. Our sociologists and political scientists and economists study aspects of our culture intensively; some study aspects of opinion change even, for example, psephologists. These are all studies in detail, relating to one or other of the tightly defined techniques or disciplines of scholarship. They are effective within their natural limits, but all these social scientists are necessarily too much a part of their own culture to see it as it really is, or to see it whole, or to see where it is going. The present writer, or his reader, is in no better position. Someone from another culture has his own cultural bias; yet anyone who returns from living in another culture, suspended between it and his own, sees, before he gets caught up again fully in his own, that it is as self-absorbed as any other. It does not seem that our culture, or any culture can judge itself, still less that it can see itself from a vantage point acceptable to other cultures. What is happening here and now is so obscure, and what is happening in the rest of the world is so obscure, that it is difficult to talk about what may be transmitted from culture to culture, and what must be rejected; and difficult above all to know what in Western culture might usefully be adopted by anyone else.

A characteristic of our culture which has some obvious appeal in other cultures is its secularism. In outside cultures one attraction of secularism has been that it aims to destroy Christianity; we have seen how Christianity has been suspected and hated, because of its intricate connection with imperialism, and with the old European claim to superiority; secularism appeals on the basis that 'the enemy of my enemy is my friend', a principle which has often given cause for regret after it is too late. Reaction against one's native religion, and against a foreign one, are quite different; and secularism in the West is part of a package of opinions which may not be of universal application. The implicit or explicit rejection of religion by the majority of the public is widespread, both in the socialist area, where it is further advanced, in that it is officially enforced, and in the free enterprise heart of the West, where the social disapproval of religion appears to be increasing, at any rate at the professional, managerial, and administrative level. Packaged in with it is a reliance on science, and as much a reliance on what science is going to do for us as on what it has done. Also in this package comes belief in progress, because scientific control over nature is the one field where there has been something like steady progress throughout recorded history. Progressive control over nature is in fact also unique in being the one point of stability and certainty left to our society. Finally, even the least developed cultures have reason to be grateful for what science has contributed to human welfare. If it is inevitable that these things should be packaged, then the techniques do have inescapable cultural concomitants. How has the West come to make up this package?

The rejection of religion has no logical connection with acceptance of the idea of progress except only on the Marxist theory that undue attention to the other world leaves you indifferent to this; from this it would follow that because it is harmful we must persuade people that it is untrue. Is this notion the product of a cultural situation or of actual hard fact? I do not know of any evidence that poor or other unprivileged people have ever been resigned to an unhappy fate in this world because of their hopes of the next, or for any other reason; and an affluent society may set store on the practice of religion. We know very little about why, or even how much, the forms of religion were accepted in Europe in the past. We know a good deal about what religious people thought about it; the thoughts of the orthodox were preserved as they stood, and the thoughts of the heretics were preserved by the orthodox, probably correctly, though only at second hand. We know much less about the beliefs of the lower classes. We know one or two things that, for example, a court official like Chaucer thought the peasants believed; when we do hear of lower class religion it is usually in one way or another a religion of protest, John Ball, chiliastic outbreaks, Anabaptists, Levellers, even Methodists. The idea that religion was so consciously devised as an instrument of government is historically quite anachronistic, and the relation of priesthood and kingship is still the subject of inconclusive speculation in various academic disciplines. Most theories are little more than gratuitous assumptions. What really did happen — and this is not historically in doubt at all — is that the Christian church made itself hated by its repression and cruelty, by the privileges and wealth of churchmen, and by the support it gave to the ruling class, over the greater part of the Christian era, and this long history has to be paid for; it is a heavy debt, and has to be paid in full. At times, as in the Spain of *limpieza*, the whole Christian society has conspired in cruelty and injustice, and the courage of individual churchmen in resisting the victorious majority has not diminished the debt as it should have; it is the successful injustice that has increased it. It is a debt that cannot be reversed in a year or two, or even a generation. Even now, as much continues to be entered on the debit as on the credit side of the account. Payment for the evil that was done takes the form of reaction against the good that was intended. Yet we have two quite different ideas — religion as a political sedative, and the church (or even the majority of the Christian people) as an instrument of oppression. It has been well said that, if religion is a drug, it is as often an excitant as a depressant. Religion can be, has been, and doubtless will be, used both to support and to oppose oppression.

Secularism in Europe is older than Lucretius, and has continued to flourish even in the 'ages of faith' (for example, the condemned propositions of Paris in 1277 may not have been Averroistic, but they were certainly secular).[3] Secularism supplies an alternation, rather than a break, in European tradition. If, however, this European secularism derives its strength from the reaction against the establishment and exercise of ecclesiastical power, *prima facie* it should be relevant to other cultures only in proportion as they have had a similar establishment. Is this why we sometimes see, also in cultures with a different history, the familiar alliance between revolution in politics and revolt against religion? If the Marxist analysis is incorrect, why do we equally see in these cultures the familiar alliance between some forms of religion and some forms of political reaction? One reason is itself the consequence of a direct cultural loan; the Communist Party because of its consistency and devotion and discipline is often in a position to set the tone of a progressive movement, and so transmits the post-Christian inheritance of Europe in its Marxist-Leninist form. This is given colour by the very fact that it forces religion into a hostile situation. Moreover, as long as it remains true that religion is inherited rather than chosen, the human instinct for conservatism will support it, and those in whom conservatism dominates will be among the religious people. Once religion has ceased to be a legacy, this factor will cease to operate, but at the present time it still affects all cultures that have not turned over officially to irreligion. The Muslim Brothers, for example, have included true revolutionaries (and in no fascist sense) and true reactionaries simultaneously. On the whole, the roots of anti-religion seem more shallow, probably because more recent, in much of the under-developed world; and even the Communist suppression of its own anti-religious propaganda occasionally seems to go beyond the purely tactical intention in which it originates. This is an area in which it is still uncertain whether the other cultures will develop in the same way as the Western.

The intercultural meaning of secularism would be clearer if we knew more about why it appeals in Europe. The relations between a society and its beliefs are complex, and perhaps not primarily a matter of reason at all. The arguments used in our own society against religion are none of them new; there is nothing obvious to explain why religion should be discarded now rather than at another time. No new argument or discovery has changed the credibility or otherwise of the existence of God, the immortality of the soul, or the Christian—if you prefer, Judaeo-Hellenic—moral system with which Europe grew up. In 1736 Bishop Butler noted that many persons treat Christianity as if it 'were an agreed point among all people of discernment' that Christianity is fictitious, and ridicule it, 'as it were by way of reprisals, for its having so long interrupted the pleasures of the world'.[4] This revulsion has taken some time to catch on, but now it is doing so fast; in England at least, it both is created by, and expresses, the culture. To men and women now in late middle age, today's newest arguments have been familiar since their childhood; only now they are becoming the orthodoxy, possibly a repressive orthodoxy. Bonhoeffer seems to have explained what we now see, though he died a generation ago, by saying that many people have believed in God just as a resort to avert trouble, and now that science looks likely to keep them alive and in comfort more efficiently, they feel that they can discard the mechanism of prayer. It is useless (though true) for religious people to say that this was never what religion was about, that this was to turn it into a kind of magic and a surrogate for science; this mistake may nevertheless be the historical explanation of what has been happening. It is likely enough that resignation to avoidable misfortune has been simply the absence of a practical hope of change.

This consideration could equally apply to all cultures, but does not do so necessarily. In Europe secularism cannot be correlated with technological advance, and even when man dominates nature other cultures may have other reasons to retain religion. Mediaeval Latin Christianity made Europe monolithic in point of ideology, but in Asia and the Mediterranean religion has often been the expression of national or communal differences. The classic example is the adoption of monophysitism by the Egyptian church, and the adoption of monotheletism by the Christians of Mount Lebanon is equally illustrative. The presence today of so many villages on one mountain-side, each a unit of one of several forms of Christianity or Islam, or of the Druze communities, shows how religion expresses the separate identity of each village community. In Asia and in North Africa we find religious political movements which, although classed as fascist or reactionary, certainly receive mass support, such as the Muslim Brothers or the Hindu Jana Sangh. The Mahdist movements of nineteenth-century Africa antedate the possibility of Marxist provocation; they were what we now call nationalist, but they conceived of themselves as purely religious. If technology released Europeans from their magical concept of religion, it could only do so because religion no longer expressed the cultural identity of Europe.

Belief is a social function. This is not to say that belief is untrue; true or untrue, belief or disbelief is a social function. This is obvious enough when we think of the way in which some beliefs have regulated the behaviour of individuals in minute detail, for example, Christianity, Islam or Marxism. Disbelief is a kind of belief; disbelief in religion is belief in a chance universe, and vice versa, and both make their demands. The demands are not less when the negative side is the predominant. We observe this in practice. In a society where everyone believes in religion, it is easy for the individual to believe. In a disbelieving society, the same individual will find the same belief very difficult. We are so used to the idea that we are rational that it is shocking for us to find that our reasoning generally conforms to that of most other people, just in one time and place; and most shocking, perhaps, for disbelievers, who like to pre-empt reason. This is one reason for the cultural arrogance which makes us think that finally all will conform to our own time and place. In a society like our own, in a state of change, even those who retain belief in religion will find that their belief is often affected by the prevailing disbelief; it becomes at least uncomfortable. Social existence demands conformity, even in change; we change together. It is obviously disagreeable to stand out against the consensus of opinion publicly; but this is as much a matter of inward compulsion as of outward conformity. Each individual in a majority sincerely and rationally reaches the same conclusions as everyone else. Minority views find their own social support, often in a small group differentiated by some peculiar fanaticism. It is harder to belong to a majority culture, and share its ways and life, while holding a minority belief.

If belief is a function of society, must a particular belief be a function of a specific society, for example, disbelief in religion of a society which is technologically highly advanced or economically highly developed? One view commonly held in England is that there is an approximate but definite line of development from the Reformation onwards: the people of Northern Europe have been eliminating beliefs steadily since that date, and they have also led the world in social welfare, political freedom, and economic advance. All these are therefore associated, and the highest technology is necessarily connected with the least belief in religion. Belief in a constantly (but of course progressively) shifting set of 'values' is substituted. It follows that other peoples and cultures should adopt the attitudes and behaviour of Northern Europe in order to enjoy the same advantages. This notion contrasts curiously with the idea of a hundred years ago that development ('improvement') ran parallel with the emergence of Protestant Christianity. No doubt the modern idea will last as long as its predecessor. If we applied this method of interpretation to English history alone, we should so far have to agree with the Victorians as to admit that the peak of technological invention and of material success in relation to the rest of the world coincided with a period of religious belief. A more convincing conclusion would be just that a successful society is often activated by some strong belief.

In our society, beliefs have fragmented into small orthodoxies. A progressive favours abortion, opposes racial discrimination and censorship. To reverse these three is intelligible, it is another known package, but to pick and choose is eccentric. Yet, although our ideas are packaged, all the different packages that belong in our society are communicated to us; and, whatever our beliefs, we are capable of feeling momentarily the whole syndrome of each belief, religious, anti-religious or anti-clerical, xenophobic or xenophiliac, progressive or reactionary, aristocratic, working-class; people even like to dress up as Victorians and Edwardians and to sing Rule Britannia with a meaningless and romantic nostalgia. The weakness is less in division than in uncertainty. The shift in belief that we see is negative. Mao Tse-Tung describes his own shift of belief, when he describes how he came to feel the workers and peasants to be cleaner than 'unremoulded intellectuals', that is, non-Communist students who washed more. He experienced 'having one's feelings transformed, changed from those of one class to those of another'.[5] This is a change into certainty and finality; its social contents would be obvious, even if we did not know that it had meantime carried Chinese society with it. It is easy to see the value and the attraction of such certainties, and correspondingly difficult to see how our uncertainties can attract any foreign culture, least of all those that are looking for stability among the problems created by the pursuit of modernisation. They may better spend their time and energy, while we seek our own solution, in looking for one for themselves.

The negative qualities in our current cultural achievement make it an unlikely model for imitation, in behaviour as much as in belief. The great difference between Western society now and a hundred years ago is in the kind of demand made on the individual; and present-day Maoist China offers the same contrast as does departed imperialist Britain. Our society has nothing more positive to offer than the removal of restraints, and so it can only bumble ineffectively along. The negative principle of selection by which we often merely prefer whatever Christianity forbade, is nowhere more noticeable than in what is required morally of the individual. All 'permissiveness' so calculated may very easily become an impermissive code of required behaviour; and the opposition that, as we saw, often develops between our own people and some 'impermissive' foreign cultures illustrates a kind of impermissiveness of our own— 'others should not forbid what we allow'— must we then forbid them to forbid, a contradiction within our own culture? Endless freedoms do not make life easier, indeed, they increase its pressures on the individual. When society enforces freedoms, there is no freedom; and there is no freedom without the power to say 'yes' or 'no'. To say 'yes' or 'no' is coming to be described by a new pejorative, 'moralistic', the error of supposing that there is right or wrong. Just as in some ages Christians have attached too much importance to sexual morality, and morality has come in consequence to be thought to be something specially to do with sex, so now it is in the field of sex in particular that 'moralistic' teaching is deplored. The whole 'permissive' society is misunderstood. If it only permits what Christianity restricted, its standard of judgement must be meaningless to people from cultures that have never been Christian. Discarding Christianity gives a lot of fun to a number of Europeans and Americans, now that it no longer requires courage, but their little self-indulgences constitute no moral system to fortify the individual against the pressures of increasing population and of economic necessity. The fuss we make about permitting does correlate with the fuss we used to make about forbidding, for example, homosexuality, which Christian societies at certain times have held in particular horror. Why should societies that did not share the horror share the reaction against it? It is admittedly just possible that all societies that have been in any respect 'moralistic' will now decide to be so in none, and to replace all morals — should we say *moralisticism?* — by compulsory freedoms. In that case, however different the various cultures may have been, all must finally come to a negative sameness which is the expression of consumer orthodoxy.

If these freedoms do not help us to survive the increasing complexities of industrial existence, ought we not to conclude that they are dictated by reaction alone, and not at all by the industrial society we regularly blame for it? A bare principle of reaction is likely to exhaust itself; is it not the characteristic and the weakness of contemporary Western culture to make no strong moral demand on the behaviour of the individual, such as Christianity and other religions and Marxism make? Even its achievement in welfare is as cold as the charity of which it is the modern equivalent. The trained welfare worker sometimes looks like the old priest writ large. It is quite common to despise voluntary efforts. At an adolescent level we hear Freud misused to justify sneers at 'do-gooding', as being a 'sublimation'. If doing good (and there is no real difference, except in the speaker, between 'do-gooding' and 'doing good') gives pleasure to the doer, it is argued, he too is a hedonist, and there is only a choice between different pleasures (doing good, eating chocolates, getting drunk, or any other self-indulgence); of course, this argument, based on a gratuitous assumption, is essentially frivolous. My point is that this level of cynical frivoloity is not in revolt against some repressively stern authority, but comes as near as anything to being itself the authoritarian dogma. It is credible that developing countries are attracted by Communism, barely credible that they choose deliberately to learn their moral system from the free enterprise side of the 'West'.

It would be silly as well as ungrateful to pretend that consumer orientation has not done as much for the welfare of the North European masses as legislation and administration have done. That is not to say that we should ignore the need to moderate our raptures. Economists seem to be saying that it is necessary to maintain a constant flow of things we make, in order that people may be employed to make them; and in order to be able to make them, we have to be made to want them, to want more things, new things, ephemeral things and different forms of the things we already have. There must be a valid distinction between the fulfilment of real needs and the creation of wants in order to satisfy them; it is the difference between the kitchen and the vomitorium. Our present situation requires us to support armies of advertisers who can boast their 'creativity' without shocking anybody. The fact is that we have come to esteem the profession of barker and the profession of pornographic tout (now so often so happily combined) more highly than our grandfathers did. The rest of the world can distinguish easily and enviously between titillated wants and want of necessities. It is 'creative' to make us want what we do not need, and buy what we cannot be persuaded to want. Yet even in our own culture we are not deprived of all reassurance; people generally are more sensible than all the parasites suppose; but there must be some danger of forgetting that satisfaction, by definition, can only be here and now, and never in the elusive hope of something else somewhere else at another time. 'Satisfaction now' has been, not the reward, but the requirement, of every respectable moral system and every religion (not 'pie in the sky'); but whether other cultures are so conditioned as to be able to resist the temptations of endless and pointless indulgence, in a consumer society — 'some jam today but better jam tomorrow' — we do not yet know. They have to raise their people above subsistence level before they can find out. Ultimately it is conceivable that they will all be glamourised by Western consumer society; already some individuals have been; but, if this is ever true of whole societies, it is likely to come about, as in our own case, by gradual erosion. Even so, new consumer orthodoxies are more likely to be shaped by the pre-existing bias of each culture.

'The layer of simmering greed and violence', wrote Nirad Chaudhuri, of Bengal at the beginning of the century, 'seemed to rest on a rock-like foundation of quite different composition never permeated or corrupted by it. We called this lower stratum religion and morality, things to which in the last resort everybody returned.' This 'primordial foundation of rock below', he said fifty years later, 'is rotting into dust'.[5] The older we get, the more we are liable to see moral decay, and the same thing has happened in every age and every human culture. Sometimes it has been justified, and sometimes not, because human affairs do fluctuate, getting better, getting worse, often some getting better, while others get worse. Let us suppose that the rocks are turning to dust in different parts of the world today. We can hardly conclude from the existence of dissolving forms everywhere that all dissolutions must approximate to our own. We may legitimately conclude that our own insecurity and instability are unlikely to help others to be secure and stable. Yet it is no more necessary for us to accept the criticism of our present-day culture from outside than it is for one age-group to accept the criticism of another. What reason does require us to do is to listen. If we think that we are judged unfairly, we must suspect that we judge others unfairly too. We have to accept differences. If we assume the ultimate maximum industrialisation of the world, we still cannot assume that other ways of living are incompatible with it; and we have not the slightest reason to wish it otherwise. Our cultural character owes so much to our history — and at the moment of writing to our reaction against aspects of our past — that there is no reason to think that our culture is specially adapted to control the technical develop- ments we have created. We use our technology to do the things we have always done; we use it culturally, and it does not shape the general outline of our culture. The differences between us in the Western part of the West and the countries of the socialist camp are enough to suggest that outside both there can be equal or greater differences. Some of the evils of our society the socialist world seems to have avoided, and we believe that they have substituted other evils; but if they have their own kind of troubles, and not our kind, it is clear that differences of culture can go with the same economic development. It must at least be open to the 'third' world to develop troubles all its own. Other cultures may make their own mistakes, but ought not to follow ours. Neither we nor they should be thinking of any one culture being better or worse than another. On the contrary, it is in the interests of every- one that there should be diversity, because only separate and indepen- dent developments will give each an opportunity to learn from the others, or, indeed, allow there to be anything to learn.

It would be better; is it possible? We have to concede that every- where there will inevitably be a great deal in common, because all cultures have membership of the human race in common. Whatever we hit on that is useful, others may copy, and vice versa, and common factors will tend to produce common consequences without any copying at all. Yet it is equally a human factor that different people should tend to make different decisions and choices; and, once differences exist, they pre-dispose people to make still more differing decisions, We have seen that these good and decent differences seem to be preserved in practice by a filter made up of suspicion and hostility. The question ought to be, can we find no better means to achieve a purpose we accept as good? We have seen reason to think that in the end that culture will fail which is less determined, less confident, less united, less spontaneous and perhaps less discriminating. It is at this point that it has seemed to me useful to look for historical parallels, and to consider some part of the vast human experience of intercultural relations.

Part Two

HISTORICAL PERSPECTIVES

Evaluation of Cultures

I FIND IT hard to believe that there is such a thing as a humble culture. I cannot think of any instance where men believe that their society is seriously inferior to another. Of course, if they are beaten in a war, they may believe that their army (or, more probably, their fire-power) is inferior, but not that their ways and customs are. If they are out-produced, they may believe that their factories are inferior; we have already seen that many cultures recognise Western technological super-iority, without conceding the superiority of the culture. It is true that when it is the fashion to imitate a foreign model, as when European youths at particular times have copied American ways, or Americans have copied British manners, imitation may seem to imply cultural humility, but it is more likely that it is a means of teasing those elders and rulers who may be hoped to disapprove of it. Whether cultural humility exists or not, there is certainly a general tendency to despise other cultures.

Analytically, we can distinguish three kinds of cultural contempt: technological, literary, and general, although in practice they may all be associated. It is easy enough to show that the sense of superiority of one society over another is absurd. Let us take first the case of a sense of superiority that is based upon a real superiority in technological achievement. We do not think less of Shakespeare because the society in which he lived, and which produced him, was technologically inferior to our own. Moreover, his achievement is—and seems to us to be—absolutely unaffected by our continuing technical progress. There is no question of its being progressively diminished as we improve our soap powders, make yet more motor cars, or travel to the moon. It may well be that, as our ways change under the influence of new manufactures, Shakespeare becomes progressively more difficult to understand, but nobody thinks that this diminishes his stature. He can be produced in the latest fashion; there have been many 'new' Hamlets in the present writer's lifetime; but nobody thinks that the current interpretation will survive longer than the production that embodies it, and yet every-body believes that the original text will survive indefinitely. Of course, I am only using Shakespeare as representative of many other greater writers. Of no time can we say that writers are better writers because the culture in which they live invents and manufacturers better machines.

It would be equally absurd to say—what no one is saying—that literary and artistic achievement are possible without any technology. Certainly, Shakespeare could have written no plays at all in a society that could not produce a surplus sufficient to maintain writers and actors. To put it crudely, if he and the Lord Chamberlain's men were scratching the earth all day with a stick in order to live, they could not have written or acted; no audience would have scratched the earth on their behalf. Even so, the most primitive society has leisure enough to create oral epics. In a society much less primitive technologically, a phase of economic depression and contraction might generate so little demand for plays that again there would be no writing or acting, and so no Shakespeare to be remembered. We cannot underestimate the function of the patron, Maecenas or the Medicis, the Duchess of Lancaster or the Despot of Mistra; or for that matter, the Post Office which allowed Trollope time to write, or any employment from which the time can be squeezed. When that has been said, it remains clearer than ever that the degree of patronage cannot measure the quality of the literary or artistic work it makes possible; nor does that quality improve at the pace of technological invention or production. Economic development encourages widespread literacy, and widespread literacy facilitates writing, but it cannot create writing, and it would be very difficult to show that our writers today exceed those of Shakespeare's day in quality, although our society is undoubtedly more literate. In fact, what we have been saying about literary and other artists applies also to some extent to scientists and philosophers. Society can only offer the opportunity and the incentive, but it would puzzle the historian to demonstrate a precise correlation between those and the actual achievement, let alone between the rate of abstract thought and the rate of material progress.

Admittedly, we can imagine a less conveniently convincing case than Shakespeare's. If we go far enough back, we shall reach completely different modes of thought about the external world, and about our relation to it. 'We cannot imagine our Sussex farmers of the Stone Age', said Childe, 'equipped with our categories any more than with our tractor-ploughs'. I shall have something to say about our sense of community with the Stone Age elsewhere; for the moment I will just say that this case does not affect the Shakespeare type of case at all; but, in addition, we cannot accept as close a correlation between 'knowledge' and the 'whole of the culture and particularly the technology' as Childe proposes.[1] Sooner or later they will interact, but I would challenge any historian— or archeologist or anthropologist— to correlate step by step the general intellectual formation and the technological discovery and practice. If we could see that intellectual, moral, and social activities advanced *pari passu* with technology in our own past, we should be justified in claiming that there is a correlation between them, but this just is not the case.

In spite of this, it happens again and again that people despise another culture because its technological achievement is less than that of their own.

Perhaps a sense of literary superiority (cultural in the older and narrower sense) is even more absurd. Our minds are formed largely by the literary content of our education, that is, by the things we read as we grow up, and we tend quite naturally to think that people who read different things are inferior people. This may be justified on the ground that our own reading teaches values that are missing in other people's reading. The idea can be extended to other arts. At the present day we tend on the whole to admire the arts of all times and places, but this has not always been so, and may not be so in the future. Our present tolerance doubtless derives from our uncertainty; but we pluck up enough courage to despise the 'socialist realist' school, and the general 'Victorianism' of the USSR. Our possession of a fine literature is part of our national self-esteem, and we are sorry for countries with a poor collection of sundry arts. On the one hand, it would be difficult to say that an accumulated achievement is not greater than it was when the accumulation was only just beginning; to add only a little to the collection is to make it bigger, and we in Britain have more in our store of literature and art and music than ever our grandfathers had. On the other hand, this does not measure our present cultural superiority; if it measures anything it measures our past cultural quality. A moment's reflection shows us that if there were any substance to the idea that this accumulation conferred superiority upon us, we should be superior to Shakespeare, because Shakespeare was not brought up on Shakespeare. Indeed, if the possession of a literature conferred any cultural superiority, the critics would always be superior to the authors.

In spite of this, it often happens that people will despise another culture because they do not like or do not understand its literature or its art or its mustic.

Thus we cannot say that a culture is superior because it is superior in one field, technological or literary; we cannot correlate technological with literary achievement and we cannot correlate literary achievement with literary potential (as shown by subsequent achievement). We can, of course, correlate the literary expression of science or technology with technological or scientific achievement, although even this is not in the quality of the writing. There must still be a close relationship between the thing studied and the literature expressing the study. There must also be some correlation between literary achievement and the development of literary techniques. Again, this relation will not extend to

quality. We do not say that Eliot's poetical technique is better than
Shakespeare's or that Eliot is a better poet than Shakespeare; we only
say that poetic technique was developing in Eliot's poetry in a particular
direction. This is an area in which we are more often capable of tolerating different kinds of things than we are in most; even here it is common to deride the artistic techniques that develop after one's own
maturity; in my lifetime people used to hate and despise Picasso; I have
absolutely no pleasure in or appreciation of some contemporary music.
What we can always expect is a change in techniques, usually giving a
run to the expression of somewhat different ideas; and in the articulate
or literary arts we can expect to see a reflection of the social structures,
and of the accepted philosophical and scientific notions of the day. All
this is normal. There is change, not necessarily either for better or for
worse. If there is an evaluation of the past achievement, it has nothing
to do with the current quality of the culture.

The sense of the total superiority of a culture is the most absurd of all.
This may or may not include a sense of technological or literary superiority, but is in any case not based principally on either. It may or may
not have to do with religion. If religion does come into it, it is of course
not a question of belief, but of the cultural expression of belief. I have
met culturally inherited fear and suspicion of Islam among unbelieving
products of a Christian civilisation; but of course religious contempt
may precede religious difference, and religious difference may only
express the pre-existing cultural dislike. In this way the disagreement
between Latin and Greek Christians has always been minimal in subject
matter, but violent in quality; and it is usually argued that the great
Monophysite and Nestorian theories were the expression of pre-existing
cultural differences between the emperors and their Syrian and Egyptian subjects. An exclusivist belief, such as Christian or Muslim belief in
the damnation of others, must tend to reinforce a general cultural contempt, but I doubt if it creates it. The Hindu despises the exclusivism
of Christianity and Islam, and the permissive moralist (moralist if he
thinks it wrong to forbid) despises the impermissive one.

The absurdity of thinking that technological superiority confers any
other kind lies in a gross over-assessment of the value and function of
technology. The absurdity of a sense of general superiority is the im-
possibility of being judge in one's own cause; we cannot judge fairly
that in which we have been brought up from infancy. Nevertheless,
some sort of arbitration might be possible, some sort of agreement of
common standards which would allow an agreed opinion. Between total
cultures, however, a common standard can never be found: the sole
standard of judgement is according to the values of the culture from
within which the judgement is made. Even a man who deliberately

tries to uproot himself and to absorb a different culture (it is very rare, but it does happen) can only do so for reasons and in terms that spring from his own upbringing in his own culture. His will always be a foreign acceptance of a foreign thing; no country reckons to absorb an admitted alien sooner than the second generation. Even a hypothetical man from outer space could only judge the cultures of the earth by their greater or lesser approximation to his own culture in outer space.

The use and history of the word *barbarian* illustrates the problem. The sense of something different and alien merges inevitably, and often unnoticed, into that of something different and inferior. *Barbarian* is a culture judgement, closely related to language, and based on a double standard of judgement; this usually means that on our side there is a high morality, and any individual lapses from it can be explained; but the barbarians (on the same evidence) have a lower morality; with them bad behaviour is typical.

Our word comes from the Greek *barbaros*, which the dictionary defines as meaning 'non-Greek, foreign'; it is not in Homer, who does use the linguistic sense, however, *barbarophonos*. The *barbaroi* were originally all non-Greek-speaking peoples, that is, people with whom it was difficult to communicate, and then the word came to mean especially the greatest and most civilised of the non-Greek-speaking peoples, the Medes and Persians. The dictionary goes on to tell us that the linguistic sense continued to be strong, so that barbarous names are foreign names, and barbarous Greek has simply the sense of *bad* Greek. The effect of the Persian wars was to add the idea of *brutal, rude*. Finally, the Jewish translators of the Septuagint used it of the Greeks (that is, Greek-speakers) in 2 Maccabees (2.21).[2]

The Latin dictionary begins in much the same way. *Barbarus* means *foreign, strange, barbarous*, a *foreigner, stranger, barbarian*; *barbaria* or *barbaries* means a *foreign country*. *Barbarus* is used to describe any people that is not Greek or Roman, and is used for *Italian, Roman*, or *Latin* in the mouth of a Greek, or in opposition to *Greek*. *Barbaria* is any country other than Greece or Rome, or sometimes Italy, as opposed to Greece. Romans, however, do not put the word into the mouth of a Roman to describe a Roman. *Barbarus* is applied to Phrygian, Persian or any hostile people, Gauls, Germans, Thracians, Carthaginians, Cilicians, Phoenicians and Cyprians, Parthians, Africans and Britons; and to Dassaretians, who spoke Greek, in one instance; and *barbaria* is used for Scythia, Persia, Gaul, Phrygia and Britain. So by transference *barbarus* means 'foreign or strange in mind and character', that is, 'uncultivated, ignorant, rude, unpolished of mind', and 'wild, savage, cruel, barbarous' of character. As the Greeks used the word of the Persians, in particular after the Persian war, the Romans, we are told, used it particularly of the Germans after the Augustan age; in terms of civilisation, ambiguous as they must be, we should probably admit that the gap between Persians and Greeks was less than that between Germans and Persians. The real point of comparison seems to be the judgement of character that the savagery of war is likely to effect. *Barbaria* by metonymy has a similar extension to *barbarus*, as the dictionary puts it, 'mental or moral barbarism, according to the notion of the ancients', 'rudeness, rusticity, stupidity' and 'uncivilised manners'.[3] The notion of the ancients does not in fact seem very different from current feelings of superiority; these lexical descriptions fit very well the experience of the present day. There were occasional imaginative exceptions. Ovid (but only in order to stress how desperate his plight) said that the Getae thought him a barbarian, because they laughed at his Latin speech, and Livy imagined a Macdeonian who called the Greeks *alienigeni* and *barbari*; but few of us see that we ourselves look barbarous to other cultures.

It is interesting too to consider what happened when the invading barbarians adopted the Latin language. At first it seems that *Barbarus* was accepted as a normal description of a non-Roman, without pejorative implication; thus a Latin Salic Law gives the penalty for killing a 'Frank or Barbarian or man who lives by the Salic Law' as higher than that for killing a Roman. For a brief time 'barbarian' became an honourable usage; but of course this was only while it was not understood. It was soon used by the Franks, especially those who spoke Latin, to designate all the trans-rhenish nations. There are any number of examples of the use of *barbarica* or *barbara lingua* for German or other languages than Latin, although those who used a Romance tongue, that is, a corrupt Latin, did not describe it as barbaric. The *Canones Hibernienses* give this penance of the Irish Synod, 'He who offers leadership to the barbarians, 14 years. Barbarian, that is, alien; who is an alien, if not he who destroys all by a cruel and savage death?' The slightly ambiguous force of the term barbarian here only emphasises the central idea of hostility.[4]

We have looked at the ideas associated with the word *barbarian* because they illustrate the mutual suspicion of cultures, their close association with the use of a different language, and so with a failure to communicate, and their implication of cruelty. I do not mean to say that the alien raiders who savagely murdered the Irish were misunderstood; but wherever we find two cultures in conflict on an equal basis we find that accusations of cruelty inflicted by others are dissociated from acts of cruelty by ourselves. For the greater part of the Middle Ages the chief 'hostile' culture, the Islamic, was designated by a special word or words (Saracen, Agarene). John of Salisbury uses 'barbarian' for 'infidel'. 'Infidel' came to carry much the same cultural load as 'barbarian' had done. The champions of the Cordova Martyrs Movement against Islam, whose sense of cultural and national superiority was the stronger for its humiliation, used the words *ethnici, gentiles,* and *gentilicia* to describe the Arabs; this reflects the Scriptural rather than classical bent of their education, but it means the same as 'barbarian'. Yet other words with the general sense of barbarian were available to medieval Europe, and expressed its sense of community in theological terms; besides the words designating only Muslims, *infideles* was applicable to Jews and Muslims, and *pagani,* applicable to Muslims and heathens. In the medieval context these words have the force of *barbarus,* of *outsider.* 'The humanity of Anselm received all men without distinction of persons. And who were "all men"? Pagans even, not to mention Christians.' This refers to Muslim troops of Roger of Sicily, serving in Apulia, to whom Anselm distributed gifts, and whom he was prevented from proselytising. The commonest way of breaching intercultural contempt has so often been through the respect paid to the fighting qualities of an enemy; this happened in the Crusades even from the beginning; the *Turci* were singled out for this sort of respect from the First Crusade till the Korean War. This is itself a comment on the nature of cultural contempt; it is tempting to say that in this civilisation shows itself barbarous.[5]

I have said that mediaeval Europe expressed its group identity in theological terms; and in fact it had no alternative. The Crusaders discovered that they were separated from each other by language, and that they could be grouped together only as Latins; thus they were distinguished, whether from other Christians or from non-Christians, by means of their liturgical and theological language. The use of the word *barbarian* tended to disuse, at least until the classical revival, but of course the 'barbarian' idea remained unchanged. It is possible even in the Middle Ages to find a cultural dislike untinged by theology, as when John of Salisbury tells us, as an example of contemporary vice which he had personally observed, that his host in Apulia brought delicacies from Byzantium, the Levant, Egypt and North Africa, when he might have found as good in different parts of Italy. In the nineteenth century, despite the strong classical influence on the education of the imperial nations, the word 'native' came to carry a good deal of the sense of the old word 'barbarian', while 'barbarian' might be used, in a way parallel to the linguistic sense of 'barbarism', to describe a young person of unpolished manners. Later chapters discuss European attitudes both in the Middle Ages and in the imperial age more fully; the best expression of the concept of the barbarian is always the Greek. The *Epinomis* attached to Plato's Laws speaks of the reception of Babylonian astrological faith: 'Let us be aware of all that the Greeks have borrowed from the barbarians; they reword it and carry it forward to a finer achievement, and so we must think the same of our present subject. Doubtless it is difficult to discover the truth of all these new questions, but there is great hope . . . that the Greeks truly will be able to take nobler and juster care of the doctrine that reaches us from the barbarians. . . . ' The classical *barbaros* and *barbarus*, perfectly express the sense of cultural superiority.[6]

We are cut off from whatever is expressed in a different language; we hate being unable to communicate, and perhaps we hate even more not being able to understand other people when they communicate with each other. We want, like the *Epinomis*, to make whatever we want or need from others into something of our own, and can do so by changing it into the terms of our own culture, which is sufficient to make us feel that we have improved it; we may indeed, as we think the Greeks did, actually improve it, although not from the point of view of the originating culture. As long as we fail to turn something alien into something of our own, we resent those whom we do not understand, and whom we cannot make understand us; and resentment is more often expressed by contempt than by the kind of fear we can associate with respect. 'Oderint dum metuant' describes the syndrome of a tyrannical regime within a homogeneous society; it does not apply between different cultural groups. The natural association of ideas is the legal one, 'hatred and contempt'. Something that is both different and alien becomes unconsciously considered as something different and inferior. The ideas 'different' and 'inferior' constantly coincide, separate, and rejoin.

The idea that one culture can hardly be judged objectively by the standards of another was well expressed, from the point of view of an overseas student in Britain, in this report by a Persian speaker:

> A newcomer from a more simple and less sophisticated cultural background is apt to misjudge your society and to see in what first meets the eye in your country symptoms of moral chaos and social anarchy, but if he stays long enough . . . he will begin to discover the solid, logical and humane order which underlies the apparent disorder. Similarly, the people of your country will surely misjudge a newcomer . . . if they insist on measuring him with the yardstick of their own social code and standards of conduct. . . . In modern times the East tries to understand the West and appreciate and emulate what is good in it, but the West either remains completely indifferent to the East, or if it does try to understand it, it is by the wrong method, namely by using its own values and frame of reference.[7]

There are several good points here; there is a good description of the difficulty a visitor of good will from another culture has in penetrating the unattractive exterior of our way of life; there is a hint of the grim effort that adopting our techniques involves; and finally there is the well-expressed warning that it just is not possible usefully to evaluate one culture in terms of another. The whole passage breathes an air of tolerance which makes the hosts' excessive cultural self-confidence seem absurd, and at the same time recognises the ease with which the visitors fall into error.

We lack the means to evaluate, and yet are constantly evaluating. The contempt of cultures for one another only repeats the reciprocated contempts of different groups within a culture. These last kinds of contempt are very familiar, occupational ones especially; for example, the writer's contempt for the plumber, or, if he holds all men as equal, for the plumber's plumbing. In turn, the plumber may despise, as well as envy, the writer; he wants the writer's rewards, perhaps, but despises his kind of life and work. Occupational contempts are transferred into an intercultural situation. A culture under the domination of an alien technology may consider that it enjoys a 'true' superiority because of its greater eminence in arts, or literature, or way of life. Some Muslim communities under imperialist domination have felt this, and Hinduism felt it for Islamic and Christian cultures alike; and it is equally illustrated by some European, including English, attitudes to America today. The opposite, or technological, contempt for the failure of a society economically less developed to maintain or manufacture machinery may even be expressed by an individual who personally is devoid of practical skills of any kind. It is only very recently that we have come to think that some competence in mechanical, electrical or radio repairs is part of the equipment of the accomplished man, even the most literary. Except as hobbies, manual skills are still associated with an artisan class. Many attitudes survive from the past; scientists inherit something of the uncertain status of the astrologers and alchemists from whom they descend. The newer disciplines, while they claim a scientific methodology, fight to occupy the dominant position from which theology, once queen of the disciplines, interpreted all the others. Even between scientists, something of the old priestly and scribal prestige brushes off on the 'pure', rather than the 'applied' scientists, and even the esteem given to applied scientists varies; we respect doctors more than plumbers, not only because we are more afraid to die than to smell, but also because medicine involves more theoretical learning, and a more complex application of theory to practice. If the diagnosis of disease ever became mechanical, the prestige of doctors would surely decline. With the exception that entertainers have always enjoyed a high regard — and the present standing of pop-singers, television 'personalities' and footballers may not be proportionately greater than that of the former fools and acrobats — it seems that brain work receives most esteem, and applied cerebration less than cerebration pure. Yet (after the acrobats), the highest rewards go neither to the philosophers nor to the technological inventors, but to the administrators or 'management', the manipulators of a technique, and even a mystique, of their own. We are not united in our assessment of the value of different functions and occupations, unless, inevitably, it is in putting management highest; and so we have no single criterion on which to base our intercultural contempt, except quite simply to despise failure and admire success.

We can gauge the validity of these different cultural judgements by comparison and analysis. It is even more obviously difficult to compare the value of two human beings. We can make some comparison by the negative method of picking out the cultural from the personal element. To go back again to Shakespeare, we should most of us expect to find him a greater man, if we could meet him, than ourselves, although we should also expect to find him technologically ignorant. Our scientists and technologists themselves are not greater scientific thinkers than their predecessors, and it is a commonplace that we may assume greater power of original thought in Democritus or Ptolemy, in ibn Sina or Roger Bacon, than in any of the myriads of schoolchildren who now know more than any of them did in his own time. We cannot assume that any of the distinguished heads of our Civil Service has greater administrative talent than Henry II, although England is more efficiently administered now than in 1189. Our greater accumulation of knowledge has conferred no increase in wisdom or intellectual power, but my point now is that no one thinks that it has. When we imagine the future, as almost any work of science-fiction exemplifies, we envisage either the best, or the worst, of current political and social tendencies, but we do not look forward to there being a different or better kind of person, only to perpetual technological progress. It is not even within our mental powers to conceive a better kind of person than our different half-discarded religions have taught us to conceive. We know that we have acquired no personal superiority over people of the past as a result of our greater accumulation of know-how; the accumulation of everything that our society has thought and made is not greater than that of past times; there is merely more of it. Yet many of our citizens suppose themselves superior to the citizens of cultures which have a smaller or less useful cultural accumulation.

To sum up at this point. One kind of cultural superiority does not imply another kind, still less a general cultural superiority. Cultural achievement does not measure cultural potential. There is no way to evaluate different cultures comparatively. We are too uncertain in our internal evaluation of skills to be able to judge other cultures by the skills they practise. No culture confers a personal superiority, even in the very field where its achievement, the product of learning accumulated over ages, is indeed superior.

We cannot evaluate our own culture in relation to other cultures, and because of that, we can evaluate an achievement within our own culture more accurately than one outside it. This is true of sub-cultures too. It is much easier to recognise the importance of something that has happened in our own history, than of something outside it. English history is easier for an Englishman to understand, not only because he has been taught more English than European history, but also because he has been taught European history by an Englishman. A Frenchman will see Italian history from a French point of view, and every European will see Europe from a particular vantage point within that continent. The same is true if we compare our understanding of European history and that of the world outside Europe. Europeans easily grasp the importance of the Carolingian age in European history, although Frenchmen and Germans still give it a somewhat different stress. Can we as easily recognise the Charlemagnes of another culture? Can we even see the importance of Charlemagne for the other culture? The Arabs have no record of the elephant which Western annalists tell us Hārūn al-Rashīd sent to Charles. We have to infer that Hārūn probably, and his historians certainly, took less interest in King Charles than Queen Victoria took in African kings to whom presents were sent in her name. We ourselves tend to give Hārūn an exaggerated importance, because he almost alone of the 'Abbāsids is familiar to us from our nursery reading.

It is hard to recognise the importance of those who shape an alien culture, because we are unfamiliar with the culture itself. We are not competent to judge within it. It is little use to teach more world history in school, unless time is available to steep the children (and their teachers) in different cultures. It is barely possible for specialists. A few points appear firmly to result. Hārūn did not foresee the pattern of the future for the Arabs, still less did he recognise the future of Europe or pick out the formative influences in it. Just as what ultimately developed in the Europe that Charlemagne had a part in shaping was not a new 'Abbāsid world in a European setting but something quite different, so we cannot expect that what will finally develop out of other cultures than our own, contemporary with ourselves but economically less developed, will be anything like we are now.

Another kind of difficulty in judging comes from the tendency of every culture to be inward turned and self-regarding. It is a standard

joke to metropolitans when they visit the country that every small town
and village seems to its own inhabitants to be the centre of the world.
In this case the judge, the man from the big city, fancies that he escapes
the same fault, because his horizons are further off. He forgets how
many big cities there are, and though some of those that are near each
other share some, but not all, of the pre-occupations of the others, the
further apart they are, the less they share. Each is the centre only of its
own particular world. Its own world, moreover, is not the total catchment area. The population of each centre is recruited from a national
area around it, and this preserves its distinct character, and checks the
growth of internationalism. The city often shows little interest even in
its own catchment area. Its culture is inbred and self-generating. The
great centres of population are particularly vulnerable to the fever of
ephemeral enthusiasms, including intellectual fashions. A glance at the
London Sunday press for the intelligentsia any week will illustrate this
point, and if any doubt remains, it is worth while to look at the newspaper files of the cultural supplements of a year or two ago. To go back
to Shakespeare, for the last time, a population explosion has yet to show
any evidence of resulting in an explosion of Shakespeares.

One reason may be the excessive importance which we attach to
being sophisticated. We are bitterly ashamed not to be *with it*, or *in the
know*, or *trendy*, or *way out*—there is a new slang phrase constantly
created, and a stream of out-of-date phrases recedes into the past. They
do not all have exactly the same sense, but they are all concerned with
the same general idea of keeping abreast of mental or emotional
fashion, and if possible ahead of it. It is very bad to be caught out in
ignorance, not of facts, which is immaterial, but of what people are
saying; it is worse by a good deal to be found out in simple-mindedness.
'Naïve' is a powerful pejorative. We call the more effective instruments
of destruction 'sophisticated' weapons. The phrase, 'had to be carried
kicking and screaming into the twentieth century', is typical of our
standards and motives. Of course, there is nothing new in all this;
satirists have pointed to its absurdity in many ages; but there is something wrong with the education of the masses if it leaves them vulnerable to this particular kind of folly. It is not only a matter of newspaper
talk which can plausibly be discounted and forgotten. We concern ourselves increasingly with techniques, to the exclusion of subjects: the
new academic disciplines are not usually new subjects, but new techniques, for example, psychiatry, social anthropology, and sociology,
social science, political science, business administration, even home
science. We are particularly good at inventing and improving techniques, computer science for example. The converse is our contempt
for the unsophisticated and the unfashionable.

If we despise those in our own society who are a year or two behind, it is not surprising that we should despise a culture which does not even try to compete with us on our own chosen ground—together of course with all the individuals of whom it is made up. It is in this context that it is possible to hear a man described as 'just off the tree'. Actually the man himself may be highly sophisticated in the things that matter in his own culture, and, although we may not realise it, and may not care about it, it is the culture and not the man that we despise, or, despising the man, we do so only because he shares in the culture. Naturally, the London intelligentsia would be hopelessly at a loss and very 'unsophisticated' in his world; this is simply the Town Mouse and the Country Mouse. We may hope that the increasing number of those who hitch-hike across the continents will modify this contempt, but there is a danger that they will pass through without understanding. There is little value in dashing through the Hindu Kush; the value in foreign travel is not in the distances covered, but in the length of time spent. Sophistication and naïvety are ideas only useful when applied to individuals to measure the extent to which they have absorbed their own culture. If 'sophisticated' has an absolute meaning, then the real sophistication may well be in knowing when to ignore the intellectual fashion. It is more 'knowing' to know the limits of knowing. There is a strong subjective element in the application of such ideas; inter-culturally they are nearly meaningless.

Even within our own culture we may fail to evaluate accurately; we saw earlier that an intercultural historical judgement is often wrong, but we can easily be historically parochial within our own history. The Victorians interpreted English history as leading inevitably to what then seemed the perfection of the age—Parliamentary democracy, the economic rewards for self-help, expanding technology, the victory of Christian religion and morals throughout the world. Perhaps every age conceives itself as perfect, not in the sense that it cannot imagine any improvement, but in the sense that it does not actually envisage any genuine change to come. We may suppose that we have reached a point of technological climax, or a society of complete stability, when in fact further discovery and continuing social revolution follow. I formed the distinct impression as a boy that there lay a long period of useful invention behind us and that we were now in a state of balance and absorption. I was quite wrong. Now we more often suppose the reverse, a perpetually improved technology and a still continuing revolution; and in fact there may be technological failure and social stagnation ahead. I am not saying that this is so, I am saying we do not know. We do not know, because we do not know what all the factors are, and whether there are factors unknown to us. We can tell that there is a

technological possibility of doing certain things; other things are subject to influences and circumstances still uncalculated or incalculable;
but even those that we know to be possible we cannot be sure will be
achieved, if social or economic conditions become unfavourable. We can
tell already that some of our technological practice is unnecessary and
uneconomic. We can say with conviction only that every age has its
own perspective of the past in relation to the present; and no age has
foreseen its own future. On that precedent it is entirely probable that
the future will not be in the direction that the leading intellects, and
the consensus of intellects, today suppose. Liberals may now be leading
or coercing the majority, as once a few early Protestants set the pace for
an England which at first was reluctant; but just as England did not
develop as the first Reformers expected, so we can predict with confidence only the unexpected.

A contrary form of parochialism is to think that conditions we know
today are unparalleled in history. This is a kind of self-dramatisation.
Earlier in this book I argued that we have experienced these phenomena before; there was overcrowding, and rapidly changing technology and social conditions, in early nineteenth-century Britain, and
yet British society was stable and traditional. I argued that the difference today is in the numbers of people affected. Although it is always
said that everything happens now much faster, there seem to have
been as few new ideas in the present writer's lifetime as at any time in
the world's history. It is said that everyone can, and many people do,
travel great distances cheaply and easily. This is supposed to facilitate
the exchange of ideas. I shall have something to say of the self-isolation
of cultures in a moment; here I will just state two plain facts. Groups
of people can live side by side in the same town and do business together for generations, and yet, if they choose to hold themselves apart,
remain in abysmal ignorance of each other's ways and ideas. Secondly,
in spite of the extended services of the 'communications media' of
which we hear so much (almost entirely from these same media),
there is less articulate explanation of the ideas of other cultures now
than at many times in the nineteenth century; the fact is that easy
quick communication has nothing to do with understanding, which can
only be constructed out of careful and patient discussion in one place
over a long time.

I do not believe that the 'generation gap' is as great as people make
out. The argument is based on the contention that our age is unique;
of course it is; every age is unique, but the process of change is not.
Now that I am middle-aged, I remember that when I was young the
middle-aged complained of just the same things as the middle-aged
complain of now; more, I remember their saying that in their youth

the older people said the same of them. I am not denying the facts of change; I am questioning our ability to estimate their importance. If we lived to the age of two hundred, we might be able to tell how important current changes are, but, as we shall not, I doubt if we can. When we were young we laughed at the elderly buffer who complained, 'the world is going to the dogs, sir'; as we grow elderly, we discover that this time it really is seriously going to the bad. Does this mean that each generation has to pass through a process of critical revolt, passing on into acceptance, and thence to disgust at any suggestion of further change? Or is it that there really is a progressive deterioration in the world over the last few generations at least? Or were we right in our own youth to reassure the elderly that they need not fear, and right again now to say that the time has come to call a stop, thus consistent enough in what we say, but reversing our role in relation to others? There is nothing inherently impossible in any of these three interpretations, and we can argue the case interminably. I will not put the possibility of endless argument to the proof; but if it is arguable at all, we have no right to claim any superiority for our culture of here and now.

This parochialism is connected with the geographical parochialism of the great cities where people think that what matters to them matters to everyone. The parochialism of the age is to think that because we live in it it is an improvement on the past, and that the way we seem to be going is the way all humanity will go. An improvement on the past in one respect which we see may go with a deterioration which we do not see; and of the future we can have no idea. The future is a complete blank. At the moment I am writing I know some probabilities for the next few hours, and I know more probabilities stretching increasingly thinly into the more distant future; but these are insubstantial guesses. I have no knowledge of the future. So with the future of the world; we have only guesses. Perhaps there have been as many perspectives of the contemporary world, and of past and future history, as there have been generations. If we think that history is going our way, we think that the future will just be a magnification of the culture of the Atlantic seaboards as it is now; but, like a computer, we can foresee only in terms of our programming. The lesson of all the perspectives is that none of them lasts. Yet if our own immediate world is impermanent, we cannot base intercultural judgements on a delusion of permanence.

All the superiorities are delusions, and they all spring out of self-regard. Each culture sets its standards by an internal clock, and we all believe that whatever is external to our own little world ought to reflect the same standard. It rarely does, of course; it is different, and so far as it is different, we think it is bad, contemptible. By definition, there is much that is different in another culture: language, politics, religion, physical appearance, aims, ideals, habits of mind, and daily customs, any or all of these. We resent difference so much that we often let a difference on the surface hide a fundamental sameness; all cultural differences cover the sameness of humanity. We preserve the difference, because what began by being resented as different ends by being kept different, in order to preserve the resentment. The usual method is the double standard of judgement. Once we have mentally rejected people because they talk and act strangely, we cannot allow that they ever talk or act like us. A cultivated Italian of the fifteenth century said of the Arabs: 'They may be as great and learned as you like, but in their ways they are like dogs'. This is invincible hostility, unless the writer is mocking his own feelings. Few people are frank about unreasonable hostility, although it constantly recurs. Even to ourselves we are reluctant to admit that we cannot confidently assess what happens in another culture; we are not sure of its implications, and we are not sure of ourselves or of our acceptance by the other group. In plain fact, we are a little frightened. When something occurs in our own culture, we can easily understand how it came to happen, we are familiar with the background, we foresee all the repercussions, and they cause us no alarm; we know just where we are and how seriously to take what has happened. In the tenth century, 'young Germans and Frenchmen, incensed by the difference of language—as their custom is—began with great animosity to provoke each other with insults'. So there was enough language in common for insult. It is the difference itself that offends.[8]

Every society enforces some degree of conformity. What it does not care about is what it does not enforce; we can judge the one by the other. Those things that are different from their equivalents in another culture, at least superficially, express the separate identity of any group, and it is for their sake that a group holds itself apart, when it is thrust physically into an alien culture. I have often quoted the chaplain of the English Factory in Aleppo who wrote in 1698, 'Our delights are among ourselves; and here being more than forty of us, we never want a most friendly and pleasant conversation'. Lady Mary Wortley Montague said that English merchants in the Levant 'mind little but their own affairs' and 'can give no better idea of the ways here than a French refugee, lodging in a garret in Greek-Street, could write of the court of England'. Always witty, often perverse, Lady Mary was no more than realistic in this. One Pera merchant boasted to Byron that he had been into Istanbul four times in as many years.[9] I quote these cases because they illustrate the invariable custom of most people

living abroad, who do so for some ulterior reason and not for the pleasure of doing it; it is true of English people anywhere over the channel,
of Europeans anywhere over their own borders, of overseas students in
Europe today. Separate European communities in Arab North Africa
are documented in consular agreements of the thirteenth century;
Italian communities in Byzantium are documented still earlier; and
the classic example of the foreign community, grown so large as to
create a whole culture, is surely Hellenistic Alexandria. At many times
in our own history it would have been only too easy to find people who
did not know 'how the other half of the world lived', even if this related to a different class living round the corner, or even perhaps to the
way of life of their own servants. Most of us know very little about the
beliefs of small sects in our own country, though some of their followers may work side by side with us daily. Over centuries, orthodox
Jewish communities have lived apart. In the Middle East, Christian
communities have lived for over a millennium in Muslim society, and
they have remained wholly ignorant of Islam, and Muslims have remained ignorant of Christian ways. It is very easy indeed for people
who are separated by cultural grouping to live side by side with others
and know nothing about them.

Exclusiveness is not a rare peculiarity; it is the commonest thing in
the world. Within a cultural group we enforce conformity, expelling or
destroying whatever we cannot correct; we cut ourselves off from those
whom we cannot expel or destroy. Islam was commanded by the
Qur'an to tolerate Christians and Jews, and that is why these isolated
communities have survived; mediaeval Christendom could not even
bear to let Muslims survive on terms of isolation, and it permitted Jews
only for fear of preventing the fulfilment of the prophecy of their final
conversion. The same instinct bands people together to resist the alien
majority. Men simply hate other men to be different. When there is
no way of forcing conformity, isolation at least facilitates contempt. The
dominating majority despises the weak, and the minority buttresses its
self-esteem by secret contempt of the way the strong behave. A community which will not tolerate dissent turns *different* into *wrong*. A
community that will or must tolerate—and this includes every community living overseas in an alien culture—makes *different* into
inferior. We began this chapter with the absurdity of a technological
culture that despises a culture technologically inferior; but, inevitably,
he whose plumbing is superior, will think that plumbing is important,
in order that inferior plumbing may mean inferior people. The more
we think about it, the more we shall see its absurdity, but anyone who
lives abroad will encounter it constantly. Any honest person will
recognise that little sensations of superiority often arise in his mind,

however quickly he dismisses them for their absurdity. So far as we can tell, this is the universal experience of humanity, and each culture is the victim and also the aggressor.

The sad fact is that although from all cultural variety the world gains, from all uniformity it loses. France M. Deng, whom I quoted earlier, wrote: 'To adjust ourselves to the values of one race' (and I should substitute 'culture' for 'race') 'will be to abandon indiscriminately a long chain of human experience with all the values of the others, most of which we have not even attempted to know'.[10] This is the very nub of the problem; we have not attempted to know, we have neglected opportunities of knowing, we have not even wanted to know, other cultures. 'That would be a loss to humanity', he rightly added; and as Donne's famous passage speaks of every man diminished by the death of another, so is every culture diminished by the loss of another. Yet this is where the innate intolerance of cultures tends; and the paradox is that it is from variety that they will benefit. We cannot be sure of the value of our own now dominant culture, or of any culture; all sense of superiority is absurd, and the best hope must be in difference and variety.

Past and Present

WE SAW IN an earlier chapter that our own culture is thought of from outside as 'imperialist'. 'Imperialism', the aggressive domination of weaker cultures, resembles other relationships of 'superior' to 'inferior'; and one of the attitudes that constantly reappears in them all is paternalism; and not unnaturally this also occurs, within any society, in the attitude of the older generation to the next. It may strike us as less natural that something of this is reflected back in the attitude of the younger generation. The paternalism of young people towards their elders may sound absurd, but sometimes they show a sense of superiority which they feel to be derived from the very fact that they are young. This must be supposed constantly to fade with the years, but to be yearly renewed with a fresh revolution of youth. The thought becomes less absurd when we extend it beyond the living to the generations of the past. A sense of superiority over the past may be part of the total attitude of our culture to other cultures, a kind of notional imperialism. On the other hand, it may be something gentler. From earliest adulthood, a son may feel protective to his parents, and want to guide them through the new world which belongs to him. The past, like the old, is helpless; inevitably it has an ambiguous relation to the present.

The past created the present; the old made possible what the young think, both the good and the bad; but the intentions of historians have shifted. Until modern times historians wanted to perpetuate the lessons of the past and the present — the past and the immediate past — in the future. They were not conscious of the past as a different society from the present, and they did not think that there was a problem of interpretation. Now historians are pre-occupied by the difference of past and present, and by the difficulty of understanding the past. They are still interested to know how it turns into the present, but they have shifted away from respect for the past, and they no longer think of projecting examples for the use of posterity. The great historians of antiquity and of the Middle Ages were writing to preserve the memory of great actions, or of processes of history, as something good to be copied, or as a warning of what to avoid, or just for the sake of preserving something notable.

Herodotus wrote to preserve the memory of the rivalry of Greeks and 'barbarians' — 'that the things done by men should not be forgotten with the passage of time'; and Thucydides wrote of the war of Athens and Sparta, because it involved the whole world. It was only with apology that Xenophon described episodes that were memorable, but unimportant to the historical sequence. A homiletic or polemic purpose might create anachronism, as when Livy imagined an ideal and distant Roman past. Tacitus sometimes leaves us uncertain how to understand his picture of a deplorable and very recent Roman past. Bede is concerned that his readers and listeners should imitate the good and avoid the bad. Yet all three were driven by the need to remember. In Livy's case it was a need to preserve 'the life and the ways that used to be', *quae vita qui mores fuerint*; and Tacitus was haunted by the thought of the many ancients who were unknown and covered by oblivion. For Bede, it was the historian's function to select 'events worth remembering'. The idea of a lesson which ought to be passed on comes out most curiously in the preface to Procopius' *Anecdota*, where he justifies his tale of scandal as a warning of retribution that awaits a tyrant in his lifetime, and as a threat that publication would perpetuate his wickedness.[1] A little more personally, Liutprand of Cremona made no bones about revenging himself on those who had wronged him, or about repaying benefits received. All are thinking of their posterity, for whom they want to preserve the knowledge of events, the useful examples and the awful warnings. Later, William of Malmesbury wrote to fill in gaps in English history; of why history should be written at all, he said: 'The lower classes make the virtues of their superiors their own, by venerating those great actions, to the practice of which they cannot themselves aspire'; Malmesbury is not preaching submission to a ruling class, but the practical value of keeping great deeds alive in the memories of men. Almost contemporary, the historian of the Latin East, William of Tyre, wrote to preserve events both admirable and otherwise; he does not preach, it is the 'disaster of oblivion' that he fears. Ancient Egyptian religious belief must be judged theologically, but even in secular terms it is touching to find that paintings in the tombs of high officials which show minute details of country life include the actual names of individual farm-workers and fishermen; during the four and a half millenia that the memory of obscure workmen has been preserved, so many rich and important people have been forgotten.[2] This is the simplest and perhaps the most successful history.

Eadmer, the biographer of Anselm of Canterbury, was conscious that he lived, as we do, in a time of change, and wrote lest the knowledge of 'many strange changes in England in our days, and developments which were quite unknown in former days' should be lost to future generations. Gerald of Wales knew what so few perceived until modern times, that cultures change: 'As the times are affected by the changes of circumstances, so are the minds of men influenced by different manners and customs'. He noted that it was the custom of the Greeks to preserve the memory of famous men, and added that no man is stimulated 'to imitation by hearing or reading fabulous records of deeds that are extravagant or impossible', but only by true virtue. There is a hint here, too, of our own contemporary attitude; didactic and controversial as Gerald of Wales always is, he means to exclude what it is inappropriate to preserve. It may be that history is to the original events no better than tinned fruit (however well chosen) to fresh; but there is frozen fruit also, and beyond the history that we write are the authors who speak to us direct. John of Salisbury is praising the use of books when he asks who would know the Alexanders and Caesars, or marvel at the Stoics or the Peripatetics, or follow the examples of the Apostles or the Prophets, if it were not for the *monumenta scriptorum*: 'For I did not see Alexander or Caesar, nor did I hear Socrates, Zeno, Plato or Aristotle'. He too seems to approach the idea of the modern historian; he does not mean to recreate the past, but he does want to be united to it, without quite realising what barriers keep him and it apart. There was a reaching out across time; another mediaeval writer said: 'I find the dead in books as if they were living . . . all the world's glory would be hidden in oblivion if God had not given books to mortals'.[3]

The classical and mediaeval historians whom I have quoted almost at random deal mostly with their own times, and only with their own cultures. Herodotus is the great exception, with his penetrating concern for all that distant past which had gone to make up the 'barbarian' cultures. It is interesting that Thucydides, who explicitly rejected the study of remoter origins, was both the more acute, and the more confined within his own cultural boundaries.[4] The Crusading chroniclers show very little interest in the Muslim world, and most, where their own resembled it. Spanish chroniclers, even when they incorporated an Arabic chronicle, appear unaware of Arab culture. One mediaeval traveller describes the Tatars in terms of his own culture ('barons', 'esquires') and criticises their funerals theologically. Then he adds that Christian funerals seem mean to the Tatars. Even such a momentary glimpse of the view from the other side, in their own age, is exceptional among ancient and mediaeval writers, and an awareness that a past age was itself a different culture from their own hardly exists. Yet, lacking our sense of history, they also lacked the 'notional imperialism' of a sense of superiority over the past. They respected it, assumed it to have resembled their own day, and strongly desired to preserve the present.

The first historian to take a different attitude was, I believe, ibn Khaldūn; he shared, not only, like Thucydides, the same method as modern historians, but also the idea of the past as strange and in need of interpretation. The historian, he said, must not trust plain historical information, as it is transmitted, but must also know clearly 'the principles resulting from custom, the fundamental facts of politics, the nature of civilisation' and 'the conditions governing human social organisation'; and finally he must 'evaluate remote or ancient material through comparison with near or contemporary material'. The originality of ibn Khaldūn was to see that the cultural difference of another age must govern the evaluation of relevant historical material, to distinguish the principles according to which it might be possible to attempt the evaluation, and, lastly, to feel the need for experience, in addition to rational principles, in order to assess a culture of the past. He realised, too, the need to inherit knowledge of all sides of a past culture, as we have in the case of the Greeks, not just the fragment of a picture; at the same time he knew that he did not want a break, but on the contrary to feel an intellectual link with the past. 'Where are the sciences of the Persians, that ʿUmar ordered to be wiped out at the time of the conquest? Where are the sciences of the Chaldeans, the Syrians, and the Babylonians, and the scholarly products and results that were theirs? . . . The sciences of only one nation, the Greeks, have come down to us, because they were translated through al-Maʾmūn's efforts.' Though ibn Khaldūn did not doubt the value of our union with our distant fathers, he saw that a mechanism was needed if their thoughts and deeds were not to be misrepresented.[5]

Our more self-conscious age sees the same problems, and in magnified form. 'The past is dead, dead as the men who made it. To sink oneself in even the recent past, then, is a hard discipline, but a necessary one if history is not to be a vast anachronism.' V. H. Galbraith, whom I here quote, continues: 'To live in any period of the past is to be so overwhelmed with the sense of difference as to confess oneself unable to conceive how the present has become what it is'. He says this although he knows very well that many men live long enough to see one single process of continuity and change over half a century or more. Perhaps it is more useful to reflect that the range of differences between our own present and our ancestors' past is probably much the same as that between different parts of the world at any one time. All societies develop, not only at different speeds, but in many and various aspects at different rates, and in different directions. At least we understand nowadays that a neolithic society and an urban industrial society can exist side by side; there has been cross-infection from one stage of development to another, in the past, perhaps less rapid than now. Yet if we imagine one steady development from a primitive to an advanced economy in each separate and integral ecumene, we shall still expect to find that differences in one place across time are comparable to differences in one time across space; and any difficulty there may be in the understanding of one culture by its contemporary cultures will be repeated in the understanding of the past by the present.

Galbraith compares his own attitude to the writing of history with that of the Victorians, quoting Thomas Arnold: 'The past is reflected to us by the present; so far as we can see and understand the present, so far we can see and understand the past: so far but no further'.[6] Thus the politics of Victorian England explain the politics of ancient Athens. This concedes a barrier between men by implication, but denies the existence of any special barrier between present and past. It ranges Arnold with Bede, and it is a point of view that we do not have to despise. It seems to mean that the past is only occasionally and partially accessible: if there must be a present parallel, in order to interpret the past, wherever none exists, the past is lost. It is a defective view, for the reasons that Galbraith gives; where Galbraith seems to lack respect for the past cultures, Arnold denies the differences. The problem, whether in thinking about the past, or in communicating with other contemporary cultures, is to recognise the differences, to accept and to respect them.

I am not competent to take part in the contentions of the philosophy of history, and I do not want to do so. I will keep to what practising historians say that they do. Arnold's attitude may be a part of what Collingwood called the 'positivist misconception' — 'the study of successive events in a dead past', whereas Collingwood believed that 'history is nothing but the re-enactment of past thought in the historian's mind'. This seems to contradict Galbraith's opinion, but in fact both Collingwood and Galbraith are conscious of the cultural barrier between us and the past, whether we deny that the past is dead when we re-enact it, or insist that, although it is dead, we must learn to live in it. If we imagine these three attitudes in terms of attitudes to foreign countries in the present day, each would equate with a recognisably common attitude among travellers. Arnold would be interpreting the foreign country in the light of British institutions, and comparing it with Parliamentary democracy and a progressive attitude to divorce and to the length of women's skirts and men's hair. Galbraith would be like the anthropologist who belongs firmly in his own urban and academic world, but who goes and lives within a different culture, learns its language and tries to understand its institutions from living inside them. Collingwood seems less like a traveller than like a man who brings the representatives of an alien culture to his own country to interrogate them. He avoids 'the cruder fallacies of mistaking historical facts of culture and tradition for functions of biological facts like race and pedigree'. This sentence is true equally of a past age and of the present moment.

Collingwood argues that a system like Plato's Republic or Aristotle's

Ethics ('the morality of a Greek gentleman') can be 'a coherent whole of ideas'; it is by understanding our past historically that we can 'incorporate it into our present thought'; historical knowledge, he said, and the definition is famous, 'is the re-enactment of a past thought incapsulated in a context of present thoughts'. The historian thinks the thoughts of many men and so he can be many kinds of men in examining the problems of his own world. He can find in history a solution to current problems. If we apply this to current cultures, we shall look to the 'inferior' cultures for some example of how to improve our own. Collingwood also says that the understanding of history changes with the 'here and now' of the historian, and every subject needs to be reworked over by the next generation. In short, the interaction of two cultures, whether living or dead, is a two-way affair; and this is most certainly a lesson we must accept for the interaction of our contemporary cultures.[7]

A mistaken attitude can dominate both our current thinking and our thinking about the past. The Merrie England school of history, based on a 'Catholic' attitude, an assumption that the Catholic church was inerrant in the sense of being right in every past or present controversy, was the direct reflection of clericalism, as exemplified in all periods and even still today. This particular school of history is not taken seriously now, if it is even remembered, but it was taken seriously once, and will doubtless be the subject of future historiographical research, from its origins in Lingard and Cobbett to its height in Belloc and Chesterton. This kind of approach compares exactly with those who love a foreign culture with passion and without discrimination.

Another view of history that we are accustomed to deride is Stubbs' idea of English history as an inevitable progress to Parliamentary democracy. The idea of an inevitable progress in any direction at all is extremely dangerous, and it suffers the disadvantages of hindsight of the past without foresight of the future: it interprets the past from the present as though the present were without a future. That is why we earlier doubted the suggestion that our own future will follow a calculable projection of the present. If we take the Whig idea of history without its notion of inevitable progress, it becomes more acceptable. Sydney Smith said of Hallam's *Mediaeval Europe* that 'the characteristic excellencies of the work seem to be fidelity, accuracy, good sense, a love of virtue and a zeal for Liberty'.[8] There can be nothing wrong with these canons, so long as we care for fidelity, accuracy, good sense, virtue and liberty. We can probably agree that it is legitimate to judge another age by universal standards; and at any rate it is legitimate to judge it by standards that are common to it and to our own. In the same way we can judge other cultures today by universal standards equally applicable and applied equally to it and to our own, at least so long as both cultures accept that these standards are indeed universal. I shall later make reservations about expressing such judgements.

To approach the past with humility is today relatively rare. A few generations ago it happened more often, but even now it is not rarer than respect for other contemporary cultures. I suppose that there are still people to read Plato and even Aristotle in a humble state of mind, and with the hope of learning from them. We would all accept that any writer of the past must be understood in his historical context, but what only amounts to an exact assessment of his meaning — of the cultural implications of what he says — should by no means diminish respect; on the contrary, if it brings out the meaning more exactly, it should increase a respect that springs from a maximum understanding. When we are at school we are bored by Shakespeare and unamused by his jokes, but the hard grind just to understand the language and the context qualified us in the end to understand at least the plays that we have studied. When no one will any longer take even that trouble, or enforce it on schoolchildren, we shall indeed be isolated from the past and drifting rudderless out to sea. It can happen. It is curious that a hundred years ago, when Englishmen were even more insular than now, everyone approached the classical authors — authors alien both because foreign and because past — with humility, and they filled and nourished their minds with them. Most people today are as ignorant of the classics as their ancestors of the early eighth century. A good example of learning from the past is in the school of modern Catholic scholars, most of them continental, who for several generations have studied mediaeval philosophers and theologians with admirable scholarship. Much of the time, most of these historians of ideas were learning from the objects of their own study, and were certainly treating them with genuine and spontaneous respect.

There can be no field of scholarship in which so many European scholars of different nationalities (mostly in Northern Europe) have tried so hard to understand a past and alien culture as the field of Biblical studies. For believing Christians especially, it became terribly important to understand the Gospel and the rest of the Bible, as soon as the techniques of historical criticism were developed. This kind of study provides the best of all examples of what we have been talking about — the idea of understanding something of absolute value by recognising and penetrating its cultural disguise; and the idea of treating a historical period as a source of knowledge and wisdom, with humility. The very theory of the *sitz im leben* is a theory of crossing the cultural barrier and inhabiting a past culture. We understand the writing if we understand the circumstances in which it originated: this is the very model for all historical interpretation; and yet it is astonishing how often the best scholars will talk about some perfectly ordinary action, or habit of mind or custom, as 'oriental', giving various universal characteristics of humanity an exotic or romantic twist. The great Jeremias describes as oriental the behaviour of the labourers waiting to be hired, in the parable of the vineyard. On Matthew 20 verse 3 he says, 'No oriental would stand for hours in the market place. Hence they sit about idly gossiping in the market-place', and on verse 7 he comments: 'the poor excuse' (that is, 'no man hath hired us') 'conceals their characteristic oriental indifference'. In the circumstances of the story, what is more oriental than occidental in their behaviour? What else can the unemployed say anywhere than 'no man has hired us'? This 'characteristic oriental indifference' is a gratuitous assumption totally unsupported by evidence. What would be relevant to the *sitz im leben* would be the situation of Jewish society at that date in that place, but the term 'oriental' is meaningless in the context; unquestionably it indicates the writer's cultural condescension. He cannot really believe that there is an 'oriental' quality which will apply to everyone who lives in the Middle East at any period of time or in any social conditions.[9]

The difficulties of crossing the cultural barrier are particularly well illustrated by Professor Barr's *Semantics of Biblical Language*. Most of this book is concerned with fallacies of historical and linguistic method, but one or two of its arguments are relevant to what we are saying. Barr strongly opposes the inference of cultural patterns from the simple facts of language, by certain schools of hermeneutics: 'An appeal to the usage of NT Greek can be discredited on the ground that it neglects the Hebrew background, and a description of a Hebrew linguistic phenomenon which does not produce the patterns expected from the thought contrast can be discredited as obviously assuming a European point of view'. Barr exposes the fallacies when the same school infers Hebrew thought from Hebrew language, and 'compares Hebrew language direct with what is supposed to be Greek thought or European thought'. If we applied this method to contemporary situations, we should compare a culture in which we had lived with one we apprehended only through a volume of grammar. Barr shows how certain syntactical forms, particularly the Hebrew tense system and the construct state, are supposed to reveal theological characteristics of the thought of the Old Testament.[10] It apparently escapes everyone that the same tense system and the same construct state are used by an urban Arab in the twentieth century and by a Hebrew in a rural community two and a half millenia earlier. There is no 'Semite thought', because there is an infinite cultural variety between different Semites (by which we can only mean, users of Semitic languages) of different historical formation and culture. This sort of fanciful thinking about different cultures might be dangerous. In Biblical studies it carries no worse consequence than being shamed by scholarly ridicule; in contemporary travel it could produce major misunderstanding.

One of the issues which Galbraith raises in his treatment of the problems of studying history is that of monastic forgery. Although forgery of the king's seal or coinage carried serious penalties, 'mere literary forgery was no more than a clergymen's peccadillo'. The tone of teasing patronage in this phrase does remind us of the tone of some travellers' accounts, intended to divert at the expense of an innocent, like a wink over the head of a child. In a present-day traveller it would be offensive; as it is about the past, it would be silly to criticise it as offensive to men long dead, but an attitude of patronage is as likely to end in misrepresentation, in the one case as in the other. 'Literary forgery' may refer to the same thing as the great French historian Marc Bloch refers to when he says, 'As for plagiarism, it was at this time regarded as the most innocent act in the world. Annalists and hagiographers shamelessly appropriated entire passages from the writings of earlier authors'.[11] The present writer regrets that he must criticise greater historians than he, but this really is unreasonable. In the first place, plagiarism of ideas continues unabated today; we are all guilty of it, usually without realising where an idea came from; and without it there would be no communication, and no progression of ideas. Copyright subsists only in the craftsmanship of an exact wording. Yet we do not think it wrong to take over someone else's building and add to it; still less does a gardener destroy the work of his predecessor, lest he plagiarise it, and start again from an artificially created desert. We do not like mediaeval anonymity in architecture and writing, partly no doubt because architects and writers now live off the earnings of their individual productions. The way a piece of writing is regarded is wholly cultural, and though I personally should be angry at being plagiarised, this only makes me a man of my culture. Plagiarism is what those writers suffer who resent being plagiarised. All the evidence is that mediaeval writers saw themselves as taking up the same work, each in his turn, adding to it, embellishing it, and of course re-using it.

The sort of forgery that Galbraith and Bloch had in mind ranges from the False Decretals, so fundamental to political theory in the Middle Ages, through imaginary or fictional history to forged charters. The Donation of Constantine long deceived everyone, perhaps because it had a kind of historical reality, in making the facts conform to the ideal. The forger may well have felt just the common attitude: 'It ought to be so (or to have been so) and therefore it is (or was) so'.

The more difficult example is that of the forged charters used to support monasteries in lawsuits which often resulted in serious injustice, not only by our present standards, but also by contemporary mediaeval standards. They are quite incongruous, except in a crudely Leninist view of religion; there is a cultural barrier between us and the monk who forges a charter to produce in court in the interests of his House, although there are parallels in the modern world. The monks felt to their monasteries just the same loyalty that Europeans, at least until very recently, felt to 'my country right or wrong'. That phrase would sound perfectly absurd if allegiance to one's country were as remote as allegiance to a monastery is to most of us. In the 'Song of the Battle of Hastings' it is represented as remarkable that the English 'count it the highest honour to die in arms, that their native soil may not pass under another yoke'.[12] In our day many people have been expected to kill for their country, and are ready to do so again, and on an unprecedented scale, although killing in private circumstances is still regarded as a serious crime. The idea of murder is repugnant to most people, but now that abortion is approved and euthanasia (named like the Euxine Sea by euphemism) recommended, both of which, not so long ago, were universally considered murder, it should be obvious that such ideas can change. As we see attitudes changing now, so we are the heirs of old forgotten changes. The monks were as familiar as we are with various kinds of legalised killing; clergy hanged men, held by military tenure, and fought in battles; if they were perfectly familiar with legalised killing, why should we be surprised that a monk thought it right to forge for his monastery? To it he owed all the loyalty that a man may owe to the community to which he belongs.

Marc Bloch argued that, if people of 'incontestable piety and even of integrity' were responsible, then it was obvious that these forgeries were 'hardly offensive to public morality'. This is not altogether true. As he himself pointed out, it was offensive to the lay opinion of illiterate landowners who were defrauded by the forgeries, but their opinion was not well organised. It was also offensive to the opinion of canon lawyers, for good professional reasons; and those most concerned to defend the process of canonical justice might be expected to disapprove. We do indeed find this; thus John of Salisbury speaks of it as shameful, and he gets Archbishop Theobald to ask the Pope for a suitably severe punishment.[13] The public opinion that tolerated this behaviour was the public opinion of the monasteries themselves, who were the most interested party. There are plenty of modern precedents for tolerating iniquity. The human capacity to justify one's own misdeeds as righteous hardly needs to be exemplified. Just because cultural barriers are a reality, it will be very difficult to feel there is a wholly satisfying and completely sympathetic understanding of monastic forgery; but I think that I have said enough to show that the explanation can be rooted in universal human qualities that span ages and places, and yet take different forms in different places and ages.

In fact, although Arnold was wrong to believe that he could understand Athenian politics in terms of English politics in his own day, he was only overstating a perfectly sound case; his experience of contemporary politics did help him to understand quite different politics in quite different circumstances. We can, and we must, use our current experience in order to interpret history. Bloch, certainly, was of this opinion. 'In the last analysis, whether consciously or no, it is always by borrowing from our daily experiences, and shading them, where necessary, with new tints that we derive the elements which help us to restore the past.' He endorses a personal remark of Pirenne's, saying that a man who does not observe the men, things and events around him is not an historian, but only a 'useful antiquarian'. Thus Pirenne began sight-seeing in a strange town by looking at the newer buildings.[14] If we are to understand history, and not just record it, the present, which is all the access we have to the human continuum, must illuminate the past. There are parallels which are a good deal more obvious than the one I have just been drawing. Sixteenth- and seventeenth-century wars of religion are perfectly comprehensible to us, because they are paralleled by the ideological wars of the present century which many now alive have seen, and which continue on a limited scale. We still have to exercise our imaginations by substituting religion for the ideologies which we have cared enough for to fight about, but with that substitution the problem becomes clear. So far Arnold is justified after all. Witch-hunting is a similar case; it is so easily comprehensible to our age that we have borrowed the phrase to describe an activity of our own. Again, we have to substitute a new subject matter, but once we have done that, the process ceases to be alien. There probably really is no great difference between the old horror of the witch, and the modern American horror of the Communist during the post-war era. There are other examples. Contemporary writers despise ancient and mediaeval writers on science and magic as credulous and absurd in their error; yet we ourselves constantly believe what 'experts' say on subjects not our own, and often repeat what they say as if we knew it ourselves for certain. Scholars themselves copy and perpetuate other scholars' mistakes. In any case, we should equate many of the mediaeval writers here in question rather with our journalists than with our scientists.

It is essential that the past event or process should be understood in terms of the age in which it occurred and in its 'situation in life'; yet

we can only form our judgement by recognising the common human
element that is always the same, despite each cultural variation in
expression. The trick is just to recognise it. If we can do so, we can
begin to respect what is different, instead of reserving our respect for
the reflection of our own selves. Just how difficult is 'nihil humanum
alienum' in everyday practice? Is there any mental distance, within the
range of humankind, that we cannot cross? Without denying the influence of technology on our general intellectual formation, I have
questioned whether the interaction is close or direct. Gordon Childe's
Stone Age Sussex farmers are not so distant that we can never meet.
Very wisely, Childe ended the lecture I quoted earlier by saying that
our present culture already incorporates 'the real thought of past
societies'. 'The best results of their thinking are already . . . constituent
of our culture'.[15] Can we not go a little further, and say that all the
results are in us, the best and the worst and the neutral?

Sympathetic magic, of course, we cannot conceive except as a curiosity or an exercise in imagination, and the Stone Age farmer could not
conceive that our science would work; but most people in either system,
magic or scientific, have had and claimed no understanding of how the
processes that the experts operate actually work. Quite apart, therefore,
from the haphazard survival of superstitious remnants in most people's
minds, the attitude that you or I may take up of admiring wonder at the
skill of the garage mechanic or the company executive will not be
different from our distant ancestor's to the abilities of his shaman. The
things may differ, but the relation be the same; although the intellectual
content of human minds differ, can we not easily exaggerate the difference in the experience felt? Those who enjoy Homer—and although
we may well find Enkidu alien, to most of us Achilles is easily familiar
—are already half way there. I suggest that we have in us still both the
thinking of those who developed in our direction and the thinking of
those who did not.

There is another useful lesson here. The differences we are talking
about now and those we were talking about before, are quite incom-
mensurate. Whether I am right or wrong to think that we can be one
with Stone Age farmers, it is immediately obvious that the differences
between us and Aristotle or Thucydides, Tacitus or Cicero, Aquinas or
Chaucer, are negligible. We need to make a very little effort to understand them, but the trouble and attention required are as slight as those
required to change residence from one European country to another.
The shared element is the greater part. We have already seen that a
man who roundly condemns a past age for its moral faults is not necessarily failing to cross the cultural barrier. If he shares standards with a
past age, there is nothing anachronistic in condemning events of that

age by those standards, provided always the events condemned have been understood in their proper context; but, if they have, it would be an anachronism not to share the contemporary judgement. Where the historian does not share the standards, he can only, of course, condemn by the standard of a *ius gentium* or Noachitic law, and in that case agnosticism will be preferable. By agnosticism here I mean a reservation of judgement on events, judgement on people always being unacceptable. I made, and I must stress, the proviso that there is always anachronism, unless events are understood in their context. This must include some understanding of the probable motivation of a kind of act. It would be anachronistic and culturally absurd to condemn the ecclesiastical forger as if he were doing exactly what the modern criminal forger does. It may not always be possible to go beyond a negative understanding. If we cannot share the feelings of the forger, we can at least make sure that we realise what they are not. It takes very little effort of imagination to share the feelings of a criminal forger. It is something just to be sure that the feelings of the ecclesiastical forger were different.

It is difficult to accept the parallel case of a man who condemns what goes on in another contemporary culture that he happens to be visiting. Logically the same principles apply: if we share the standards of judgement, we can judge. What is dangerous here is the likelihood of being unable to recognise what underlies a cultural difference, to see what would happen if the thing were transferred to one's own culture. An Englishman may be indignant about a case of bribery in a foreign country in which he is living. He may share exactly the same standard of judgement as a friend of that country. His criticism of the act may still cause resentment. If it does cause resentment, is this just mild xenophobia, which prefers to keep criticism in the family? Not necessarily; the insider will know and understand the reasons for an act that has happened in a situation more familiar to him than to the alien. He may feel that the judgement of the foreigner is right in principle, but that it makes too little allowance for circumstance. In dealing with the past, there is no one to feel xenophobe resentment, and the historian must guard against the effects of his relative ignorance; and that is the very thing he is trying to dispel. It is hard to decide whether historical judgement or contemporary intercultural criticism is more dangerous to truth. The second is more obviously likely to do harm in the course of the history now making; but history now making may also be harmfully affected by a deformed recording of the past. One wrong judgement of the past may lead to a wrong judgement of the present, and the same wrong will reflect from the one context to the other.

There are a good number of attitudes to history which we can see reflect attitudes across cultures. Kipling was fond of a character, Strickland, who could transpose himself into an Indian, and Buchan recreated the same character in his Sandy Arbuthnot.[16] On the other hand there used to be a myth about going native, and some people abroad will embrace the surface customs without any real sympathy or acceptance of common motives or even of the alternative cultural framework. These kinds of behaviour are similar to the unreflective appreciation of an historical period. Again, the interpretation of history in terms of our own day resembles the kindly imperialist authority who insists on developing a country in a direction it does not wish and which it bitterly resents. All these attitudes, which are singularly unprofitable either in living abroad or in writing history, can be avoided only by learning to recognise the universal quality or factor in all its many possible cultural variants.

This looking for resemblances between historiographical attitudes and the attitudes of travellers and residents abroad is not a parlour game. It is very necessary for all of us to be able to recognise these attitudes, so that we may know what we are doing. We are not all professional historians and we are not all overseas residents; but most of us are amateur historians when we interpret a past that for all of us extends across our own lifetimes, and often across the periods our parents and teachers have discussed with us. The history of a few years ago is very close to what may concern us at any moment. We are also amateur travellers, and the different cultures of the world are close and accessible. It is obvious that they are constantly misrepresented to us —obvious not only to someone who happens to have the local knowledge that reveals that the newspapers are wrong, but obvious because the written sources contradict each other. The attitude to other cultures is put in front of us all the time: other religions, peoples, classes are on our doorsteps. The interpretation of everything that is different is one complex whole, and back across time or over the boundaries between places, perhaps only the boundary of the next street, is all one attitude. Every thought of something different about people is a leap of the imagination.

The classical and mediaeval historians did not say that they wanted to project their own personalities into the future, and as far at least as the mediaevals are concerned, their indifference to plagiarism, their communal treatment of the writing of history, ought to acquit them of the wish that we have in our age to perpetuate the personality of the author. What they wanted was to perpetuate the example of their time for the use of the future, and, quite simply, because it was worthy not to fall into oblivion. This motive is hardly ours at all; perhaps we feel too sure that we shall be remembered, either because so much is published, or because we are so sure of the importance of our age. It is true that the mediaevals venerated a past of which they often had a very imprecise knowledge, and Bloch pointed out that this veneration was actually the reason why the forgers had to invent a past that had not happened. We know more about the past, and have less respect for it; it is the future we want to dominate, and we like to believe that it will extend the present along predestined lines. We invent the future — not only in science fiction, but in our ordinary assumptions — as the forgers invented the past; but at best, and inevitably, we are more inaccurate about the future than any mediaeval poet about King Arthur or Charlemagne or Alexander the Great. For us there are two great railway termini: the past arrives at one, in the present we transfer by bus to the other, and from there the train sets out into the future. These are false certainties. We know little enough about the present, less about the past, and nothing at all about the future. The classical and mediaeval historians were much simpler in their approach; they took it for granted that humanity was all one, had always been and always would be. We whose techniques of interpreting the past are so much more highly developed lack this awareness of the whole human race of past and future, and so, instead of accepting as harmless or useful the various cultural differences, we try to impose our own upon all.

The history of our own culture, as strange to us as any other culture living today, ought to teach us to accept some cultural barrier as normal. The only impassable barrier consists of not recognising the differences of attitude that a strange cultural origin or background causes. Once they are recognised they are on their way to be understood. The danger is to fail to recognise across the cultures that the same things are the same, however much the cultural differences disguise them. We can diagnose symptoms: lack of understanding (very obvious when we are dealing with the barrier to the past); lack of communication (we cannot communicate with the past, but when or as far as we achieve understanding, the past can communicate with us); and lack of sympathy. Sympathy is a pre-condition that must develop step by step with understanding.

In the case of our relation with the other cultures of the present the same factors apply as in relation to the past, but communication, of course, is even more important, when it is capable of functioning in two directions. Communication is often blocked wilfully by the deliberate cultivation of cultural prejudice. There are ways in which the past barrier is less serious. The past cannot feel resentment; in the present every failure adds to the barrier, and every attitude that is resented — patronage, interference, even, sometimes, being useful or right — is a failure to communicate. The more we widen the range of our study of cultural prejudice, the better we can hope to understand it. That is why it has been useful to think about the historical barrier. This dual consideration has a dual advantage: it helps us to understand better both the present of other people and the past of our own. It opens whatever communication is possible in either case.

No one really questions the need for tradition and continuity. The Maoists at the height of the cultural revolution had to appeal constantly to Lenin; for us it is as useful to rescue every generation, our past, and ourselves, who are the future's past, from oblivion, as it is to communicate across our own present world, in which many different futures exist potentially, the sequence of events already under way. It is good practice to keep our ears open to whispers, rather than ourselves to shout into deaf ears. In a culture devoted to the values of the rat-race it is probably pointless to add that the solidarity of the human race — its common experience in so great a variety of forms — is a good in itself.

Transmission of Ideas

UP TO THIS point we have discussed some of the aspects of cultural difference which impede communication. We have taken several historical examples, but we have not reviewed the historical conditions of cultural interchange. The present chapter identifies some historical settings which proved unpropitious, and the chapter following is concerned with an age of successful transmission. I want to know how ideas are transmitted, what prevents their transmission, and how the ideas that are transmitted and received are selected.

We have seen that cultures outside our own have wanted to preserve their separate identities. Historically they are a series of already overlapping ecumenes: there are a number in the African continent, some of which overlap with Arab cultures; these overlap in turn with the Persian, and the Turkish overlaps with both these; the Persian overlaps with the Islamic culture of India, which has also its own Hindu culture; and the Indian and Chinese cultures overlap at their points of common penetration in South East Asia. Even China, traditionally turned inward, has expanded by emigration. These over-simplifications at least remind us that none of the cultures which are now subject to the technological domination of the West and North, and to cultural pressures accompanying it, have ever been isolated identities, but are the products of cross-fertilisation, and often the result of invasions and aggressions now long past. In spite of this, they feel their separate identities and feel that these are threatened and are worth preserving. Mostly, they think that 'Western' domination is the product of a series of fortuitous circumstances which enabled the technologies to develop where and in the way they did. What are the historical precedents, if any?

I have to select a restricted part of the world, and consider only the area of the conquests of Alexander and the conquests of Rome. It is the area where the liturgical languages have been Arabic (with Syriac, Chaldean or Coptic for most Christians), Greek and Latin, the area where the dominant religions have been Islam and Christianity. The most ancient stratum in its inheritance is Sumerian, Babylonian, and Egyptian, the more recent Hellenic and Iranian. It has seen a cultural continuity survive political and military, ethnic and linguistic changes, but we do not know the mechanism which preserved it. We know a little about the transmission of ideas from both Egypt and Babylonia to the Greeks, and the history of astrology is well enough documented for us to infer something about the transmission of late Babylonian astral religion, not only to the Greeks themselves, but to Ptolemaic Egypt. There is not the documentation to tell us about the mechanism of transmission. We know much more about how cultivated Romans came to adopt the Greek language and literature, but the case is in no way parallel to our present situation; the Romans chose to adopt the ways of a conquered people. We also know about the dissemination of Jewish thought in the Hellenistic and Roman world; we can tell a good deal from Josephus and more from Philo, and something earlier from Maccabees. The spread of Christianity in the Apostolic age tells us still more about the transmission of ideas through the diaspora; but again, there is no real parallel with the present day. That situation had nothing to do with techniques; and neither Greek nor Jew was dependent on the other. Another transmission of ideas occurred when the Arabs adopted Greek scientific culture, classical, but more especially Hellenistic, from the eighth century of our era onwards; the Arabs interposed a cultural filter, and took only the scientific and technical literature that interested them; they had their own poetry and did not want Greek poetry or drama. Yet this also has no modern parallel, either to the partial transmission of Greek through Syriac, or to the relation of 'Arabs' to 'Greeks' — Arabic-speakers were increasingly descendants of Greek-speakers, and genetically were predominantly neither Arabs nor Greeks.

There is never a perfect parallel, of course, only a parallel in some respects; but I think the most useful parallel is the adoption of Arabic scientific culture by the mediaeval Latin West. This was the same corpus that the Arabs had taken from the Greek, with their own developments of it. The parallel is close in that a distinct and vigorous culture, in its recent history more limited, technically less developed, needed and took scientific knowledge from a more highly developed society. Moreover, as we shall see when we look at the story in more detail, the borrower did exactly what the technical borrowers of other cultures would like to do today: it rigidly excluded the cultural elements it did not want, while freely taking all it did. We now know that the society from which it borrowed was in decline, culturally and technically, and that a successful future awaited Europe; but whether there is a parallel in that respect to the modern world, whether our culture is on the verge of decline, the speculations of a Spengler cannot tell us.

The area with which we are concerned has had a remarkable history. It has been devoted to internecine war. In some respects, some parts of it have enjoyed a parallel cultural development, and the cultural attitudes of separated parts of the Mediterranean are similar even now, after much more than a millenium of division between Islam and Christianity. On the other hand, a shared technology for long did nothing to prevent new and divergent cultural developments. The invention of the stirrup created or was absorbed into, a different kind of society among the Turks, among the Arabs, among the Byzantines, and among the Franks, in spite of superficially 'feudal' resemblances. Moreover, different techniques of fighting were based on the same technology. This area has twice erupted outside its boundaries. Islam spread further than the army of Alexander had marched, and it continued at intervals to extend itself. Then from the beginning of the sixteenth century until very recently indeed was the period of European imperial expansion. The area has warred greatly within itself. Apart from the invasions of the peoples who settled Europe, from the Viking raiders to the last world war, Europe has constantly fought within itself, and Western Asia has hardly done so less.

We can speak of this as one cultural area, because it has had no lasting frontier to divide it, but it is a commonplace that the Western and Eastern halves have been fighting each other as long as history has been recorded. From the Old Testament we are familiar with the swing between Egypt on the one hand and Assyria, Babylonia, and Persia on the other. The wars of Rome with the Parthians, and of East Rome with the Sassanids, were a see-saw apparently perpetuating itself indefinitely into the future. It is the classic irony that Khusraw's sweep across Syria in 613, and Heraclius' dramatic recovery of the True Cross fifteen years later, immediately preceded the total destruction of the Sassanian world, and the Byzantine loss of Syria, in the Arab invasion. The see-saw of warfare continued between Muslim Arabs and Christians, but after this the boundaries had changed. The Arabs took into the 'East' not only Syria, but the southern and western Mediterranean; and the 'West' came more and more to be divided between the Byzantines, fluctuating between weakness and strength, and the Latins, who grew steadily from great weakness to a position of power. The geographical division now became North and South, and on the whole it has remained so up to our own day.

From that time to this the shifting frontier has also been the frontier of Europe. The invasion of North Africa and Spain was completed early in the eighth century, but the victory of Charles Martel in central France did not end Arab attacks. The Aghlabid conquest of Byzantine Sicily was a century later; the ninth century also saw the sack of the Roman suburbs, and quasi-permanent Arab settlements in southern Italy. The tenth century is rather a period of equilibrium, despite the Arab raids on northern and southern Italy and the Alps, and the long occupation of military settlements. In Anatolia it marked Byzantine expansion. In the earlier eleventh century the equilibrium was perfect, and then with the Norman invasion of Sicily the return swing began. The same century marked the growing impetus of Spanish reconquest, and ended with the First Crusade. The failure to capture Damascus in the twelfth century is already the beginning of the reverse trend; the victories of Salah al-Dīn at the end of the century mark this more clearly. There followed a progressive swing against Europe, although the Arabs increasingly disappear from the scene; in turn the Seljuks, Mongols, Mamluks and Ottomans advanced against, and the latter deep into, Europe. The impetus against the 'East' continued in the West, however, until the obliteration of Granada and the expulsion of the Moors from Spain in the sixteenth century. The seventeenth century seems to be another period of equilibrium, and the eighteenth saw the beginnings of Islamic dependence on Western power. The nineteenth, of course, was the great period of European expansion, which over-flowed the Islamic world into India and China and four continents; and the mid-twentieth is one of equilibrium. What comes next we have no means of knowing. These periods of backward and forward movement with intervening periods of balance are not a neat sequence; the imperial expansion against Asia was a by-passing of the Ottoman attack on Europe, and the Portuguese were massacring Arab merchants in the Persian Gulf while the Ottomans were enslaving the populations of Eastern Europe. The whole series of wars seems more like an international sporting event, until we remember the endless cost of lives and suffering. It hardly seems a propitious setting for the exchange of ideas.

Except in Spain, where there was early a well-documented cultural conflict (described in my next chapter), the early centuries of Islam seem to have been devoid of any intercultural exchange of thoughts. To the educated ruling classes, to the Popes and the Abbots of Cluny, to articulate men of affairs like Luitprand of Cremona, the Arabs were dangerous; but they wasted no time, either on controverting or on learning from them, and would have shared the culture of the ordinary masses to the extent of lumping together all infidels, Saracens, Vikings and Magyars alike. A man from Mars might have found it difficult to disentangle the Arab and Latin rulers, in Italy often in alliance, and the Byzantines, vaguely suzerain, sometimes enemies, sometimes allies; it is likely that he would have found the Mediterranean all one. Northern Europe was more obviously different. The rise of Islam roughly coincided with the conversion of England to Christianity; it is food for reflection to recall how far both had travelled in different directions before the industrial revolution. The greatest writer for many generations in Europe was an Englishman: Bede as an old man was contemporary with the first Arab harassment of France, of which he heard; as a young man, he was contemporary with the beginnings of scientific translation into Arabic under the Umayyad caliph Marwan I, of which he did not hear. The science of the ancient world had not begun to pass into Arabic on a substantial scale when he died. The expansion of Christianity in Northern Europe coincides with the great era of Abbasid rule; Bede and Boniface and the Carolingians seem very distant from the later Umayyads, the first 'Abbāsids and the 'Abbāsid prime; northern Europe was a remote province of the great world.

In literary terms, Latin Europe was self-generating. Until the twelfth century there were only the patristic inheritance and limited classical sources. The nadir is a Merovingian text where Venus appears as a masculine, and he is an incestuous lover of his sister 'Junae-Minerva'.[1] The Carolingians restored to Western Europe its own Latin culture. John Scotus Erigena is one isolated figure of Greco-Roman thought, and although he shows no Arab influence, he is interested in the theological problems which come close to Muslim preoccupations; he was a man of Mediterranean culture, although he did not come from it. There is an actual awareness of the Arab world implicit in Gerbert's mathematics, of the very last years of the millenium, implicit also perhaps in the later magical myth about him. Europe was beginning to catch up; Indian numerals were at this date still not in universal use among the Arabs themselves. The inbred Latin literate culture was thirsty for new sources of thought. Europe was intellectually famished and profoundly provincial; and yet it had not developed away from the ancient world, merely fallen behind. It still belonged to one Latin-Hellenic-Arabic world, divided by religion, divided politically, but not yet developed irrevocably in new and different cultural directions. Conditions were really propitious for the transmission of ideas at the moment of equilibrium before the Latin expansion of the Middle Ages. It is interesting to contrast conditions in the equivalent period of the seventeenth to eighteenth centuries.

The modern study of Arabic grew out of the urge to understand the Scriptures better; it was an attempt to support the study of Hebrew, and was linguistic and, in a primitive way, anthropological. It was rapidly dissipated in a miscellaneous interest in cultural bric-a-brac; there is no sort of planned order in the English or French translations of the mid-seventeenth century, comparable to that of the mediaeval translations we shall be looking at later. Finally, at the end of the century Galland discovered gold when he published his translation of the *Arabian Nights*. A later translator of Galland into English analysed his appeal into three points: the picture of foreign manners and customs; the machinery of magic—jinns and magic lamps, the matter of pantomime; and the knowledge of the human heart. It is difficult to make any scientific investigation into the impact of the *Arabian Nights*, but it seems as though the first and last of these two points did make the Muslim world seem less the enemy, more 'us' and less 'them'. Until that date, the popular picture of the Arab world had been as seen by the Barbary Coast slave, a stereotype of savage cruelty, although one French consul thought the Arab slave in Spain or Sicily a good deal worse off. Indeed, in those days the defector to the Muslim world could hope to rise to political eminence, and this was realised. Both then and in the Middle Ages, Christian Europe was hierarchial and monolithic, like the USSR today; the place for eccentric enterprise was the Muslim world, but just as the West gets a bad press in the USSR today, so the tyranny of the Turks or the Barbary Coast was an accepted image then. This was changed when Galland brought Harūn al-Rashīd and Ali Baba into the nursery and the drawing-room.[2]

The serious love interest, not only of Galland but also of other 'Persian Tales' and similar material published in the fashion, brought together the satirical fashion of the day in Europe and the old tradition of lascivious Arabs: 'The Turkish ladies don't commit one sin the less for not being Christians' said Lady Mary Wortley Montague. Now Islam was reproved for being repressive, where the traditional attack was for its sexual laxity. Montesquieu used his Persian hero like Goldsmith's Chinaman, as a man from Mars, to satirise Europe, although also to sentimentalise sexual freedom for Persian ladies. The second of Galland's three qualities, the exotic appeal, created a tradition which could produce things of great but eccentric beauty, like the Brighton Pavilion, as well as turgid and obscure fantasies like Vathek; but it was no bridge between cultures. A vague good will by itself is a very small achievement. This literature was not about anything serious; it taught European readers no skill, or technique, or anything they wanted to know. It did not even bring them a representative literature that Arabs themselves admire; William Jones' *mu'allaqat* (which did) was never popular. Their minds were opened, but only to an unreal world typified by Disraeli's complaint that he had to give up a Greek servant dressed like a Mameluke in crimson and gold, with a thirty foot long turban, for a barefoot Arab in a blue shirt: that is, he had lost the picturesque bogus orient and gained the plain reality of the actual East. A mind opened to a world of the imagination was closed to what was actually happening. A mind closed to the light of day was as closed as that of Peter the Hermite to the virtues of another culture. The romanticism of the exotic was a new divisive factor. Those who in our century saw the desert Arab as the true and romantic Arab and could not come to terms with an Arab who lived in large cities were the victims of one of the most impenetrable, mental barriers ever constructed.

The long literary tradition of oriental romanticism teaches lessons of practical use in our present investigation. The sort of imaginative cult that we are talking about is like dangerous driving; it is the expression of an internal dissatisfaction and instability which is more the affair of the student of abnormal psychology than of the historian; it is a mere yearning that has nothing at all to do with communication; it is an adventure of the Western mind within itself. A genuine link requires us to want the same thing for the same reason. The Englishman who yearns for Samarcand, for Isfahan or Bukhara cannot see that for the Persian these are Nottingham, Northampton, and Leicester. A real communication can only take place if both sides are looking for the same thing. I remember that, at a time when I used to have to do with foreign visitors to Scotland, I noticed how people from the Mediterranean wanted to see the cold grey haar, and were truly disappointed when the islands of the Firth of Forth, as quite often happened, lay in a golden sun and a blue sea, and the Bass Rock looked like Monte Cristo. The Southerner who wants fog and the Northener who wants sun are looking for the same exotic satisfaction, but they cannot find it together. Far from communicating, two cultures in this situation are like neurotics too absorbed in their private fantasies to notice each other. Although this romanticism has survived into the present day, whenever, as often happens, Britain conducts its oriental policies in an *Arabian Nights* fantasy, more sensible conditions capable of transmitting actual ideas were in fact created by the imperial situation.

In the first place, many of the administrators were sincerely interested in the history of the cultures in which they were working. If sometimes they glamourised and romanticised their roles, and seem to put themselves in pseudo-oriental postures, there is a considerable bulk of serious literature by men like Metcalfe, Munro, Malcolm and Elphinstone in the early years of the nineteenth century. Sir William Jones, Sir Ouseley Gore, even Warren Hastings, a generation earlier, had combined scholarship, or a genuine interest in scholarship, with their imperial duties. The tradition continued more than a century later: anyone who cares to consult the run of *Sudan Notes and Records* will see that, at however uneven a standard, the amateur anthropology and amateur linguistics reveal a wholly disinterested love of the subject. For many, in short, colonialism created an opportunity for research. Travellers did a real service in the interpretation of one culture to another; Burton and Livingstone were outstanding. One of the most remarkable, because utterly dispassionate and endlessly informative of books, Lane's *Manners and Customs of the Modern Egyptians*, is not exactly the product of colonialism, but it is certainly a good advertisement for the capacity of the imperial age for intercultural scholarship. I have given English examples, but the French produced serious studies of Algeria, and later of Tunis and Morocco. We have to realise and accept that although colonialism generated the contempt of the rulers and the hatred of the ruled, it also created knowledge and understanding. It gave the opportunity to the writer and generated the interest of enough readers to make publications possible. Its weakness was that it was one-sided. Indians writing about Britain and Algerians about France are usually products of the decolonisation era.

Another shared interest which made for real communication was that very technology of which I have written so much. It is closely linked with neo-colonialism, and of course it was closely linked with classic imperialism. It is also the theme of proto-colonialism, the supply of experts which preceded colonial interference, just as now it is the substance of multilateral and bilateral aid. We have yet to see one of our contemporary experts publish a book which bridges a gap between cultures. The *Memoirs* of the Baron de Tott, a French officer under Louis XV, Hungarian by birth, who was an artillery adviser to the Ottoman sultan, is not a serious study, such as I was talking about just now, but it illustrates how the technical weakness of other cultures created personal links. It is evident that such a man lived in a way that was not wholly cut off from the life of the people. Another Western technique in demand at about the same period was the medical. When the Florentine Dr Lorenzo was murdered, apparently by no less than the Capitan Pasha, in 1815, he had practised medicine in the Seraglio for forty years under the diplomatic protection of the Austrian Emperor. We can set this sort of life against that of the merchants who held themselves aloof. We may believe, whether we are Marxist or not, that the overwhelming technical superiority of Europe made the imperial movement inevitable, but if the gap between the technical achievements of Europe and the rest of the world had been a little less drastic, these loans of experts might have led to more fruitful links.

The situation of superiority in which the European was put, whether he liked it or not, made it difficult for him to compare his own culture with the one that he visited. We find, of course, an occasional healthy reaction against the jinns and the magic, although that too could be overdone. 'As I rode along the narrow streets, I was assailed by scents far different from those of fairy-land'; and there were complaints about modernisation: 'Cairo is being rapidly Haussmanised'. Attempts really to penetrate into cultural differences that yet show what is common in humanity are of two kinds. Serious published works are rare. I would suggest that Morier's *Haji Baba* books, both of course fictional, are quite a serious attempt. The first, and best known, does fail in this way, because it was, and was seen by the Persians to be, however light-hearted, a laugh at the expense of the other man, and the absurdity of his little ways; but the second, *Haji Baba in England*, tries to laugh equally at both the cultures, Persian and English. The other, less well known, and less easily illustrated, is the reaction of hundreds of ordinary sensible visitors, whose minds were sufficiently open to their actual experience to overlay the childhood fairy stories. 'Although this day's entertainment had no way answered my expectations, as to splendour or female beauty', wrote an Ambassador's wife in Constantinople in 1815, 'I was yet extremely pleased at having passed so many hours with a Group of Turkish Women and to see enough of their characters and manners to enable me to form some idea of their humour and mode of life. I found them much more cheerful happy and good natured than I expected—The visit of a Foreigner was an amusement . . . but I understand that they are pretty much occupied—the lower Class in Cooking and in making Confectionary . . . and the upper ones in making their Clothes and in Embroidery'. There was a real gain as a result of travel and the mixing, however limited, of cultures.[3]

Communication suffered most, of course, from the intolerable imperial relation of conqueror to conquered, which only imagination of an exceptional quality could mitigate. Napoleon was the teacher of the lessons of modernisation, not only to the people of Egypt, but, indirectly, to all Afro-Asia, and the first lesson was the victory of a highly de-veloped armed force, which later convinced Jamāl al-Dīn al-Afghāni that it was science rather than any imperial nation that ruled. Napoleon was so clearly 'insincere' in ordinary European terms that we forget his genuine cross-cultural insights. In retrospect, at any rate, he believed that he had been anxious to enlist in his support both the 'Arab national spirit' and 'the religion of the Koran'; in practice he had made a better show of the latter than of the former; he was, after all, in command of an army of occupation. Was it absurd that he should write to Muslim rulers 'in the name of God, the Compassionate, the Merci-ful', adding the *shahada*, 'there is no God but God, and Muhammad is his Prophet'? When his general, Menou, became a Muslim, under the name of Abdalla, Napoleon said that this had made a good impression on the Egyptians, but had made Menou ridiculous to the Army. Napoleon never allowed himself to choose between the Army and the Egyptians in this way, but it is irrelevant to think in terms of 'sin-cerity'; he enjoyed 'being' a Muslim to Muslims, a Catholic to Catholics, an atheist to atheists. It is absurd to say that he 'was not' any of these. He was a Catholic; he had grown up one, and had the senti-ment, and even some reflection of the doctrine; he was an atheist, because he felt, and could almost share at will, the attitudes appropriate to the Revolution through which he rose to greatness; he was a Muslim, because he loved the grandiloquence he associated with the East—surely another legacy of Galland—and because, as he understood Islam, it gave a special place to a man of destiny. Yet he was not three men. In his mind, at least—and his mind was sound—there was a real communication between Catholicism, Islam, and Revolution. He was not insincere when he described the Cairo diwan in the *Moniteur* as 'a Directory of five members', implying as revolutionary a body as the Directory at Paris; this was no more insincere than to carry revolution by force to Italy or Germany. This is what he was doing for the 'Arab national spirit'. His private idea of destiny and his idea of Islam came very close: 'There is only One, Father of victory, Merciful, Compassionate . . . who, in His wisdom decided that I should come to Egypt to change its face . . .'. Here we have it all, Islam, the man of destiny, and revolution too. Napoleon's idea of Islam was absurd, but it was a courteous gesture for an imperialist to make, and in a way it succeeded. If revolution is more than a technique it is the one great cultural borrowing from the West that has worked.[4]

It may not seem immediately appropriate to compare Charles Gordon, who had a much clearer idea of Islam. No Englishman in the nineteenth century, and no recorded Christian, set so high a religious value on Islam; he thought it was a saving faith, and he actively promoted it among his troops. He was also aware of popular feelings. Before Arabi Pasha's bid for national rule in Egypt he had written: 'Our Govt seems in Egypt to be on a very dangerous incline, with a troublesome abyss at the end of it, they scarcely seem to think the people of this country are capable of an opinion, whereas there is a mass of pent-up energy in the people and it would need a large force to keep the population down'. He saw that reforms must be 'the spontaneous desire of the mass of the people'. Yet he became the object of a cult which was anti-Islamic and was made into an imperialist symbol.[5] This reversed Napoleon's story. The imperial situation prevented Gordon from linking the cultures; it constantly distorted attitudes. Wilfred Scawen Blunt, by temperament a martyr and yet by vocation a spokesman, was too eccentric to carry conviction. He and Gladstone were like repelling magnets; and how can we explain the working of Gladstone's mind? How could he not respect the nationalism of Egyptians as he did that of Greeks, Bulgarians, Armenians, Irishmen and Sudanese; how could he work himself into such hatred of Arabi; how could he believe 'orientals' incapable of the same political feelings as Europeans? More consistently, Radical opinion pointed out that 'we who so much pride ourselves on our popular institutions appear to be the last to recognise anything of the kind in other countries'. It was characteristic of the age to interfere persistently in the affairs of the less developed countries of Africa and Asia, even when there was no actual military conquest. The man who interferes, to direct affairs from a superior position, and with greater efficiency, for the good of all, tends to close his mind to the subtleties of the culture in which he interferes. To Gladstone, Stratford Canning in Constantinople, 'the great Elchi', seemed a tremendous Turk. It may sound contradictory to say that Canning had only a profound knowledge of the surface. When we find an ambassador setting the secretaries of Embassy at work on the Qur'an, to see if it in fact required the death penalty for apostasy (a subject of obvious interest to the Christian missionary lobby) the amateurishness of his approach to the culture, in which his long career was devoted to interfering, contrasts with the professionalism with which he did so. In all this age, interference never occurred, but with the best motives: 'The French brought us here, and we should not in honor abandon this Country to be ravaged by an unfeeling Turk'. The imperial facts were known right across Africa at an early date: in 1825 the Sultan of Sokoto prudently objected 'You have subjugated all India' to Clapperton's trade proposals, and the Englishman disingenuously replied, 'We merely afforded it our protection, and gave it good laws'. It was taken for granted that to superimpose an alien good was a good thing to do; as the French said when they took Tunis: 'We can offer it all the benefits that we enjoy'. Every imperial victory of Europe was an extension of what the French called the 'mission civilisatrice'.[6]

Interference began because Europeans refused to see the rest of the world as, like Europe, entitled to its own cultural expressions. There was a general conviction that material advance was bound to European culture. No one grudged the economic development of the Middle East, for example, at least until Ismail Pasha proved so inefficient at finance (various of the failures would make a useful study for developers today); but in his time Muhammad Ali was considered to have 'well earned the eulogiums of civilised man'; and Bowring, in a public report, praised him because 'Nothing more awakens his attention than the progress of the mechanical arts'.[7] Yet there was no hesitation about imparting culture with technology; it was this that Thackeray satirised in an early *Punch*, making Viscount Pumicestone instruct Her Majesty's Ambassador at the Sublime Porte to recommend inter alia 'gas-lamps, Trial by Jury, Weekly and Sunday Newspapers, Harvey Sauce, two legislative Chambers and the Ten Pound qualification for voting'; and most of this, or its equivalent, was indeed exported.[8] The technology was seen as the natural product of European literary tradition: 'Eastern literature is at best very deficient as regards all modern discovery and improvements'; and Macaulay, who certainly did not grudge education to Indians, recommended to the public mind of India 'those intellectual pursuits on the cultivation of which the superiority of the European race to the rest of mankind principally depends'. It is obvious, not only that such cultural intolerance must provoke extreme resentment, but also that it must inevitably arise in a situation of ruler and ruled.

To the general cultural intolerance was added a religious and moral issue. The attack on the non-Christian religions was quite fierce: 'All these Shastras were not composed by God, men wrote them for private gain'. These were Christian words, which their enemies would soon turn against the Christians. Indeed, we read that the doors were opened 'at once to the cotton of England and the truths of the Bible', and this is not a criticism, as it would become at a later date, but a complacent boast by Christians. There was a long controversy, mostly between missionaries and administrators, about the moral and social value of Islam, then spreading in Africa; and in India the dispute about 'neutrality' (of Government towards religion) was endless. 'A Christian nation', said the missionaries, '. . . is bound to commend the true religion to its subjects'. In Sudan in 1905 Gwynne (later bishop) preached that God seemed to have a favour for England, expressed in freedom, justice, and imperial success, a 'genius for colonising' which was contingent upon 'the foundation of character, the feeder and supporter of the moral fibre of the race'; British prosperity must be used to spread 'the highest civilisation' and 'the best knowledge of all, the knowledge of God'. Christians today may doubt the national appropriation of God, but Gwynne was reflecting accurately enough a reality of morale; and this attitude was not peculiar to the British or the Protestants. The French Government justified, and the French church celebrated, the victory in Algiers in 1830 as one of Christendom over Islam; and some fifty years later the conquest of Tunis, formally in the name of 'a sacred duty which a superior civilisation owes to populations which are less advanced' was still accompanied by talk of Crusade. K. M. Pannikar in our own day wrote of evangelisation as a renewal of Crusading, and we have earlier seen how he considered the work of missionaries a kind of cultural onslaught on Asia by the people, as distinct from the governments or capitalists, of the West. The Hindu leader of the early nineteenth century, Rammohun Roy, wrote: 'It is true that the apostles of Jesus Christ used to preach the superiority of the Christian religion to the natives of different countries. But we must recollect that they were not the rulers of the countries where they preached.'[9] The tragedy of the Christian church has been the confusion between religious and cultural certainties.

It is obvious that the close union of technical superiority (especially in armaments and military organisation), political interference and often military conquest, cultural intolerance and religious and moral self-righteousness, inevitably closed possible channels of communication between the Europeans and the rest. As might be expected, the situation was reflected in the attitudes that Europeans adopted. This classic comment reveals a moment of transition from one cultural superiority to another; it comes from the British Ambassador in Constantinople in 1794, and refers to the behaviour of two young men who had been representing the East India Company at Basra: 'Europeans who have resided for any length of time in Indostan are in danger of carrying into other situations the ideas imbibed in that country. Accustomed to consider the native Inhabitants of the East as an inferior race of men, and to treat them accordingly, they are apt to indulge the same feelings with respect to the uncivilised Turks, on their arrival in the Dominions of the Grand Signior. But as the Mahometans of these Countries entertain similar sentiments of their own superiority over all Christians, it is easy to conceive the collision and discord that must be the consequence of this contrast.' An Indian visitor to London a little later found that he was attacked and ridiculed for the notions of his own culture, and yet could not get people to see that he could say exactly the same things of theirs.[10]

Crucial to the sense of superiority, now that people were actually travelling, and seeing the despised cultures with their own eyes, was the application of that double standard of judgement of which I have already had occasion to speak. This was essential if rulers were to sustain their ruling attitudes. A typical cultural judgement is to say: 'Asiatics are not from habit or education accustomed to take large or liberal views' (1807); a hundred years later the same cultural attitude was expressed by Lord Cromer: 'Orientals do not reason very closely'. This was not just a professional approach by practising imperialists. Let us remember that Friedrich Engels wrote that he did not believe that Arabi was anything but 'an ordinary pasha', who objected to the international capitalists 'because in the old Oriental fashion he prefers to put the taxes into his own pocket'. The facts were quite different; but, lest we feel any doubt that Engels writes simply out of cultural prejudice, he goes on: 'We West-Europeans should not so easily be led astray as the Egyptian fellahs or all the Romanic people', and he finally decides that only 'we Germans' will 'preserve our theoretical superiority through criticism'. Pasley, the writer of 1807, argued that Asiatics are 'too much inclined to ascribe to their own personal importance, those honors and attentions, which are alone paid to their Representative Character'; at just the same period and in the same area, we find

British authorities refusing to pay for the extravagant state super-fluously adopted by their local representatives. As Byron remarked sarcastically of Greek independence, 'Shall we then emancipate our Irish helots? Mahomet forbid'.[11]

When we consider the barriers to the transmission of ideas in the nineteenth and twentieth centuries between Europe and the rest of the world, it is clear that all are aspects of the absolute conviction of superiority which was the mark of imperialism. The rules were not the same for all men, because not all men were the same. Political and cultural domination of this character was compatible with actual living among other people, only by means of not mixing with them, at least on social terms. This produced the idea of an irreducible difference between West and East; Dumas said an Arab told him, if you boil a Frank and an Arab in the same pot for three days, two separate soups will come out. Dumas was too wise, and in too ambiguous a cultural position himself, to put the joke into the mouth of a Frenchman. It is a curious fact that 'never the twain shall meet' is always quoted as though it stood by itself, when the point of the verse is actually, 'But there is neither East nor West, Border nor Breed nor Birth,/When two strong men stand face to face', etc.[12] The ruling relationship could only tend to exaggerate the differences between cultures, and to strengthen the tendency we have seen so much reason to regret wherever it occurs, to equate difference with inferiority.

The relations of Europe to whatever parts of the outer world were at any time known to it are compounded of devastation, harassment, con-quest, war; this is true whether Europe is the aggressor or the victim, and over the course of history Europe has filled both roles. As the pendulum swings to and fro, it seems at this moment to be poised at the central point where the continuation of its swing is unpredictable. It is clear enough from the history of modern times that a relationship of ruler to ruled is, as anyone would expect, inimical to the free trans-mission of thought. Yet this is not a decisive factor. Mediaeval Europe, though highly suspicious of Islam, and able to look back on some three hundred years of Arab aggression on European populations, found means to receive a whole body of ideas from the very culture it most suspected; this may have been the easier, because the open policy coincided with Europe's turn to be the aggressor. The open policy in one field was in any case circumscribed by a closed policy in other fields; this is what we shall be looking at in more detail in the next two chapters. Modern Europe also derived a cultural benefit, unconnected with exploitation, from serious studies of academic value, undertaken by colonial rulers, and in any case made possible by the imperialist system. Whenever individual imagination and scholarly industry were able to function, and this was often, there was a real service to the understanding of one culture by another. The weakness was that this advantage was almost always confined to the 'oppressor' culture; it is only in the last thirty years that the 'oppressed' cultures have had adequate access to information about the 'oppressors'. A good deal of what the colonial scholars 'discovered' was, although news to their compatriots, everyday knowledge to the cultures studied; it was like the scholarship of our own day, which we have seen also sometimes exploits what is familiar abroad as unfamiliar at home. In early days, however, the application of new techniques of historical criticism to the colonialised cultures was a real advantage for them. Now they can apply the technique themselves; but then the work was new, and useful both in itself and as an example.

Europe in the twelfth century needed scientific knowledge and method, all that I have classed as technique; it was desperate for new material and new methods, and found them, as we shall see, in Arabic. Europe in the seventeenth century wanted nothing from other cultures; its own momentum was building up, and they had nothing to give it of the technical kind. It sought only a leisure occupation, and in order to titillate the imagination of the idler members of a wealthy class, re-used alien cultural material in a way that seriously, and for a long time, distorted relations between Europe and a large part of the oriental world; its only useful function was to mitigate hostility. It may have played a part in preparing the greater seriousness that prevailed in the nineteenth century. I think it follows that one of the controlling factors in cultural relations must be the internal need of those concerned. If this is true for Europe, we may assume it is true for other cultures too, until someone can identify a difference. Relations must fail, or at best will fall short of the best, when the internal needs of cultures cannot usefully combine together.

What stands out at every stage of history is the invariable necessity of a shared interest; genuine borrowings come from wanting something the other culture also wants. Cultures can communicate if they have a common purpose. When this is lacking, there is a blockage of understanding, such as happened between the Byzantines and the Latins in our Middle Ages. There was no serious technological divergence: they forced their religious quarrel out of nothing; it was just that no common interest prevented different traditions from clashing: 'Byzantine diplomacy seemed chicanery to the new baronial societies of the West', as Gervase Mathew said.[13] The equally violent clash with the Arabs did not obscure an area of common interest; the Arabs themselves wanted the knowledge that the Europeans acquired from them for no different reason than the Europeans; knowledge could be shared for a common purpose. The same situation exists today, when all the world wants to make use of techniques that derive from the culture of Western Europe. My aim in the next two chapters is to see whether the mediaeval experience is relevant to the present problem. I am only looking to see whether the example of Europe's borrowing from the Arabs will tell us anything about the process of borrowing from Europe today; I am comparing, not the things, but the relations of things. In investigating the possibility that A is to B as C is to D, I am not arguing that A is like C or that B is like D. There is no question of saying that mediaeval Europe is like the developing countries today, or that the classical Arab world resembles our North and West today; but the mode of borrowing in the one case may bear on the mode of the other. Although we in the West may go on getting richer faster than anyone else, the rest of the world has also greatly improved its status since 1870, just as Europe was improving its status in 1170. No historical similarity can be taken literally; there is no photograph of the future; but we know from our private lives that existing experience enables us to acquire more. New experience is a variation of the old.

A Cultural Filter in the Middle Ages

THIS CHAPTER IS about a cultural filter that worked well and that is well documented. How did the people concerned think? How did their thinking begin and how did it develop? What were they consciously after? And were their conscious ends the same ends as the technique served in practice? At first glance the attitude of mediaeval society seems to be quite different from that of our own, because the Middle Ages followed the classical and Patristic traditions in thinking no man free who was not master of himself. Perhaps the antithesis is not as great as it seems. Earlier we argued that freedom may in practice exert great pressure on people who lack the support of a structure of belief and of required behaviour. Even when ideals conflict, achievements fall short of what is intended and may differ from each other a good deal less than either from what it aims at. We best compare the two societies by saying that the ways in which pressure was exerted were differently organised then and now, although in both cases exerted with popular support.

In mediaeval society the attraction of orthodoxy soon began to take a negative form — the discrimination of heresy. The unity of their thoughts seemed important to Europeans who found their identity in a positive conformism to express a common urge. In the eleventh and twelfth centuries the negative aspect appeared as a quarrel among theologians, the zeal or the jealousy of a Lanfranc against a Berengar, of a Bernard against a Porretanus or an Abelard. Then it became the destruction of peoples, of a rival church, like the Albigensian, or an anti-church, like the Waldensian. Later it became the oppression of odd individuals accused before the Inquisitors of casual blasphemies or anticlerical expressions. Finally it became the means of destroying outside races, Moors and Jews compulsorily converted in Spain. All these cases, however, were problems of internal absorption, even the Spanish case; and, although there were many signs of social dissatisfaction, and although this was sometimes expressed in terms of religious dissidence, there is no evidence that uniformity was not the wish of the effective majority. For understanding how pressure was exerted on the individual, in order to protect him and his society as a whole from outside pressure, there is no better area to study than that of the way Islam was treated. Europe's problem was how to deal with ideas that were incompatible with its own orthodoxy but that were securely based on

an external society well beyond the possibility of effective destruction
by force. Our particular purpose is to examine the means used in these
circumstances to exclude the unwanted ideas, in order to admit the
wanted.

THE FORMATIVE PERIOD

The story begins in ninth-century Cordova when some two score
martyrs forced the reluctant Qadi to execute them, because they insisted on attacking Islam and the Prophet scurrilously in public. The
story is particularly well documented on the Christian side, though
with a number of significant gaps, by two of its leaders, personal friends
since their school days, a priest, Eulogio, and a layman, Alvaro. Their
writings express the ideology of the movement, and betray something
of its social setting. Although they so greatly admired and encouraged
the self-immolations, Eulogio did not court the martyrdom he finally
received, and Alvaro, so far as we know, was not a martyr at all. What
were the motives underlying the movement? In what terms was it
expressed? And so what social attitude did it signify?[1] Neither the
protomartyr, a monk who was publicly executed at the celebrations of
the 'Id al-Fitr, nor a merchant who was severely beaten and paraded
through the town on a donkey, seems to have set out to be provocative;
the interest of these two cases lies in the reaction that the publicity
aroused among the Spanish Christians of Cordova. The next martyr
best exemplifies the movement. Isaac was the child of wealthy and
noble parents; he was 'accomplished and learned in the Arabic language' and held the office of *exceptor reipublicae*, a katib or secretary,
working for government. His name was one of those that may equally
be Christian, or Muslim in the Arabic form, Ishaq. Suddenly he was
seized by a spiritual ardour, gave up his job and became a monk, in a
monastery maintained by his family in the mountains; after three
years of ascetic discipline, he left the monastery and returned to the
town where he had once enjoyed honours and cultivated pleasures. He
went to the Qadi and said he wanted to be a Muslim and asked him to
explain the religion rationally. Then he interrupted him, called him a
liar, abused Islam, invited the Qadi to turn Christian. He was committed to prison and finally executed. This behaviour suggests the survival of the tradition of publicly attacking the State religion which in
pagan times had been condemned at the Spanish Council of Elvira.
Ishaq was the first of 'those who came really of their own accord', of
'our spontaneous martyrs'. Ishaq's family and friends were great seers
of visions; Ishaq himself had spoken three days before he was born, and
when he was seven a virgin saw a ball of light descending on him from
heaven.[2] There is a plain history of instability, verging on religious
mania, and Ishaq was evidently given to periodic exaltation, but his

behaviour was infectious; and six other monks, including his uncle, immediately followed his example, and formally denounced the Prophet in court. Others followed them. When the movement died down, the final tally included two distinct classes of martyr. Some were monks with the same background of exaggerated ascesis as Ishaq. Others were lay people, many the children of mixed marriages, nominally Muslim, but who had been brought up secretly, more or less loosely, as Christians, and who, by returning to their Christian allegiance, became formal apostates from Islam. This was a capital offence; it would be superfluous for these people to abuse the Prophet. Others had to depend solely on provocation. Many of them were related to each other. They included a number of women, and notably a girl called Flora, whose sufferings inspired Eulogio. He encouraged her in her martyrdom, and his own account of his cult of her, in life as well as in death, sometimes makes strange reading. There is an incongruous note, as if of Victorian romance. Some might think that his sentiments, innocent at the conscious level, at another level were 'kinky', as when, after her first encounter with the authorities, he caressed the convalescent scars of the executioner's whip on her neck.[3] When, long after her death, Eulogio himself was executed, he was helping another girl in a situation which must vividly have recalled Flora's to his sympathies. He had hidden his encouragement of the martyrs from the authorities who believed him to be a moderate and a co-operator, and had welcomed his election as archbishop of Toledo.

Islam seemed to these people the antithesis of the ascetic ideal that they had embraced, and death, the natural fulfilment of their ascesis, seemed doubly appropriate at Muslim hands. This asceticism added a strong cultural colouring to their basic Christian belief, but it was cultural also in the literary sense; and it was cultural in the stronger sense of the national expression of a communal identity. Ninth-century Spain was not a united or stable society; Toledo was notoriously rebellious, and the mountains of Regio were a refuge of disaffection. The national community consisted of Arabs who were an aristocracy, although not exactly a feudal aristocracy, as well as merchants; of Christians, whether descendants of Visigoths (and themselves a displaced aristocracy) or of their Roman predecessors; and of Spaniards, of the same origins, whose parents or ancestors had become Muslim. The Islamic conquest had taken place five or six generations before, and these scattered elements had lived side by side long enough for local as much as sectarian grievances to motivate them; but in Cordova, the capital, the separate identity of dissident or discordant groups could be preserved only by maintaining cultural characteristics within the wider community, and normally by peaceful means. It was one distinction of the martyrs to have discovered an infallible means to violence, by provoking it from others upon their own bodies. Yet they were in revolt as much against the acceptance of Muslim rule by ordinary Christians, as against that rule itself. A Christian might live freely as such, and still enjoy senior employment under government, as at first Ishaq himself had done; he might acquire the cultural character of his conquerors and live very much like them. It is surely relevant that the two groups from whom the martyrs came were the old families (whether Visigothic or Roman) and the mixed marriages, those who most proudly remembered and fiercely resented the loss of power, on the one hand, and on the other those whose upbringing placed them at the point of intersection of the two religions, disoriented in their loyalties, and uncertain of their social identity.

Eulogio refused to accept an inferior position in society; he thought it an intolerable humiliation for a Christian priest to be laughed at by little boys, or even stoned by them, or to be thought by some Muslims to pollute them by contact. It is likely that his resentment at subordination, and all it involved, was shared by others, and that it subsisted in the Christian community, and even accumulated with the passage of time. We know that two centuries later, at least, Spanish-speaking girls sang Arabic love-songs for their masters, and Arab girls were forced in turn to sing for Christian conquerors. Yet we cannot doubt that there was always a majority for accepting the situation. Alvaro wrote his *Indiculus Luminosus* in order to defend the martyrs from the criticism levelled at them by other Christians, which was that they provoked their fate by unnecessary aggression, 'proceeded without any hostile stimulus'; and his purpose was to show how oppressed they were. He describes nothing that we can seriously agree to be oppressive, and Eulogio specifically resented 'the liberality of the king' which made Christians indebted to the patience of Muslims for their freedom of worship. The conscious aim was to prevent any *modus vivendi* for the Christians. In a furious passage of satire, Alvaro imagines the party of moderate Christians, as repenting their attitude to his own extreme party: 'Woe to us; we have used the Gospel against the Gospel, for whoever forbids cursing also orders blessing. They are the persecutors of the Arabs; we are the persecutors of the worshippers of Christ.' The angry minority among the Spanish Christians communicated their feelings to the rest of Europe. This sense of the persecution of Christians would persist throughout the age of the Crusades; but 'persecution' was as neutral as 'fight'; it was right or wrong only in respect of who uses and who suffers it. The Cordovan episode is also representative of later traditions in the way some of the Christians and the Arabs could live side by side and yet, because of their hostility, remain totally ignorant of each other. The existence of Arabisers among the Christians shows that this was a matter of cultural choice.

Alvaro is best remembered for his complaint against the handsome young Christians, articulate, of good character, who are outstanding in their knowledge of Arabic literature and their power of expression in Arabic, and who meet to discuss 'Chaldean' literature enthusiastically; they know nothing of the beauty of the church, or of its rivers which flow from Paradise. He and Eulogio substitute a fanatical latinism, which speaks of the Arab rulers as 'consuls' and of court functionaries as 'lictors' with 'fasces'. The Spanish church was in touch with contemporary Europe, and this fanciful style resembles some Carolingian and sub-Carolingian writing, but it is much more extreme. Eulogio brought copies of the *City of God*, the *Aeneid*, of Juvenal, Horace, Aldhelm and Arrian back from a visit to Pamplona. He compared the style of the great classical writers unfavourably with that of his friend, Alvaro; no doubt this is an academic exercise. The real interest of both writers is in the Scriptures and some Fathers, in Gregory and Augustine, but most of all in the interpretation of Old Testament passages as prophecies against Islam. Both Eulogio and Alvaro attack the Qur'an, Alvaro explicitly for its style (*inter alia*); what they say could equally well be said of the Biblical texts they quote. This is one of the polemic lines that these writers initiated in the West. Eulogio described (and shared) his grandfather's violent dislike of hearing the call to prayer; yet his language might just as well be used by a Muslim to describe the Christian priest at least. This is characteristic cultural failure, to see differently from outside and from inside; understanding and ridicule give the same thing a very different appearance. It is curious, too, that writers who attack the sexual morals and use of armed force by Islam should employ imagery which is predominantly sexual and military. Certainly, if a death-wish is a kind of aggression, here is the *locus classicus*.

Both Alvaro and Eulogio supported their attack upon Islam with an attack upon the personal life of the Prophet. This also would become a standard aspect of Christian polemic in the Middle Ages, and for long afterwards. Much of their material derived from a little anonymous history of the Prophet which Eulogio found in the neglected library at Pamplona. It has its analogues in oriental Christian writing, and the material it contained would continue to be used in the West for many centuries after; indeed, into modern times. We need not assume that it is the direct source of so much later writing, especially of the twelfth and thirteenth centuries, but we must suppose that it represents a living tradition of the Christian population of Spain which survived to emerge again in a later period. In support of the suggestion of cumulative resentment, we can compare a history in Latin of the Arab conquest of Spain, written a century earlier under the name of Isidore of Beja; it was hostile enough to Islam, but it had none of the inexhaustible virulence with which Eulogio and Alvaro look upon the Islamic scene.[4]

The methods used by this small group to resist the pressures of worldly success, and of the cultural influence of a dominating Arabic-speaking community, were much the same as those that later the whole of Western Europe used in order to exclude the external Islamic influence. It is extraordinary that so many characteristics of so exceptional a movement should recur in one form or another. Its terminology did not survive, but its rejection of Arabic and Islamic culture found new expression. For example, even in pre-Islamic times, Latin writers adopted the Greek usage of calling Arabs 'Saracens', a word of doubtful origin, but in the Middle Ages always explained as though it were an Arabic word, and an Arab claim to descent from Sarah. Many Latins preferred to use the word 'Agarene', to demonstrate that Islam was Ismailite in descent, in accordance with Genesis.[5] In practice the two words were interchangeable, and 'Saracen' quickly acquired a pejorative connotation. 'Ismaelite' was also used. *Pagani* and *infideles* were ways of saying *non-Christian*, and Muslims might share the first of these with the heathen, and the second with the Jews. Sometimes the chroniclers of the ninth and tenth centuries will say whether raiders came from Sicily, Africa, and Spain, but normally the Arabic-speaking world was seen and treated as one, as hostile, and as unknown. If the Cordovans could shut out the Arab culture amid which they resided, so very easily could the whole of Latin Europe.

For something like four hundred years the relations of Christians and Muslims in the Mediterranean were confined to raiding and warfare, particularly in Southern France and Southern Italy. This was the age in which the Arabs sacked St Peter's and the suburbs of Rome; and as they settled in Provence and in the South of Italy on the Garigliano, where they 'kept in security their wives, children and captives', they became a fluctuating force in politics, and soon were partners in temporary alliances with Christians. For the Arab settlement at La Garde-Freinet Liutprand of Cremona blamed the people of Provence themselves: 'One faction . . . called in the help of the . . . Saracens . . . and in company with them proceeded to crush their neighbours'. A similar situation in 881 had brought forth the condemnation of Bishop Athanasius of Naples by Pope John VIII. These alliances do not seem to have resulted in fruitful communication. The commonest words in the chronicles are 'depopulaverunt' and 'devastaverunt'; settlers from North Africa were said to be the most destructive. At Monte Cassino, Peter the Deacon, a 'forger' whom we may better think of as a writer of historical fiction, invented a Sicilian martyr killed by Muslims in the sixth century, before the time of Muhammad. His tale was credible because it reflected a state of continuous warfare. The stories of these periods are full of murders, captures, and rapes, which suggest considerable interchange of personnel, without the least interchange of thought. We know that Arab emissaries to Charlemagne's son spent a whole winter in the North as guests of the Emperor, but there is no hint of any communication of ideas. We have to imagine an isolated household in the cold winter of Aachen; it does not seem likely that they were asked, or can have wished, to share the royal hearth. Certainly isolation was the pattern of embassies by the middle of the tenth century, whether Liutprand's in Constantinople, or that which John of Gorze headed for Otto I in Cordova. When Abbot Maieul of Cluny was captured by Arab raiders in the Alps and held for ransom, we read that he refused unfamiliar food, but that one of the Arabs recognised that he was a holy man and made bread for him that he could eat. Another put his foot on the manuscript Bible that the Abbot carried with him, but was rebuked by his fellows because this was a Book of the Prophets. Here the Latin source concedes or implies some understanding of the Muslim doctrine of revelation, as given to the prophets in turn, including Jesus. It is a meagre result for four centuries of warfare and alliances, but it is about all there is. We see again how communities can live side by side and know so little of each other. The medical school at Salerno derived some teaching material from Arab sources, tenuously linked with Monte Cassino through the translations of Constantine the African, the monk who was supposedly an Arab convert from Islam. French medicine was professionally jealous of Salternitan practice. It is something that the myth of Salerno was of joint Latin, Greek, Arab and Jewish foundation, but the school, of course, was exclusively Christian.[6] There seems to have been no other Arab scientific influence on the Italian mainland. Mediaeval relations with Islam were rooted and grew up in frustrated violence; but it would be a gross over-simplification to say that anti-Islam was just the product of those centuries when Muslims burned, sacked, raped and killed over parts of what are now Italy and France. They did so in an age of constant war, when the cultural differences between Mediterranean peoples, apart from language, were slight. The Arabs were no exception that their case should stand out. As raiders, they were no worse than the Magyars in Northern Italy and central Europe or the Vikings in the West and in the Mediterranean itself. The raided populations had many of them been raiders once: Lombards, Goths, Franks; Saxons whose ancestors had raided the British, and Danes who had raided the Saxons, both fought the Arabs in the capacity of Varangians in the Byzantine service. The Arabs were different in just one way: they did not, like the rest, become Christians, and so they never entered the conscious unity of European society.

THE CONSCIOUS REJECTION OF ISLAM

Christian and Muslim communities were kept apart by something quite different from geographical space. Partly this was each community's sense of identity, and still more it was its sense of purpose. Both were expressed in terms of religion. It proved quite possible to exclude a whole range of ideas from the European public, and the system of exclusion by suspicion was theological, because this was the natural mode of cultural expression of the day. Europe began to receive ideas from the Arab world, in the twelfth century, partly in Palestine-Syria, more in Sicily and Italy, but chiefly in Spain, at a time of aggressive war, fought not only by arms, but also in words. At this date a clear and unshakeable doctrine, which has largely survived into the present day, of what Muslims must be believed to believe was formed in the West. In essentials it was the same as Eulogio had taught, but writers who were totally ignorant of Islam, and others who came to have a genuine and detailed knowledge, all set out their material in such a way as would support the constant Christian polemic, of which the Cordovans give us the earliest example. Everything was forced into a single pattern: if Islam were no true revelation, it must have been maliciously contrived; the emphasis laid on its different sexual morality, and the violence supposedly implicit in the doctrine of holy war (jihād), was endlessly re-iterated. It was not suggested that contemporary Muslims were worse men than the Christians; in fact, a number of stories circulated which satirised Christian moral practice by way of contrast. It was the idea of an alternative system of sexual morals that aroused the anger of the clerical polemists and caused them to present the alien system as designedly self-indulgent from the first. Perhaps they feared that it might attract the Christian faithful; more probably they were simply offended by anything that opposed the centuries-old swing of European opinion, then still very far from being exhausted, in favour of an ideal of total sexual continence. Nor was there ever any doubt that Crusade, which rapidly came to follow the same rules as jihād, was as violent as anything that Christians had suffered, but for the whole European community it seemed a case of kill or be killed. Persecution was still conceived as bad, if it was applied against Christians, and not by them. We meet again the characteristic of cultural conflict, that the same thing has one complexion when it is done against us, and another when we do it.

The detailed Christian presentation of Islamic religion was intended perhaps to deter Christians who might be curious about it, and perhaps to strengthen the pressure against Muslims living in Christian territory, in Sicily and later on the mainland at Lucera, and in Spain as the Reconquista advanced; but primarily it served to fit Islam into the total orthodoxy with which Latin Christendom expressed its sense of identity. None of it could be used, as much of it was ostensibly intended, against free Muslims in the world, who, even if they can be imagined listening to it, must have derided its crude misrepresentations of what Islam really taught.[7] The relevance of the usual themes would have been unintelligible to them, the errors of fact would have aroused their contempt, and the vicious abuse their deep anger. At the end of the thirteenth century Ramon Lull never understood the failure of all his efforts to proseletyse in North Africa, where his 'unanswerable reasons' aroused popular indignation, but official indulgence; at Bijaya the authorities seem to have recognised him as a good sort of man, but judged him quite irresponsible.[8] He was killed in the end by an angry mob. The most interesting period was the mid-twelfth century. The *chansons de geste* are notoriously as crude in their hostility to Moors as they are wild in their suppositions about Islam. Their philosophy becomes fully explicit in the closely related historical fiction, the *Chronicle of Turpin*, attributed to a bishop contemporary with Charlemagne. Two religious discussions in it are not altogether ridiculous. In spite of the consistent misrepresentation of Muslims as polytheists, we can extrapolate some phrases that are put into the mouths of Muslims and that are quite compatible with an actual Muslim talking, but the discussions are inconclusive and end in an appeal to arms, or, more exactly, in an appeal to God to show the truth by means of trial by combat; and invariably the Christians win.[9] Naturally this was not a reflection of actual events; God's vindication of Christian belief by battle was the perfect fantasy of what 'ought' to happen. In the Levant it did not happen for long, and when events in Spain came to correspond more closely to such day-dreams, the demand for that sort of fiction evaporated. The most interesting point is the recognition of the failure of debate or argument to convert. It is an oversimplification to think of the polemic against Islam as simple war propaganda, although it is true that most of it was written for clerical or knightly consumption, theology or songs, for the two classes most interested in Crusade. When we consider that the attitude to Islam is historically continuous from the Christian attitude to the Roman pagan world we must recognise that a more complex analysis is needed.

There was effectively no presentation of Islam in its own words. The earliest North European literature about Islam is wildly absurd, but it follows the same polemic line as the rest of Christian writing on the subject. That Peter the Venerable, visiting Spain in 1143, employed professional translators to turn the Qur'an into Latin is rightly famed, because it represents a new and at the time unique undertaking. Peter seems to have believed that Islam would prove to be self-refuting and so had a sincere interest in the search for facts. He based a polemic treatise on the translation of the Qur'an, and a draft summary of the usual Spanish anti-Islamic polemic, sent by his secretary; but not only did he apparently fail to realise that his premises were unacceptable to Muslims, in fact no effort to reproduce the text in Arabic is known to have been made. His text of the Qur'an is hardly better than a paraphrase, and translated with it were some eminently refutable, popular Arabic religious works, in no sense representative of reputable Muslim thought. For purposes of controversy with Muslims they were chosen ill, but for Christian home consumption, well enough. In the same body of translations there was also a work invaluable for future polemic use, a well-informed but malicious attack on Islam by a pseudonymous Christian Arab. Later, a better translation of the Qur'an was made by Mark of Toledo, and he translated in addition devotional pieces by a genuinely influential Muslim religious thinker, ibn Tūmart, the Mahdi of the muwahiddin, the Almohads. Mark's work is represented by few manuscripts, and seems to have been almost unknown, whereas the Cluniac Qur'an, with most of its satellite literature, was enormously popular, and continued in serious use long after it was printed in the sixteenth century. In the thirteenth century, the author of the *quadruplex reprobatic*, possibly Roman Marti, had a considerable knowledge of hadith, which, however, he quoted only to justify his own polemic. St Peter Pascual knew the *sira* of ibn Ishaq well; it is an early Arabic life of the Prophet, but Pascual could not bring himself to prefer it to traditional legendary Christian material. The work of Roderick of Toledo and the historical material used by Alfonso the Learned reveal the same distortion of increasing, and increasingly accurate, information. Ricoldo da Monte Croce, who reached Baghdad, and at least visited the religious schools there, derived his material from a Christian Spanish Arabic source. Islamic material was never allowed to stand by itself. There was no serious publication of it that was free of accompanying distorting propaganda; even Mark of Toledo appended a polemical preface. Nothing that European writers disapproved of was allowed to appear, other than in a context of pre-fabricated refutation.[10]

The distinction which separated thought about Islam from every cognate idea is well illustrated in the greatest of all scholastic minds. In the *summa contra gentiles*, which is largely concerned with the contemporary problem of the unity of the intellect, raised by the commentary of ibn Rushd on Aristotle, St Thomas Aquinas discusses Islam very briefly indeed, with very little attention, and more or less in passing; he recapitulated briefly the familiar lines of Christian propaganda.

The contrast with the seriousness with which he discusses the philosophical cruces of the common tradition, which we may call Hellenistic-Arabic-European, is very great indeed. It is fair to say that the reverse process on the Arab side is not dissimilar; al-Ghazāli's refutation of the divinity of Jesus Christ is a case in point.[11] Both religions, and Judaism too, operated a filter mechanism: each one saw the other two as perversions of its own pure form of the same revelation; each therefore wholeheartedly rejected the others, and was interested in a selection of facts to strengthen the faith of its own adherents, by means of greater verisimilitude. Each community would give the 'authentic' picture of what the others 'really' said or meant. A firm conviction that other people's beliefs are absurd and disgusting makes it possible to discount whatever another culture claims to say. It is no wonder that communities could live side by side and not communicate. Whatever the other said would be understood in terms of an inherited interpretation.

THE EXCLUSION OF IDEAS IN PRACTICE

We shall rightly conclude that Christian teaching about Islam, whether well informed or ill, was a defensive operation. A sense of being put upon persisted among Christians, although they were physically the aggressors throughout the Mediterranean from the middle of the eleventh century until after the middle of the twelfth, and, if we include unsuccessful aggression, until much later. It was only the successful advance of the Ottomans that put Christendom again on the defensive. In the meantime Sicily was thoroughly Latinised, and the reconquest of Spain continued with steady if uneven success until, after the last long delay, the fall of Granada in 1492. Latins, even in the twelfth century were aware of Arab resentment at European aggression, both in Syria and in Spain, and argued that true religion conferred the right to conquest anywhere. Land that had once been Christian remained in a special class. It was generally accepted that the capture of such land was a restoration.[12] The First Crusade itself was considered to be a defensive war, not only for the recovery of Jerusalem (and it was as the *Recovery* that the event continued to be celebrated liturgically) but for the defence and restoration of places where Christians were being 'persecuted'. Any notion of popular self-determination is anachronistic; what the 'Christian people' — Greek and Syriac speakers — had once possessed, the 'Christian people' — Latins — had the right to take again. The basic populations concerned were Latin (in the ecclesiastical sense) in Spain, France and Italy, and Greek, partly Latinised, in Sicily; in Spain there had been a large, and in Sicily a considerable, Arab (or Arabised Berber) admixture; they were wholly Arab or Arabised in North Africa and the Levant. It seems to have been long before the Latins realised that they could live only precariously in the Levant, or that their strength was confined to areas where their own population was solid. Theoretically, there was no difference of status between Toledo and Jerusalem, between Damascus, Antioch, or Edessa and Palermo, Bari or Messina, except only that Jersusalem was the most Christian of all, and so should belong to the Latins as a spiritual suburb of Rome. It is understandable, however little justified, that there should always have been some sense of outrage in Western European thought about Islam.

All the best informed polemic of the Middle Ages, notably Peter the Venerable's, Marti's, Ricoldo's, Pascual's, Lull's, derived its material from Spain, and, as we shall see shortly, Spain was also the site of most scientific translation. Where communication was greatest, polemic was most sophisticated. The two came side by side, sound information in all things, but communication in some, and occlusion in others. The Alfonsine *Cronica general* incorporates Arabic historical material, but for the most part the Spanish chronicles and the poem of the Cid take for granted a mixed society of professional soldiers. Within this framework an intelligent clergy was free to develop as it saw fit. If Spain became the home of anti-Islamic thought, Sicily was the home of indifference. Monastic landlords would accept a serf's oath on the Qur'an, without interest in the content of the Book. Norman encouragement of the tripartite culture, Latin, Arabic, and Greek, produced no considerable monument, except al-Idrisi's geography, and that was not translated out of the Arabic. The Norman monarchs found viable institutions of government, and viable customs, in all three cultures, and useful servants, both artists and statesmen. They were attracted by a tradition of monumental art that was Mediterranean, and predominantly Byzantine. They could put up with Byzantine religion until the Latin was widely and strongly established. They could tolerate Islam for as long as was useful. Ultimately it was Frederick ii, in papal propaganda the friend (and certainly an ally) of al-Kamil the Ayyubid, and apparently possessing no personal animus against Islam — accustomed in fact to flaunt his Arab interests and his dislike of the Popes — who transferred the remaining Muslim population to the mainland, where it could function wholly in dependence on the Crown as a mercenary reservoir and was to be broken up by the Angevins. There were more translations from Greek than from Arabic. There was never a blended culture at all levels in Sicily; at best there were different cultures side by side in uneasy co-operation, temporarily tolerant, and united only in the reigning dynasty.[13]

Lastly, in Syria-Palestine there was a Latin state, occasionally and ineffectively reinforced overland, and more closely linked to Europe by sea routes that the jealous cities of Italy operated; it was surrounded by the Muslim Arab world, and made up of Latin lordships— including ecclesiastical lordships — set over an Arab population, both Christian, of various persuasions and communities, and Muslim. The situation might be supposed ideal for the absorption of different cultures into a new amalgam; and something of this sort occurred at a local level. For example, the baths flourished as they had done before the Latin conquest, only now women appeared in them publicly. This seems to offer a kind of adaptation to, and of, the existing culture.[14] If we come to consider the evidence for a literate knowledge and understanding of the surrounding world – and we are thinking of a period longer than separated Warren Hastings from Lord Mountbatten, longer, that is, than the effective history of the British imperial rule in India — we have to conclude that it was almost non-existent. About mid-point in the history of the Latin States of the East flourished one of the best historians of the Middle Ages, William of Tyre, a writer of wide sympathies, civilised tastes, broad interests, narrative ability and sound historical judgement, a wise and tolerant ecclesiastic. We might compare his position with that of Kipling in the British Indian Empire, although he came relatively a little earlier in relation to the mediaeval colony. He compares very unfavourably as to knowledge. His ignorance of Islam is astonishing, particularly if we compare him with his contemporaries and near-contemporaries in Spain. His *History of the Oriental Princes* is missing, but, as far as the evidence goes, it would have added nothing to its Coptic source, or shown knowledge of Islam the religion, beyond the little educated gossip that we find in the same writer's existing *History of Things Done Overseas*. William's famous summing up of the character of al-Malik Nūr al-Dīn Mahmūd ibn Zangī is the furthest that we know he went towards appreciation of a Muslim ruler, and the tension between personal admiration and the obligations of communal hatred is obvious: 'the greatest persecutor of the Christian faith, and yet a just prince, subtle and far-seeing, and religious according to the traditions of his people'.[15]

In Crusading literature verisimilitude and fantasy are constantly intertwined. There is often a genuine appreciation of the qualities of an Arab ruler, sometimes stated at length, sometimes allowed grudgingly to slip by. Some of the literature about Saladin shows an almost exaggerated admiration; and Richard I of England certainly wanted to be admired by him in return. Crusading material about Islam dates largely from the early thirteenth century, and is represented by James of Vitry, whose work is a good example of what I have called the educated gossip of the Latin states. His and other accounts of Syrian origin found their way into Western chronicles and other writings; they appear to represent an oral tradition; the Latin States produced nothing comparable to the genuine learning of contemporary Spain. We saw that Ricoldo travelled to Baghdad, yet turned to Spanish source material. Fidenzio of Padua, writing in the bitterness of the last days of the Latin States, had only gossip to offer, but he recognised that the sultan 'had a certain piety, and loved to do justice on others, although an infidel and evil'.[16]

One of the most interesting writers of this epoch, William of Tripoli, a little earlier, did indeed write, and very appreciatively, of Baybars. His contemporary history is excellent; he knows a great deal about the establishment of the Bahri Mamluk dynasty, and about the murderous circumstances of the accession in turn of Aybak, of Qutuz (including the interval under al-Mansūr 'Ali) and of Baybars. Baybars he compares for military ability to Julius Caesar, and for malice to Nero; by 'malicious' he means 'unscrupulous'; he admires Baybars as a ruler, and particularly for his severity in public morals, his detestation of prostitution and drunkenness, and the favour he showed to Christian monasteries, as well as to his own monks, the *fuqara'*. In William of Tripoli, more perhaps than any other writer, we get an impression of something like assimilation to a common Levantine culture. Yet the part of his book that deals with contemporary history begins with the recapture of Damietta; there is a long gap between that and the immediately preceding chapter, which takes the story of the rise of Islam from the time of the Prophet to the invasion of Provence and to the gates of Arles. His story of the Prophet is legendary, and wholly objectionable to Muslims. All this part of his work has a marked Western bias, and clearly does not derive from the Latin East at all. (He himself is Mandeville's main source.) There seems no exception to the rule of cultural exclusion.[17]

All the evidence is that, throughout the Mediterranean area, except for short periods and a few people and only partially, there was a nearly total separation of Christian Latins and Muslim Arabs living side by side. Canon law, from the twelfth century onwards, increasingly extended to Muslims the legislation intended to isolate Jews from the ordinary life of Europeans. Friendly intercourse with Muslims was effectively forbidden, even in Arab countries, where European merchants and pilgrims were dependent on the good will of Arab rulers. Consuls and religious superiors dealt as strangers with the authorities. From the thirteenth century the papacy attempted, with only very partial success, to boycott the trade in war commodities, including foodstuffs and raw materials. There were anomalies: the sale of a Christian as a slave did not involve the same automatic excommunication as the sale of a simple weapon. Yet it was not the canons that kept apart people of two religions who habitually transacted business together; it was rather their mental preparation. The same accounts of Islam recur monotonously, and pilgrims in the later Middle Ages learned from the merchant communities of Alexandria and Cairo the same 'facts' as circulated centuries earlier in Spain. The Christian interpretation of Islam made communication in any point of religion impossible, and the records of those who travelled in dar al-Islam, and tried to communicate about religion, a Raymund Lull, a Ricoldo, a William of Rubruck even, illustrate the inevitable failure.

Personal contact with Muslims posed problems, even for the greatest polemists. When the Moorish slave who had taught Ramon Lull Arabic made an attempt on Lull's life, Lull was reluctant to put him to death, and thanked his Lord to be relieved of the responsibility, when the slave hanged himself with the rope that bound him. What is most theological here is the assumption that any Muslim's damnation was so sure that his suicide could not matter. Yet it is clear that Lull was distressed. Lull, obsessed by his methods of 'proving' the Trinity, could not escape the narrow circle of his thoughts. Ricoldo perhaps better illustrates the problems that a cultural barrier can create. He was warm-hearted, intelligent, and reasonably humble; he appreciated the constant kindness he received, yet he seems almost as distressed by heresy as by Islam. He admired the Jacobites for their long and strict fasting, and the prolixity and devotion of their prayers; but he feared lest all those great good works should only end in damnation. The Nestorians, whose guest he was at first in Baghdad, he saw as crypto-Muslim: 'They think about Christ nearly the same as the Saracens'. With the Muslims he claims to have disputed, but it is doubtful whether this is serious. 'We were astonished how works of such perfection could be found in a religion so far from truth' (*lex tantae perfidiae*). For Ricoldo there were two unsolved problems: how could there seem to be so much virtue among the damned, and how could God give the victory to Muslim armies. Above all he illustrates surprise when wrong belief and good behaviour go together. Of course, this attitude to Islam is only a part of his attitude to heresy.[18]

To suppose that the resistance to a fair presentation of anything Islamic was the biggest element in the movement to suppress unorthodox thought in Christendom would be quite mistaken. The European longing for orthodox uniformity was much wider than the European rejection of Islam. Islam was indeed of special interest: apart from questions of sex, which are of interest to every age, there was its teaching about Christ. To many it seemed to be the 'sum of all heresy' and its genuine devotion to Jesus and Mary inexplicable. It was also associated (as in Ricoldo's case) with oecumenical tendencies, in that re-union with the Orthodox might renew Crusade. This was the case at the Council of Lyons in 1274, as well as at the Council of Florence. In spite of all this, internal heresies were more important as catalysts of European feeling, and particularly as symptoms of unrest. Mediaeval society was highly sensitive to all deviations, and increasingly so from the eleventh century onwards, very roughly during the period when European expansion in the political, economic, and geographical senses began to gain momentum, and a little before the age of translations from Arabic changed the content of learning. Internal heresies were rarely linked with Islam. None of those examiners who were able to elicit confessions from their Templar victims by torture stimulated explicit confessions of secret Islamisation, although there were accusations of idolatry and sodomy, both of which, however mistakenly, European folklore has associated with Muslims. It is true that the early Pastoureaux, true revolutionaries, were thought to be in the Muslim interest; and, later, when a number of lepers were found guilty, by French inquisitors, of a grand conspiracy to infect France, they confessed to the complicity of Muslim monarchs in Granada and North Africa, who certainly had never heard of them; but this was exceptional. Then, with Wycliff, a new idea of Islam entered the game, that of internal or moral Islam, of which it was easy to accuse one's enemies, and when the Reformation came, both Catholics and Protestants did so, in many million printed words.[19]

The dogmatic filter excluded every Islamic idea, except deformed to 'prove' a Christian argument, so successfully, that the only cases of Islamicising that came before the Inquisition were those of unhappy Moors who had been forced or tricked into Christianity. The period when the mediaeval West absorbed much Arabic learning coincided with the period of military expansion, but only with the earlier stages of the long development of inquisitorial condemnation. The graph lines of the survival of Arabic science in the West and of inquisitorial processes of all kinds, however, do roughly co-exist, but they do not exactly coincide. They are both part of the European experience at about the same time. If we take only the periods of active polemic against Islam, we shall find a closer correlation; the great interest in attacking Islam may correlate with the translation of scientific learning. A second period of interest coincided with the Ottoman invasions and with the European Renaissance and with the printing of much of the mediaeval corpus of translations from Arabic.

It is clear that the capacity to recognise and reject anything Muslim was highly developed and never in doubt. The technique of rejection could hardly be faulted. In spite of the inquisition, the system of pre-censorship ('nihil obstat' and 'imprimatur') was late to develop. So far as Islamic tendencies were concerned it was superfluous. Hidden heresy and later hidden witchcraft were sources of fear, and even panic, but crypto-Islam, although ultimately it became a subject of recrimination, never gave rise to real fear. Everyone knew without doubt or hesitation that Islam was to be excluded. The interesting thing was that it was possible contemporaneously to borrow a great deal from Arabic culture.

THE ADMISSION OF WANTED IDEAS

We have surveyed the area of rejection, and examined the method; we come to the area and method of admission. Especially in its beginnings, the translation of Arab science is properly described as a movement; and, although the method of admission was negative, simply allowing as much as did not offend to pass, the choices and attitudes of the translators were positive enough. They were enthusiasts for the material that now they exploded upon the Latin world; although never heretics or accused of heresy, they hated the traditional scheme of studies. They were revolutionaries, and conscious that they were. The late classical period had bequeathed a meagre legacy; in the twelfth century, when Latin literature of the best age enjoyed a revival, the scope of knowledge was widened enormously, and deliberately, by the translators from the Arabic.

The revival of dialectic and the appearance of new modes of thought date back even into the tenth century; the line of teacher and pupil runs continuously from Gerbert (becoming pope as Sylvester II, in 999, he died in 1003, but his main influence was at Rheims) to the later schools of Chartres. The line was thin and insubstantial. Of European geometry in the period between Gerbert and the reception of Arab mathematics Paul Tannery said: 'This is not a chapter in the history of science; it is a study in ignorance'. Latin scholars of the eleventh century were debating what was meant by 'internal' and 'external' angles; but, as Tannery remarked, thinking at once of eleventh-century Europe and of XIIth Dynasty Egypt, 'A very advanced state of civilisation may be achieved, imposing monuments may be raised, arts and literature may blossom, while practical geometry is still in its infancy; for arithmetic it is very different'. In other words, no technical mastery confers a total superiority on a culture; yet certain minimal techniques confer cultural advantages. As far as arithmetic goes, Europe would still use the abacus when scholars had become familiar with al-Khwarizmi. Yet in a strictly technological sense it is doubtful if Europe was much, if at all, behind the Arab ecumene; it had already begun the long haul which would finally take it ahead of the world; but it lacked, and lacked totally, the more theoretical techniques. In spite of commercial and diplomatic contact, the main lines of thought in Western Europe were isolated from either the Arabs or the Byzantines. There is no evidence that Gerbert had any first-hand knowledge of the Arab world, but he was the first Northern scholar (he was an Auvergnat) known to have visited Spain. He brought back the Arabic numerals, although without the crucial nought; his mathematical and dialectical studies make no direct reference to the Arabs or to Arabic learning.[20] In his life-time the miniature Christian kingdoms in the North of Spain were active, but they did not yet support centres of translation.

The growth of the medical school at Salerno, the 'Hippocratic City', cannot be accurately dated; we have seen that by legend it was an inter-cultural foundation, and certainly the Cassinese, Constantine the African, apparently a converted Arab merchant, who died in 1087, and probably his successor Afflacius, introduced (without acknowledgement) the medical teaching of 'Ali ibn al-'Abbās al Majusi. We cannot speak of any considerable absorption of Arab scientific work until the twelfth century. In 1127 Stephen of Antioch translated the work of 'Ali ibn al 'Abbās methodically, and his attitude contrasts with Constantine's. He stressed the need for accuracy, and, untypically in this, insisted on a correct attribution to the author. He had learned Arabic in order to acquire 'the naked beginnings of philosophy', and hoped to go on from the philosophy of material things to 'the excellence of the soul'. We have the impression of a deliberate movement, comparable to the Renaissance of the Romantic Movement, of an open society of spontaneous 'philosophers'. New disciplines, and new methods in old disciplines, came into being as they fed on the material from Arabic documents. We might compare the effect in our own century of the development of psychology, psychiatry, social-anthropology, sociology, economics, political science and others on the world of learning.

Adelard of Bath, an English contemporary, travelled to Southern Italy, perhaps to Sicily, and apparently to the Latin states in the Levant. In some points he resembles Stephen, whom he could in fact have met, although there is no indication that he did so. Adelard made a number of mathematical translations from Arabic, although his earliest work shows signs rather of the Greek influence. In his best known work, the *Questions on Natural Science*, the Arabs are deliberately claimed as his mentors. He is contemptuous of knowledge found North of the Alps, and goes out of his way to attribute methods of rational investigation to the Arabs. He represents a tendency in contemporary opinion, the excitement at something new and the rejection of the old methods as inadequate. Adelard seems to intend a kind of deculturation: 'For I am not one to be satisfied by the picture of a whore', he says, and makes my point about culture-transferable techniques, in less pompous language than mine. 'Indeed every bit of writing is a prostitute, accessible to the affections now of this man, now of those.'[21]

Enthusiasm for Arabic philosophy did not imply sympathy for actual Arab cultures. Dislike was sometimes expressed as criticism of Arabic as a language. Often this was purely technical, a boast of having overcome difficulty, but Hermann of Carinthia and Robert of Ketton, friends who worked together in Spain in mid-twelfth century, were both incorrigible paraphrasers who explicitly disliked the style and construction of Arabic. Mark of Toledo, a better translator, would later say much the same, but Hermann and Ketton rejected, more explicitly than most, both religion and culture, while embracing passionately the techniques that interested them; like other translators, they were motivated by the ignorance of astronomy (astrology) among the Latins, and Hermann recalls how hard they had worked to extract knowledge from the 'innermost treasures of the Arabs'.

At this date 'Arab' begins to be taken to imply a culture that is not really distinct from the Greek, or even the Indian; it does not even seem to imply a race or a people with a religion of their own. Al-Khwarizmi's correct attribution of the 'Arabic' numerals to the Indians ('the twice five signs of the Indians', written from right to left and including of course the nought) may have contributed to the general confusion of mind. Another translator, Hugh of Santalla, also chiefly interested in astrology, was equally confused about the nations, Arabs and Indians and Egyptians. The Egyptian setting of the Hermetic corpus was little understood, but Hugh was above all conscious that he was recovering the knowledge of the ancients, and making public things that had long been hidden. It is hard to think that there was any definite chronological or logical distinction in his mind between Greeks — Hellenistic writers in Greek — and Arabs, or writers in Arabic; only through Arabic did he know the Greeks at all. This murky confusion contrasts, to the modern eye, with the sense of excitement over the new studies that gripped Hugh, and many others: an 'insatiable thirst' to 'philosophise', that is, to taste new subjects and disciplines. At about the same time, the astronomer Raymund of Marseilles was able to prepare planetary tables, because 'we were the first of the Latins' to benefit from the translations from Arabic. He too failed to distinguish between Indians and Chaldeans and Arabs, but he welcomed the exotic names; he wrote poetry about the different peoples and cultures; evidently he saw himself as a citizen of the world. A little nervous about orthodoxy, he stood for the new culture which was made up from the Fathers of the Church, from Hellenistic and Roman authors, and from Arab scientists, al-Zarqali, al-Battani, abu Ma'shar and al-Qabisi. These three distinct groups (to us) seemed to him to be two: the Fathers, and the rest. There was a strong feeling for foreign sources of knowledge, and in 1140 Peter the Deacon wrote the life of

Constantine the African, then half a century dead, claiming that he had studied with the Chaldeans, Arabs, Persians, Saracens, Egyptians, and Indians. These are just names.[22]

Most or all of the translators were inspired by the sense of having been restored to a world of learning, or of themselves restoring Europe to its intellectual inheritance. They were often generous in their appreciation of the 'Arabs', not as actual people, but disembodied and dissociated from everything but a library of 'philosophical' techniques. In 1187, the greatest of the translators, Gerard of Cremona, died aged seventy-three, and his pupils published a little bibliography and biography, lest his work be forgotten or attributed to others. This recurrence of individualism is worth noting; it suggests both that the translators felt the work to be memorable, because revolutionary, and that they felt it to be outside the communal spirit, the joint effort of all people. The biography explains that Gerard came to Toledo, to study medicine, and Ptolemy's *Almagest*; he stayed there to the end of his life, to translate the vast number of Arabic books into Latin, because he was sorry for the Europeans who needed them. The list of translations consisted of seventy-one titles, and is very incomplete; they cover a wide range of subjects, classified as dialectica, astrologia (including astronomy), philosophy and medicine. Daniel of Morley, an Englishman who returned home from Toledo, explained philosophy to his patron, the Bishop of Norwich. His intellectual formation was like that of his master, Gerard. He too had gone to Spain because he had been disgusted by the teaching at Paris, and his aim was to pass on to others the teaching of the Arabs, that is, the philosophy. Late in the century, an unknown writer laments the low state of learning in Europe, where it has few friends and many detractors. There is always some sense of a lost inheritance, now only to be recovered from foreign reservoirs. Dominic Gundisalvo, in the preface of his *de essentiïs*, which is based on al-Farābi, talks nostalgically of the past, when many were philosophers and the title of wise was reserved for few; now the world is getting old, there are few philosophers, let alone wise men, and people are preoccupied either with literary hopes or with career ambitions. I do not think he is talking about the immediate known past of Europe, but about a vaguely conceived time of the great philosophers.[23]

Although the whole movement of translation was dominated by the aim of restoring Europe to the main stream of the world's thought, those who took part in it realised their isolation. In their devotion to their purpose they remained aware of opposition, and perhaps even more of indifference. The great theological controversies of the age passed them by, although the use made of dialectic in theology and philosophy, which provided the steam behind the entire scholastic development of the future, was only made possible by translations from Greek and Arabic. The West was ultimately influenced by ibn Sina's (Avicenna's) metaphysical thought; and ibn Rushd (Averroes) whose Aristotelian commentaries would in time contribute more to Latin than to Arabic thought, was himself alive during the heyday of the translators. The other products of the translations, mathematical, chemical, medical, meteorological, astronomical, were destined to constitute an increasingly important layer in Western culture; and an improved astrology had a long and practical future. The translators, however, in restoring the heritage of Europe, were reuniting it to its natural roots in the ancient and Hellenistic past; they were not seeking to discover any connection at all with the contemporary Arab world. Confusion about 'the Arabs' continued into the thirteenth century. That most of the translations, and the more popular and successful ones, were from the Arabic, was not hidden, and it was perfectly understood that some of the greatest writers who now came to be read, ibn Sina, 'Ali ibn al-'Abbās, al-Farābi, for example, were Arabs, meaning, at least, writers in Arabic. That in fact many were Persians was not known; and even if we take 'Arab' to mean 'writer in Arabic' it remains obscure how these Arabs were seen in relation to the Hellenes. There was particular confusion about Hermes Trismegistos, who was naturally taken to be a single author; but so there was about other Hellenistic writers, and even about Plato and Aristotle. As long as Arabs were not identified as Saracen (or its equivalent) they were not treated as Muslims, and they and their culture shaded off into that of the pre-Islamic world. The taxonomy was not chronological but logical; the relatively little known Greek Fathers were classed with the Latins, and non-Christian Greeks and Arabs were classed together, whether they came first or last. In one account, when the King of the 'Romans' wants to foretell the harvest, he consults the 'philosophers', and the treatise resulting has to be translated from Arabic into Latin. Over a long period, the word *paganus* is used by a wide variety of authors, and the more educated may be thinking rather of Plato and Aristotle than vaguely of idolatry.[24] If Aristotle and ibn Sina are not often described as pagans, that is only because they were rightly admired, and 'pagan' was pejorative. There did, indeed, come to be a notion that they must have been touched by revelation. This vagueness about chronology, and the indiscriminate use of ethnic and cultural terms, indicate an interest in these aspects that was emotional, even romantic, rather than precise. One thing is beyond doubt. In no single case did the dependence on Arabic sources, on Arab writers, or on Greeks in Arabic translation, stimulate in any Latin writer a kindly or a tolerant thought for the religion of the Arabs, or even for their proper culture.

The attempt to return Europe to its scientific inheritance succeeded; the subjects included in Latin writing from the middle of the twelfth century represent an enormous widening of interest and technique. The new tradition was integrated quite happily into the existing patristic one. The preface of Gundisalvi's, which I quoted earlier, cites the psalms, Isidore's Etymologies, Isaac Iudaeus (Ishaq ibn Sulayman al-Isra'ili), ibn Sina, al-Ghazāli and al-Kindi. The blending of Europe's old self-generating culture and the new restored learning comes out curiously in Philip of Tripoli's preface to his translation from Arabic of the *secreta secretorum*, a short compendium attributed to Aristotle, supposedly his advice to his old pupil, Alexander the Great. The translator says in his preface that 'no one in his right mind would resist' its teaching. In fact it is a compendium of subjects with which mediaeval science was most concerned, science, medicine, astronomy, astrology, the duties of kings and the qualities of justice. It translates an Arabic text which expands a version in its turn adapted from a presumed Syriac original; elements are Greek and Persian, and it is fitting, however fictional, that it should be associated with Alexander. It is a great tribute to a common civilisation; and it was as popular among the clerics of Europe—over two hundred manuscripts are known—as it had been at the court of al-Mansūr.

Arabic Aristotle and Holy Scripture would henceforth happily combine; the thirteenth century harvested the sowing of the twelfth. Roger Bacon saw the history of philosophy as extending from the Latin Fathers to the classical Latin writers, Cicero, Seneca, Pliny and Josephus; and from the Hellenistic scientists to abu Ma'shar, al-Farābi, ibn Sina and ibn Rushd. A peculiarity of Bacon's was to insist that the pagan writers had found their inspiration in the Hebrew prophets. Plato, for example, must have heard the preaching of Jeremiah. He sees a gradual extension of knowledge from its Old Testament sources across the civilisations of the world. After Aristotle he thinks he sees a break in the tradition of learning, which ibn Sina and ibn Rushd restored 'after the times of Muhammad'. Bacon is not nearly so confused chronologically or ethnographically as the earlier translators of the preceding century, and yet he still, for the most part, treats Muslim writers in the same way as he treats the ancient Greeks.[25]

Compared with Bacon, Michael Scot presents a more confused but equally interesting historical perspective, an astrologer's world-view. His is a story of a special skill handed on more or less secretly from the sons of Noe, who learned magic arts from the demons. Scot has a clear picture of a gradually expanding population in an empty world, and the growth of magic commensurate with urbanisation. Finally, the secret art is passed to two Alexandrians, Demetrius and Alexander, and

Ptolemy, King of Egypt learns it from them. Probably this is a confusion with Claudius Ptolemy, the geographer and astronomer. Zoroaster also figures in Scot's story, fire worship being another demonic trick. The Art reaches France from Spain through the ingenuity of Gerbert, apparently already skilled in necromancy and who discovers the use of the astrolabe by this means. We are dealing with authentic Mediterranean traditions of magic actually practised, often in primitive and persistent forms, and common to the Christian and Muslim worlds. The confusion of philosophy, astronomy, astrology and magic is inextricable. A list of the great astrologers is interesting: the Biblical Solomon and the Sybil (perhaps the Jewish Sybil?); then Thabit ibn Qurra, Mashalla, Dorotheus, Hermes Trismegistos, Boethius, ibn Rushd, John of Spain, Isidore, abu 'Uthman Sahl ibn Bishr and al-Qabisi, a wide range across the spectrum of Hellenistic and Arabic writers and including both Muslims and non-Muslims.[26]

A third glimpse of the width of erudition and the broad perspective of knowledge is given by the translations done at the court of Alfonso x in the later part of the thirteenth century, many with the personal interest and intervention of the king. Here there is a very clear division between the scientific material derived from the Arab world and the history, which is strongly oriented against Islam. It has some oriental Christian source material, and even some that is Muslim Arab, but it never deviates from its anti-Islamic stand. The *Kalila wa Dimna*, which in origin is an Indian collection of fables (Bidpai), is a rare example of cultural borrowing; the book of the game of chess is as neutral as the science. Another way to judge the literature of mediaeval science is to take one author in one field: Arnald of Villanova, spanning the thirteenth and fourteenth centuries, reminds the reader of the great Arab medical writers in his breadth of interests. He himself cites principally Galen and al-Razi as the masters, but all his writings, often largely adaptations, reflect the width of the Hippocratic inheritance; his interests extend across the whole field of medicine and public health, even to female cosmetics. His enormous output illustrates an amazing vitality in both the author and his many themes, a vast extension of knowledge since the tenth century, but still more, the capacity of a culture to absorb neutral material.[27]

VESTIGES OF ISLAM AND ELEMENTS IN COMMON

All this acquisition of knowledge from Arabic, Arabic originals or Greek originals through Arabic, was dissociated from Islam. A sceptic might question whether really nothing Islamic survived in these translations. A frank reply would have to be both 'yes' and 'no'; yes, in that recognisable Islamic formulae were used, but no, nothing was used that would seem Muslim to anyone who did not already know that it was.

Forms like *in nomine dei pii et misericordis* (in the comparable English convention, 'in the name of God, the Merciful, the Compassionate') occur quite often, but there is nothing in the bare words to startle the most orthodox of Christians. The same may be said of *si deus voluerit*, an obvious Muslim formula, and also 'on whom the Creator be merciful'. Avicenna's *Canon of Medicine*, popular alike in the Middle Ages and in the European Renaissance, begins: 'Let us first give thanks to God . . . whose mercies are manifest upon all the prophets'. Sometimes there seems to have been adaptation. When al-Zarqali is made to begin, 'in the name of the Lord', or al-Razi, 'in the name of God', without addition, it looks as though 'the Compassionate, the Merciful' has been suppressed. There are other elisions and praaphrases: Michael Scot curiously begins a translation from the Arabic Aristotle, 'in the name of our Lord Jesus Christ, almighty, compassionate, merciful'.

A very popular Latin translation that can easily be compared with its original is Bacon's edition of Philip of Tripoli's *secreta secretorum*. The opening paragraph of the Arabic is 'In the name of God, the Merciful, the Compassionate. May God prosper the Commander of the Faithful, and may He help him to guard the faith, and may He preserve him to cherish the fortunes of the true believers'. This becomes: 'May almighty God protect our King, the glory of the believers, and strengthen his rule to guard the divine law and his own, and cause him to endure, for the exalting of the honour and praise of good things'. The sentence, 'Truly God compensates every one according to his faith and action, either in this world or the next, and truly He does what he wills' is rendered just *laudes Deo*, much as the English versions of the East India Company's Persian correspondence used to begin conventionally 'After Compliments'. The ending of the book, not only the prayer for the Prophet, but also the characteristically Qur'anic, 'Praise be to God, the Lord of the worlds' is omitted.[28] The Latin translator knew that the work had been translated into Arabic by a Christian, Yuhanna ibn al-Batriq, and may have felt that he was re-Christianising it.

One field of learning where what was held in common by the Arab world and by Christian Europe was particularly important was astrology, the ancient and traditional science that the Hellenistic world had developed out of its Babylonian origins. In our Middle Ages its hypotheses were still in process of being disproved—no doubt in this respect there are sciences of our own with which it might be compared, if we were in a position to know which they are. Obviously such natural sciences as astronomy (in the modern sense of the word) presented no cultural difficulties in transmission, because they were merely technical. All that was necessary was to correct the planetary tables for the new latitudes. The astrology from which astronomy was rarely disentangled implied more, a large common sociological area, because the occasions on which astrological advice might be asked and given were likely to occur equally in Christendom or Islam, as they had been in the Hellenistic world to which the two others had succeeded.

The translation of the astrology of Abu al-Hasan 'Ali ibn abī Rijāl by a Jew at the court of Alfonso into Castilian, and thence by a Spaniard into Latin, is a good example of the common Mediterranean culture. Ibn abī Rijāl, known as al-Maghrabi, went from Spain to establish himself in Tunis. His sources of course are Hellenistic, but naturally all trace of astrology as an institutional religion has disappeared: there are no priests of Thot, and astrologers are professional men like doctors. The gap was not great between eleventh-century Tunis and thirteenth-century Toledo; indeed, if we project ourselves from those two into their future, our present, it is obvious that even today many of the problems on which 'judicial' astrologers were consulted are as important as ever they were, sometimes more important; travel and letter-writing are incomparably less important, because so much easier; on the other hand, rumours, which now appear as newspaper reports and television newscasts, are probably more of a hazard than they were when the astrologers studied them. All these fields fell outside the forbidden area of religion. If there is no great dissimilarity between our problems and those of the Middle Ages, it is obvious how closely Arabs and Europeans shared like conditions. Yet from all this area of judicial astrology, too, the forbidden subject of Islam was excluded. Religious expressions in ibn abi Rijāl are even more interesting than those I have cited from other sources. They sound strange in Latin dress, but, while they are clearly not of Christian origin, they are never inescapably Muslim; this product of three religions even makes 'Ali ibn abī Rijāl specifically give thanks to the Lord Jesus Christ.[29]

Much more was common to Christianity and Islam than Christians wished to admit; it took constant vigilance if two such similar religions were to seem unlike. In the wide area that lies on the margins of theology and philosophy there was considerable reliance on what in fact were Muslim sources. To take only a well-known example, St Thomas Aquinas depends often on ibn Sina, al-Ghazāli and ibn Rushd. Bacon used Muslim philosophers in order to make polemic points against Islam, but seems genuinely to have liked what he quoted. He argued that our apprehension of the future life is like that of a deaf man's of music, and supported this from ibn Sina. He was fond of this passage: 'A man shall not be freed of this world and of its deceptions until, wholly taken up with that other heavenly world . . . the love of the things there draws him altogether away from thinking of anything lower',[30]

It is so impressive that all the writers of the twelfth and thirteenth centuries who were concerned with the translation or use of material from the Arabic knew just what they were about. It seems that a writer will come to the very edge of an exclusively Muslim formula, and yet never cross over the edge. They believed, of course, that any genuine theological correspondence between the religions must be *praeparatio evangelica* or *preludia fidei*, that is, some approximation to a Christian position, an anticipation of revelation. Islam could not anticipate Christianity, chronologically, and yet the great Arabs were often treated as if they were ancient Greeks. We notice, too, what was in fact translated from Arabic. Just as the Arabs never translated the poetry and drama of ancient Greece, which would have been hard to absorb into their own literature, because of its very different style, so the Latins never translated the poetry and other typical literature of the Arabs, and for the same reason. Perhaps this had nothing to do with Islam; the Syriac translators of scientific Greek texts had not translated poetry or drama into Syriac either; we see effective cultural filtering of the unwanted, in both cases. We earlier noted the very partial success of translations of Arabic and Persian literature into European languages at a much later date. What little Arabic literature was accepted in the Middle Ages was properly absorbed. *Kalila wa Dimna*, itself foreign to Arabic, was exceptional, but the genre of the fable was welcome in West Europe, and the analogues of 'oriental' plots in Western literature prove only that good stories are popular, whether we believe in diffusion, or in spontaneous generation. The exact part played by Arab literary practice in Provencal poetry and in the conventions of courtly love is still controversial; but it seems clear that much original stimulus came from the Moors; macaronic Arab and Romance love songs unequivocally indicate a common world of singing girls, but there is no later development of Arabic literature parallel to that of Latin and Romance. Similarly in architecture there is a considerable interpenetration of Byzantine, Arab, and Frankish, characteristics. We cannot really say that the later development of Europe would have been very different if it had acquired scientific knowledge from Greek without the Arabic influence.[31] European development has never been anything but wholly European in both direction and style. At the same time, the borrowing was durable; although it has been constantly overlaid, still it has never been outgrown. With the new techniques, it is difficult to see that Europe could have made any progress; with them, it is equally difficult to see that the progress made was in any way alien.

The rigid exclusion of the specifically cultural and Islamic, the acceptance of the technical and universal, is surely the means by which this was achieved. There was a spontaneous and determined general agreement about what to take and what reject; what was taken was always either culturally common, or culturally neutral. The body of scientific knowledge (whether right or wrong is irrelevant) was culturally neutral. Its cultural bearings were easily absorbed, because they were part of the common inheritance of the Arab world and of Europe. Theological sensitivity was perhaps only the index of this mediaeval allegiance to Europe. It remains for us to see whether the non-Western cultures today can utilise Western techniques—culturally neutral or culturally common—in their own way, with the necessary determination; whether anti-imperialism can be as effective a filter now as anti-Islamic discrimination was in time past.

A Cultural Filter in the Modern World

I EARLIER ARGUED that it should be possible for a society to exploit anything 'culturally neutral', without being deflected from its own characteristic cultural development. This seems plain common-sense, and the ability of mediaeval Europe to exploit Arab thought and skills, while maintaining its own undeviating direction, shows that it can be done; but is it certain that this is what is happening today in practice? For a century and a half 'colonised' or foreign-dominated countries have been claiming that they can take modern European techniques without the associated culture; but are they succeeding? It may be that the experience of mediaeval Europe was unique. Does the mediaeval precedent encourage us to hope for the survival of different cultures today, or do the favourable conditions then prevailing no longer exist?

An essential preliminary question is, are we flogging a dead horse? Has anti-imperialism, which was so powerful a sentiment for the first seventy years of this century, finally exhausted itself? I said earlier that there are signs that might be so interpreted. If this were the case, all that we are saying might still be interesting, but it would be recent history, not contemporary analysis. The world, however, is still divided into richer and poorer, and it is unlikely that resentment at the consequences will disappear. Some developing countries are becoming rich by selling natural deposits, oil in particular, but there has yet to develop any significant diminution of cultural discrimination, one group against another, whether internally or between nations. A more likely interpretation of what is happening is that anti-imperialism is being refined into a more sophisticated complex of ideas. It is inevitable that oversimplifications, which made up much of the anti-imperialist theory, should disappear under criticism, or more simply under the pressure of a more careful analysis, but of course the theory can be re-stated to forestall opposition, in either a Marxist or a non-Marxist form. Anti-imperialism will continue to be re-stated so long as any national group seems not to determine its own affairs. We might compare the process of re-stating these ideas to that which went on in the Middle Ages, when a more accurate knowledge of Islam forced Christian polemists to deploy inescapable new knowledge to support their inherited theories. In their case, this meant distortion of the facts, and I am not suggesting that anti-imperialist theory is as false as the anti-Islam in the Middle Ages; I am saying nothing at all here about the truth or untruth of the theory. The important point is that the process (true or false) follows the same path.

In any case, there is no indication that anti-imperialist sentiment has lost popular support at the xenophobic level. Moreover, although the countries which maintain systems rigidly hostile to imperialist foreigners change from time to time, there continue to be countries which do so. Techniques of isolating resident foreigners from normal relations with the people of a country may be borrowed from the socialist countries, or may be spontaneously devised, or may be both in part. They are rather like the mediaeval canons which isolated Muslims from Christians by regulation; but they seem to be less durable, because they have not up to now been maintained anywhere for a really long period. This comparison would suggest that the modern situation is like the mediaeval, but only a pale reflection of it. If so, anti-imperialism would be too weak to repeat the mediaeval experience of cultural resistance.[1]

A resistant culture must at least be able to satisfy the minimum conditions of the mediaeval situation: the material techniques that it wants to absorb should not be alien to it; there must be a single-minded determination to achieve a conscious end, and the will must combine with knowledge and judgement to produce unambiguous action. When I argued that Western disarray ought to save borrowers from taking our cultural uncertainties with our technology, I may have made too rational an assumption; the lame may really want the blind to lead them. Mediaeval Europe long succeeded in keeping uncertainty under control, but uncertainty, which erodes like rust, is equally hard to prevent. The mediaeval example tells us that the will to resist, if present, can succeed, but not, of course, whether in fact it is present in any particular case today. Of the pre-conditions of success, the first is present, almost beyond argument. The new body of knowledge is in no sense alien to the cultures that want to absorb it. It is a matter of technology and other techniques, and no one who has reasonable experience seriously considers that techniques cannot be learned by anyone. The ingenuity of mechanical workers in developing countries is often praised. What is usually criticised is a failure to maintain machines. This is not a question of ability; it is a question of organisation. Even the technique of organisation is fairly easily acquired. The will to exercise it is the crucial factor, and the will is not only a question of motivation. Certainly the motivation is there; all the countries of the world are pressing hard for technological, and every kind of technical, advance, and when this is combined with a determination not to accept outside direction, the will is there. There are two unsolved questions. Is there always a genuine determination? And, when there is, do the

ability and the will result in the third condition: the power, by discriminating, to take effective action? Discrimination in the Middle
Ages was achieved by anti-Islamic prejudice, usually even in conflict
with the facts. Is anti-imperialist feeling an equally effective filter?

A survey, or series of surveys, of the extent to which culture resistance has been or is being successful is badly needed. I have no space to
attempt it here, but some facts, common to a number of countries,
seem clear enough. In no single case can we in any way yet be sure that
a final choice has been made; it is certain only that we can nowhere be
sure that cultural resistance will succeed, and we can equally certainly
recognise always and everywhere a temptation to give up resisting. As
in other questions of contemporary history, when we think we recognise tendencies, they are reversed; a country seems committed to a
particular trend, and suddenly it turns round and goes the other way.
At any given moment, we are unable to tell which of various incompatible tendencies is going to win, or where the pendulum will come to
rest. The uncertainty of all contemporary interpretation of events has
been a recurring theme of this book. We cannot see the finish. The
danger of making mistakes in the analysis of present-day history remains, even when much of some particular process is clear enough. In
the resistance of cultures to dominant outside influence, we are never
sure that a case of apparent success or failure is final. Partial and temporary success or failure is what in fact we most often see. Often there
is a compromise, and intrusive new customs are modified, without
being rejected outright; and then, even so, persistent erosion by the
passage of time turns partial success into total failure. Total success or
failure would be final, but there may be only a deceptive appearance of
either. Our difficulty is not how to recognise emphatic success or failure;
but to distinguish the elements of each in a confused situation, and to
tell whether a situation is deteriorating or improving. The key problem
is to tell an indigenous development from the copy of an alien pattern,
modernisation from 'Westernisation', a natural cultural development
from cultural intrusion. A spontaneous development sometimes resembles a borrowing from outside.

Although there is no necessary correlation between technical advance
and cultural achievement, it would be folly to suggest that the two do
not get confused. Economic development has much influence on cultural process, of which the nature is an accident. Even the crucial
difference between a culture that controls its economic development
and one that is controlled by it is often accidental. Much may depend on
a very small group of people. When a country is developing, the classes
that first benefit set the tone for the whole, and, if they are not 'anti-
imperialist', this continues until 'progress' and foreign ways have be-

come inextricably associated. The behaviour of a 'progressive' class in a culturally imitative society closely resembles the classic behaviour of new-rich individuals. These are usually derided for trying to assimilate their behaviour to that which a traditional wealthy class acquired in childhood. In a developing country where anti-imperialism is not a governing principle, the leading class often copies foreign ways, as though imitation might establish their position by magical assimilation to the successful and wealthy foreign culture. This is most pathetic when we see, as sometimes and in certain countries we do, not the acceptance of technology and the rejection of cultural intrusion, but an inability to acquire the technology combined with imitation of the culture. So far as this point has a general application, it shows the value of anti-colonialism. At least this excludes open imitation and assimilation, whatever seepage of alien ways there may be.

Yet seepage is important. I shall begin by taking one small but informative example. The attitudes of revolutionary regimes, whether 'left' or 'right', 'nationalist' or 'socialist' and in whatever sense 'democratic', have usually included popular xenophobia, some attachment to folk-lore and local language, sometimes an enjoyment of religious difference (Muslim, Hindu or local Christian against foreign Christian), and usually a desire for economic autarchy. This last has often necessitated consumer austerity, which can only be disliked by a middle class, even a new middle class that it has itself created; in contrast, the 'workers and peasants' are grateful for anything that raises them above subsistence living, but what satisfies them is deprivation for the bourgeois. Different countries in turn have been willing at different times, over the last twenty years or so, to 'cut off their noses to spite their faces' by rejecting 'imperialist' help for the sake of national independence. This has always much annoyed the wealthy aid donors, who find the pursuit of an irrational (that is, unrewarding) ideal particularly irritating. Their own concept of freedom, is individual, not national, freedom, and the latter seems meaningless to them. The primacy of individual freedom is a doctrine that may itself be a 'Western' cultural intrusion; or it may be one of the luxuries of wealth.

There is tension, not only between 'imperialists' (or 'donors') and 'nationalists' (or 'xenophobes') but between the first wave and the new wave of nationalism, and between nationalism and a new wave of anti-nationalism. In particular, successful revolution has tended to create a middle class that rejects austerity. There really is a tension on this very point within each resisting culture.

For example, this comes out in the difference of generations within these countries. One generation makes a revolution and imposes frugality in order to achieve real independence, but frugality is not, of

course, an aim in itself; independence is supposed to be the way to a
higher standard of living for everyone. When foreign capitalism is seen
to produce better results quicker, there are many who react against
austerity, and prefer immediate to future comfort, indulgence to independence. For quick results, however, they do not conceive of a
counter-revolution back to capitalism (or forward to capitalism, which
many countries have never enjoyed, except in the capacity of buyers);
they simply demand better living for a relatively small number. There
is a return of privilege, and those concerned may even be the children
of the leaders of the original revolution, whose own state of privilege
derives from their contribution to society, not from their parents' position. The children of old revolutionaries may form a kind of *jeunesse
dorée*; but, of course, this is only one possible symptom. What is
general is the growth of a movement away from austerity for the sake
of independence. It may be associated with 'liberalism', and is likely in
any case to be associated with disillusion, relaxation of controls (whether
good or bad) and a lack of public spirit. Another likely result, when a
revolutionary party retains the apparatus of power, is corruption. This
in turn creates further dissatisfaction, and in all such cases the anti-
colonialist filter loses its effectiveness.

The situation of an unresisting minority in a resisting culture is
crucial. The case of divided generations is only one example, but it is a
very revealing one. In Western Europe and America in the sixties
middle-class younger people wished to enjoy no privilege more than the
working class, and tried to copy the ways and appearance of the workers
as well as they could. Their motive was egalitarian, and the intellectuals from among the workers who were declassed by their education
were happy enough to accept a position in which they could set the
pace, and in which they escaped from seeming to be class defectors. All
alike were glad to be told that students were a kind of worker, a proposition which is either self-evident or blatantly untrue, according to
definitions and circumstances. A good deal of artificial behaviour resulted, a copying of the superficial and less typical characteristics of the
workers; the former, because the middle-class could only observe from
the outside, and the latter because the declassed workers taking part
were sharing a middle-class experience, not the experiences of their
own class.

The impact of this on developing or resisting cultures of the 'third
world' has its ironies. A young privileged class, in the capacity of a new
aristocracy, can be seen to copy the clothing and fashions of the Western
youth, for exactly the opposite reason: in order to dissociate themselves
from the masses in their own countries. They do it because they see it
as smart and international. The pop culture in its superficial character

means egalitarianism in its area of origin, but élitism or privilege in areas where it is adopted by an affluent minority, and so the original attitude is reversed; precisely, dissociation from the workers and peasants replaces the will to associate with them. Yet, although the intention is reversed so neatly, there is less opposition between the two attitudes than appears at first glance. Both are middle-class attitudes. The adoption of working-class manners by a middle-class ashamed of not being workers, or for some other reason wanting to be or seem like workers, is self-evidently a middle-class objective, and so is the attitude of those in developing countries who copy them; on the other hand, the poor in countries still poor do not have the time or the inclination to copy the ways of the wealthier peoples. These two attitudes are also alike in being poses; the middle-class European adopts the posture of the worker (as he sees it) and the middle-class, or privileged class in the developing country, adopt what they see as the posture of the inter-national wealthy class.

Any imitation of the 'West' is based quite simply on wealth. Many simple people in a developing country do not believe that there can be communists in capitalist countries, because how can there be capitalist communists? This looks naïve, but in fact it goes to the heart of the problem. Any rich or well-to-do individual in a developing country tends to assume that he shares a class solidarity with anyone, not obviously a poor man, from a rich country. It used to be common for the landowning or money-owning classes in a poor country to treat any European, being a member of a master-race, as one of themselves. The European might often be an official on a limited salary, augmented temporarily by allowances for overseas duties, but not enough to allow considerable savings; yet he was expected to sympathise with the rich when they were expropriated or lost part of their wealth, although they remained very much richer than he. There is sense in this. All the people in a rich country belong in the privileged band of the human race, and the poorest of them may be the envy of most people in a poor country; the privileged few in that country rightly recognise that they are speaking to privilege, when they deal with anyone at all from the richer society. A single word, such as the Arabic *khwaja*, can denomi-nate almost any rich man and almost any foreigner. It is when people recognise that whole societies are wealthier than their own that anti-imperialism takes shape. The revolutionary rejects colonialism for the same reason as his rich compatriot associates his personal condition with that of a rich country; and each reacts appropriately, either renouncing, or else copying, the ways and cultural manifestations of a dominant wealthy society.

The Americans are in a position unlikely ever to be repeated elsewhere. They were the first to experience a problem of unassimilated wealth, and they also have no long single cultural tradition. Even so, they may well emerge from their cultural impasse by their own efforts. It is only at first sight that prosperity seems always to wear the same appearance. It is obvious that it does not in the case of individuals. Some men may over-indulge when they become rich, but not all, and those that have done so may not so continue. The same applies to whole societies. Prosperity actually means freedom to choose an occupation; we observe that both societies and individuals that become rich without preparation or understanding find themselves with nothing to do; even so, most individuals choose different occupations, and most cultures still tend towards different patterns of life. As in the mediaeval example, continuity of development is the test of whether a new pattern of behaviour is imitative or spontaneous. This can easily be applied to arts and literature. When a West African writer, say, uses English to express West African ideas, continuity is unbroken. When a writer in, say, Arabic, uses his own language to express Western ideas, or to practise foreign literary forms, there is at least some break in tradition. In some countries, writers envy the prestige of journalists in the West, and would gladly borrow at least some of the culture that honours them.

The rule that improved machines do not make a cultural revolution is, however, everywhere exemplified. There was no fear of techniques in the mediaeval example, and some of them have a direct parallel to-day. A man, an ox, a horse, a tractor, each in turn has done the plough-ing, providing increased power without changing the purpose or the function of the operation. Now, the skills of looking after motors have replaced the skills of looking after horses, but that in itself has meant no greater change than there is when we turn from one book to another: we are still reading a book. Even in countries that do not produce the machines themselves, there is no great cultural change so long as the machines do a familiar job. In the case of computers, a non-producing country has sometimes developed uses that are as 'advanced' as any to which they have been put on their home ground, by following the natural bent of its own culture. Import of machines sometimes results in economic dependence, and that in turn in cultural imitation, but we have only to look anywhere in the world to see that there is no revolu-tion just in using a tractor for farm power, or a computer for calculat-ing. The real cultural revolutions came long ago, when farming and calculating began.

A few examples of cultural sameness obtrude. To most people today, architecture seems much the same everywhere. Yet this is probably a sameness induced by unfamiliarity with new techniques, and an area where we can expect cultural differences to develop as character of any sort begins to appear. This does not mean that the copying of ancient themes would give distinct cultural character. Victorian Gothic has come to be recognised as a style of its own, with its own beauty; Moorish style buildings in the Arab world may in due course be seen to have a similar character and beauty; but they will not be a natural development of Moorish into modern Arab. We may rather look for regional differences with no obvious stylistic links with tradition, except as much as Gothic has with Romanesque, or Mameluke style with Ayyubid. The local differences should have this regional difference, and this traditional continuity, that each culture's different needs should be served by buildings with different stylistic emphases. If, as with international hotels, the needs are the same, no doubt the architecture will be too. Few people would agree that any developing country has yet thrown up a living local variety of modern architecture; neither, on the other hand, is there any obvious reflection of regional differences within the West, even in proportion to surviving cultural differences in the area. This seems to bear out the 'one culture for the technological age' theory, although it is too early to judge whether localised traditions will develop, and there has always been an architecture and style of clothing, decoration, furniture, and so on, typical of each age, within which local styles are englobulated. We can recognise the styles of the eighteenth and nineteenth centuries wherever European influence reached, in spite of great individual differences. Again, Krak des Chevaliers and Caernarvon are not less alike than the Nile and London Hiltons. The verdict must be *not proven* — or 'not yet proven'.

It is not difficult to distinguish genuine cultural borrowings that are fully and easily assimilated; as, long ago, chess travelled westwards, so now football has been naturalised, alike on the playing fields, and in the back streets, of every continent. Again, like the apologues of European stories that scholars find in oriental sources, so cowboy legend has been widely absorbed in divergent cultures without anything that could be called, or mis-called, Americanisation. Such cases need not detain us. Neither should the real loss of craftsmanship that necessarily accompanies industrialisation be mistaken for more than it is.

Resistance often comes from the conservatism of the masses that sometimes militates against improvement, whether technical or cultural, but just as often frustrates exploiters. The same thing happens in the West, of course, but perhaps less effectively. It is as much a triumph of common-sense as of reaction or inertia. Then there is further resistance from revolutionary feeling of varying kinds, which rejects all 'Western' solutions, just because it is suspicious. By revolutionary sentiment I mean a spontaneous reaction, which may find differing shades of expression, many of them largely home-grown, though rarely wholly free of outside influence. The attraction of orthodox Marxist-Leninism is also felt, more or less strongly, but throughout the different cultures there are far more who feel a vague attraction, than there are convinced, trained, and dedicated Marxists. Probably this attraction comes from the fear that the home-made filter will not prove effective, sometimes from an almost child-like longing for outside protection from cultural intrusion, for a third party and a second choice. Such thoughts are natural, but they can lead nowhere useful, and self-reliance is more easily admired than achieved.

The anti-imperialist filter seems to be ineffective against some of the positive attractions of wealth, although the copying of the superficial characteristics of the wealthy is more negative than anything else can possibly be. It is also pointless, unless acting rich can make a man rich. It may, indeed, persuade others that he is rich, and so make fraud possible; in the same way a small class acting rich can delude a nation into supposing that there is economic development when there is not. The third condition of mediaeval success was the capacity to discriminate. Western manufacturers and advertisers would naturally like to bring their export markets into the pattern that they have imposed at home. In theory, anti-imperialism should at least be effective negatively, and able to eliminate the powers of the foreign manufacturer to determine what he will sell in the export market. Why, then, are the fashions of Europe and America very largely followed in cultures outside those two areas, even where direct advertising is relatively ineffective? It is surely because they are associated with an enviable bourgeois life, illustrated in films, papers and magazines, seen by those who travel, and depicted in or represented by products which the manufacturers sell throughout the world. Why do new fashions take a local form so much less often? Apparently because the industries concerned are so dominated from the West that whatever is not actually produced there is produced to look as though it was. Sometimes a local industry, even in a country trying to break free of alien influence, will imitate the brand labels by which particular Western products are best known. We may be underestimating the power of local traditions to recover and to reassert themselves, but, if the process of imitation goes on too long, a total failure of cultural resistance is likely enough. If local traditions survive as a tourist travesty — we might instance the 'oriental dancers' who flavour the floor-shows in some countries — or even as an artificially cultivated folkloric performance, they have not survived at all: at best we are seeing their fossils. A tradition survives only as a living and changing process, unassimilated to any intrusive or foreign taste.

When the preservation of local tradition, if only under the guise of folklore, is seen to be part of the behaviour of successful nations, and adopted as if to attract success, self-conscious preservation is part of the imitative process, and represents a clear failure to discriminate the essential requirement of a healthy society. A tradition in such a case is necessarily interpreted by intellectuals and professionals, whose training has cut them off from the very tradition they are setting out to preserve. However sympathetic, they cannot be spontaneous. Artificial preservation is lifeless. The filter is not an embalming instrument; the wrong one is being used, one which admits only what international opinion has endorsed. The filter that is the only means to the desired end is one that protects the society from contaminated imitation; to change the metaphor, a culture needs a wind-break that will allow natural organic growth in its lee. Just to forbid imitation and to put a stop to artificial preservation is not, of course, a way of escape, and when it occurs it shows as certain a failure to discriminate as the reverse. A certain amount of imitation is superficial and altogether harmless, especially when it is something of a joke. My example of the brand names might be a case in point; it is more serious to find Western techniques of packaging more successfully copied than the manufacture of the article packaged. Prohibition can be seen to be useful, in any case, only when it favours a living alternative. There is no way out of the cultural dilemma for those who do not enjoy a flourishing and spontaneous indigenous development. Let us put it that the cultural barrier should act both as a filter and as a shelter, but it cannot provide actual growth, and we nowhere see it do so.

The simultaneous appearance of certain common tendencies over the whole world does not of itself imply that cultural characteristics are dying out, and it would be another failure of discrimination to think so. The same thing may happen to many individuals at once, without their ceasing to be themselves, and so it may to many cultures, each reacting in its own way. Outbreaks of violence by young men and women are universal today, but this varies in its expression from, say, urban guerillas who have dignified themselves with a cause and a sense of righteousness, to the muggers who are too inarticulate to know how to justify their sense of dissatisfaction. The guerillas at best utilise violence for a purpose, like the Cordovan martyrs or the Crusaders, and they are unlikely to be more successful. Quite a different example: the demand for more education for more people, to a limit not yet reached, is universal. Because it arises from a human want, it was likely to develop everywhere, if it developed anywhere, and this has indeed happened. Some consequences are inevitable, and equally universal, such as a certain lowering—or at least varying—of academic standards. We shall find the true cultural differences in the kind of education that results, not necessarily in the educational techniques, but in its general tendencies, and sometimes in the social purpose underlying it. Those experiences that are common to most societies of the world fit perfectly into the mediaeval model; they represent the first condition of success, that there should be some common tradition that can assimilate new techniques without self-distortion; things that happen spontaneously everywhere prove that there is a large shared area, which, often unacknowledged, in fact underlies the whole experience of cultural rejection, as much as that of cultural toleration or intrusion.

If little tends to disprove the survival of different cultures, positive indications are also rare. Earlier in this book I argued that many cultural differences are capable of surviving industrialisation, and up to now this has happened; of course, the process is not far advanced. The indifference of spectators to acts of criminal violence against individuals, which now characterises Western industrial society, is still inconceivable in other cultures, even in populous cities. Cultural differences inevitably penetrate new contemporary techniques. For example, all psychology that is based on an early inculcated sense of shame must be different from culture to culture, in so far as each one has chosen different things to be ashamed of; it is not that morality differs between cultures, but that more shame is arbitrarily attached to particular actions. This process carries ancient cultural differences forward into the future. One measure of successful cultural resistance is the irritated reaction of outsiders—usually Europeans or Americans—to points of difference. The fact that some countries are particularly disliked or greatly criticised in the West is a fair indication that they have managed to maintain some viable alternative to what the West admires. There is also a Western suspicion, which is rationalised in Western cultural terms, of all cultural differences. I have heard bitter criticism of the strict observance of Ramadan, as if it were the survival of some evil practice with sinister fascist implications for the present. Similarly Europeans and Americans often believe stories invented by those people in a developing country who have assimilated Western standards. A totally unimportant matter is sometimes blown up into serious conflict. Thus objections to short skirts, and even a mere preference for trouser suits, have more than once been inflated into an issue, in which Western observers get caught up into the argument between 'Westernisers' and resisters. Foreigners involved in this way resent the implied criticism of Western ways, and seem almost to resent even the survival of alternative cultures. If these points seem patchy and inconclusive, we live in a patched society, nowhere near any apparent conclusion.

It is not easy to point to a contemporary society that has a high cultural achievement totally unrelated to technical advance, although we were able to do so quite easily in the pre-industrial past. Having admitted so much, we can claim that some societies still seem sufficiently vigorous to follow a path of their own; only we cannot be sure how long this will continue. Weak cultures certainly collapse; in practice, we watch cultural intrusion succeeding wherever there is no sufficient attachment to a living local tradition, and just as far as that is so. Because of the cultural weakness associated in the West with some technological development, the result of a successful intrusion is always disarray, rather than the substitution of anything positive.

We saw how easy and how dangerous it is to 'colonise' our own future or our own past. The future will take care of itself, of course, and will be determined by what we do and are, not by what we think we do and are. The past cannot take care of itself so well; what has happened is final, but its effects continue to work themselves out, without our being able to interpret or understand them. A sense of superiority over the past, and a present-day disorientation, go together, alike in dominating and dominated cultures; in the latter, the opposite, an exaggerated esteem for their own past, may usefully protect them, unless it is so unrealistic as to cause reaction through ridicule. In all this there are consolations and reassurances. When representatives of a dominant culture resent the independence of those on whom they intrude, they provoke a greater resistance. Over the ages, healthy cultures have survived, and what would die anyway has quickly disappeared under pressure; a survey of the world today does not suggest that things are otherwise now. Inherited tradition continues to judge innovations, and those who intrude crudely are crudely rejected. The hard test is what actually happens, but, so far, what has happened is less than decisive. We do not yet know. At least we can accept some general principles as a guide, and we can certainly apply them to the problems of personal behaviour in cases of cultural conflict.

Part Three

PRINCIPLES

Theorica

WE HAVE SURVEYED a number of problems, all related, none in very great depth, but some more thoroughly than others. My arguments would not be more convincing if I multiplied the authorities I quote, and, if I did so, they might easily be smothered. Nor can I claim to have proved propositions that by their nature are not susceptible of proof. I can and do hope that I have managed to illustrate a few propositions well enough for the reader to recognise that I am talking about things in his own experience. Some people may experience cultural differences more (or more often) than others, and some by habit or nature are more aware than others of what they experience, or more sensitive in their response. Yet everyone has some experience of cultural differences in everyday life, and everyone makes some response to them.

I summarise the propositions that I think spring out of the discussion in the two first parts of this book, and I hope that they may be accepted.

Good academic relations between peoples of different cultures, like other relations between them, are constantly spoiled by interference, misunderstanding, and suspicion. This is my subject; this process is the cultural barrier.

By cultural differences we mean that different groups of people do things in different ways, or do different things or think about things differently. National differences, regional differences, racial differences, class differences, even those social differences which are based on the sexes, all the differences that groups of people gradually develop through circumstances (and often through the exploitation of the weaker group) are cultural differences.

Other cultures than our 'Western' or 'European' culture want to share the benefits of our technical advances, but only if it is a necessary condition of doing so do they want also to take over the cultural accretions that our techniques have acquired. One method of filtering out these cultural accretions is suspicion, and anti-imperialism, a doctrine expressing suspicion, is at least partly effective as a filter.

The different habits of mind that individuals have acquired constantly prevent useful co-operation and even communication. People who have no language problems at all still cannot understand each other, or, understanding in part, they misinterpret. I do not mean immigrants in Birmingham or tough British sailors in the tropics, or engineers or business managers on desert and jungle projects; I take my examples from the academic and professional world, from our own academics overseas and from foreign students at an advanced and mature level in Europe, all people whose occupation, permanently or temporarily, is made up of discussion and reflection. My examples are of the British abroad and of foreigners in Britain, but the British are in no way different from all the other cultural imperialists, American, Swedish, French, Russian, Italian, and the rest; in this book the British simply stand for all the culture which has spread out from Western Europe. My examples are not taken from the ignorant, the malicious or the base; they are taken from the best.

People find it difficult to live in a strange culture; it imposes an emotional strain. If any inclination to emotional unbalance already exists, it is quickly laid bare. This, too, applies both to those who go to teach and to those who come to learn.

We can separate the cultures. Modernisation need not be Westernisation. Our own cultural situation is not the only conceivable product of our technology. It does not help us to control or use our techniques, and so in fact fails to provide what we ourselves need. Other cultures would be rash to take our cultural solutions without first scrutinising their value—to them or to us; we might even retrace a few steps of our own to recover our cultural losses, or borrow techniques of living from those whose cultures are technologically so much less successful than our own. In any case, a cultural loan is distinct from a technical loan.

We can test our present problems and our search for solutions against past experience; and in so doing we shall test the cynic who says that we learn nothing from history, except that we learn nothing from history.

There is no superiority of one culture over another; in any case there is no one in a position from which it is possible to judge. Technological superiority has no cultural significance, and is transferable from culture to culture. Every man should be proud of his own culture, but should not believe it must be better than others. If he does think it is better, it only wants that he should develop a missionary spirit, and then he will start to impose it on others. We must learn to accept, or, better, to welcome, that something is different, without thinking it either better or worse than what we have ourselves.

To learn nothing from history is to learn nothing from the experience of other people; and it is the same negative attitude, whether it is applied to other people today or to other people of the past. Many who are proud to forget their forefathers are equally glad to ignore their contemporaries; to the undifferentiating, there is nowhere beyond the horizon and no time before today. We do not need to cut ourselves off like this. Admittedly it is possible to look at the present with minds overloaded by the past, but we are actually in no danger of this. It is more fashionable to off-load the past completely, and to come to the present with an innocence indistinguishable from ignorance. If 1170 and 1870 are irrelevant to 1970, then so is 1960 irrelevant today, because there are always new men of affairs. The corollary of ignoring the past is to accept that today will be forgotten tomorrow.

History offers a number of useful lessons in the difficulties of transmitting ideas from culture to culture; there have been unequal exchanges and exploitation, there has been falsification, and apparent transmission that was really misleading. Cultures are genuinely and profitably linked by a shared purpose, to satisfy a spontaneous, internal need of each.

One aspect of mediaeval European history, looked at in some detail, provides a splendid example of a cultural filter successfully at work; if everyone concerned is agreed about what to exclude and what admit, filtering is done almost effortlessly. It even suggests the hypothesis that it is the exclusion of certain ideas that makes possible the admission of others.

Whereas exclusion, irrespective of whether or not it be enforced by authority, works because it springs from a consensus of opinion, admission is dictated by separate needs rather than by consensus. The mechanism is one piece. Admission is not the residue after rejection is complete; what is rejected is what is not needed (and the rejection itself disposes to unity), and what is needed is not rejected. A well-instructed literate community can judge very delicately between the 'useful' and the 'harmful', but a cultural filter that functions efficiently in a unified and reasonably harmonious society may not work in a society divided and uncertain.

These are principles, but their application is not obvious. We cannot say immediately, 'Modern anti-imperialism serves the same purpose in the developing world as anti-Islam served in mediaeval Europe', because the contemporary evidence of what is actually happening is ambiguous. Neither can we say the opposite: 'The developing world is in such disarray that the comparison with mediaeval Europe only emphasises that the same story is unlikely to be repeated'. The developing world is disunited, but we just do not know whether its various constituent societies retain the organic tradition, character and vitality needed to resist industrial pressures. If it is all so doubtful, has history after all been any use to us? Surely, yes. It can no more determine our future than a horoscope can; but if we believed in the influence of the planets, we should be foolish not to make what plan we might of it. With history it is as with any experience, even individual experience.

Each time we cross a busy road we encounter a situation like, but never wholly the same as, many situations of the past, and we can face it with some knowledge of the factors that go to make it up. There are — as the next chapter will examine — practical conclusions to be drawn: to the 'developing', 'go on and act with determination; do not believe those who say it is too late'; and to the 'developed', 'try not to destroy anything because it looks different; do not believe those who say that this is inevitable'.

To the questions with which I set out, I have found answers that go some of the way to satisfy me. Of course history is useful, here and now, as it always has been. Of course we can distinguish techniques from cultures, as well as we can tell a spade from a garden; spades remain much the same, but of the gardens they create, no two need be alike. As for the cultural barrier, partly it is definable in practical terms, and these make up my last chapter. Partly, not the cultural difference, but the failure to see the cultural difference, constitutes the barrier.

Several times I have referred to the advantages of being different, and to that extent, the barrier is no bad thing. It is bad when we cannot see or speak across it, but that happens most often when we are unaware even that it exists. The actual differences between cultures, when they are seen, most people do in fact accept. We saw that even those who expect that there will be one world culture want at least to ensure that all the different ecumenes that survive into the present world should contribute to this solitary culture of the future; it would be easy to reduplicate examples of this sentiment. To think as much immediately concedes the value of past differences, and, if these differences have been valuable in the past, we must think that they would be equally valuable in the future, until someone disproves it. Those who want all cultures to contribute to the monster future culture have just given up the hope of the separate survival of cultures, not the wish that they should survive. Those who really do welcome the monster must realise that there is only one alternative to wanting a variety of cultures to survive, and that is to say that what we and no one else think, here and now, is alone valid, and will remain valid forever. If we believe in any change, we believe in some variety of culture; and if we do not regret it, we must regret the loss of other forms of variety. The fact is that very few people would welcome the monster if they did not think it inevitable.

I have said as much as I can usefully say to show why I think that we need not accept that inevitability; but it may be worth saying a little more about why we should want variety. Differences have always stimulated human beings to effort, and sameness has always dulled ingenuity. No society has ever had enough momentum to go on for ever. Every importation, whether rejected or absorbed, has been productive by reaction: rejection stimulates replacement, absorption nourishes organic development. This may be questioned less by the societies that lack technology than by those in our own society who are too 'sophisticated' to fear the natural consequences of hubris. We have talked of the danger of over-stimulation in societies that have to borrow so much that they cannot retain their identities; we must equally fear under-stimulation, and the loss of identity through inanition. For our own sake we in the 'West' must look forward to a more balanced exchange than is possible now, one from which both sides will benefit equally; but already we benefit from outside experience, and we could benefit more than we do, if we chose. A tendency to a fancied self-sufficiency is very dangerous to any culture, and particularly so to ours, because of our natural tendency to infer superiority from technological dominance. A letter to *The Times*[1] recorded the failure of a commercial enterprise to recruit for overseas service at twice the emoluments offered by the Diplomatic Service; but surely it is naturally those people whom only money will induce who are the cells of the cancer of self-sufficiency. For the 'developed' countries, all interchange with countries economically weaker is a question of long-term, not short-term, self-advantage. Educational interchange, of its nature, would in any case be only of long-term advantage. Our Western interest is to derive the advantage of equal exchanges with different societies that serve as stimuli; the road may yet be a long one, because first the others must achieve the technological equality that constantly recedes and that must come before a true cultural exchange. It will always remain true that for those who believe in communication between cultures there must be separate cultures to communicate with each other.

This book is about the barriers to communication. We have seen that a barrier at a certain point can divert water into a useful channel. The cultural filter successfully applied in the past can be applied again in equally propitious circumstances. Are these present? There are in fact many points of similarity between the situation of the developing world today and the situation of mediaeval science. People in Europe then, as now in developing countries, were enthusiasts for new disciplines. They were conscious of, perhaps over-estimated, the power that the new knowledge could confer, and could not see clearly the natural limits to the application of the techniques; they were quick to resent the opposition of old-style learning, which they deliberately ignored as incompetent to satisfy their current needs. They were totally satisfied with their own cultural development, into which they were able to absorb outside notions, and these did not deflect them from the direction in which they were going. They were above all sensitive to the need to catch up with the rest of the world, to recover for their own society a place in the total development of the world, its ideas, its sources of knowledge and its skills. These points are often closely parallel in the two situations, and as the dilemmas of the two seem to be much the same, so may their solutions resemble one another. Conditions of admission are more easily satisfied than conditions of exclusion. Selection of what to take should be a natural choice that follows need; and, as it was so in the twelfth century, so may it most easily be in the twentieth. But selection for rejection is less easy: it cannot follow an obvious course; it must be more rigorous, because more arbitrary; it is much harder to recognise what will be disruptive than what will be useful.

Although so much that applies to Europe as a debtor culture in past times applies equally to the debtor cultures of today, it may do so to different degree in different places. The answer is not necessarily the same in all the ecumenes that survive outside the European. Each of them may want to borrow different things, some to borrow more, some less, from the technologists; they may want to take more or less of technique, and more or less of cultural loan in addition. Even different parts within each ecumene — all as different from each other as within ours are the Americans, Britons, Frenchmen, Germans, Poles, and Russians — may all want to make slightly different use of the foreign material. True cultural borrowings apart, those who receive the transfer of a technique are free, as we have insisted, to make what cultural use of it they please; but they must make some cultural use of it. It is best to assume that all adaptations will tend to be different, within approximate and sometimes overlapping ecumenes, Latin America, Africa, the Muslim world, India, China, Japan, the rest of South-East Asia. We may expect, and I believe we should hope, that all these will make something culturally different of the same techniques. Cars will everywhere result in getting somewhere faster, although we can exaggerate the effect of this; they will also always create classes of drivers and mechanics, but the way these are absorbed into society can easily vary. The cultural adaptation of the radio is obvious. The cultural adaptation of critical method is more interesting. All scholarship has passed through stages of being totally uncritical, and within one culture this can fluctuate from age to age. Both Thucydides and ibn Khaldūn were succeeded by scholars with less critical acumen and technique than theirs. There is nothing essentially Western in the critical methods that were developed and in some fields are still best practised in the West: these methods, themselves neutral but effective, can be used to correct Western bias. Panikkar's fine achievement, *Asia and Western Dominance*, was a reversal of bias. Macaulay, a savage critic of Eastern literature, wrote magnificent but biased history. Historical method is capable of continual refinement, but at any stage of its development can be used in different cultural senses and ways.

We do not know how far other cultures will, like the West, get rid of their religions; we could in any case expect that their religions would develop (if only, on the principle of Newman's conception of Christian development, by bringing out what is latent), even if there were no foreign influence or example. The same is true of these various cultures taken generally; they are likely to develop by drawing out what is already latent. I have insisted earlier in this book that, if the traditional religions do not maintain themselves, the post-Islamic or post-Hindu cultures will still be different from the post-Christian, either because they would carry forward different emphases in secularised form, or if they were formed, or if they characterised themselves, on the analogy of our own present culture, by negation of what went before, we should expect to see quite different sets of contrary reactions to the different sets of belief. I recalled the differences in absorption of Marx-Lenin in Russia and China, according to the antecedent characters of the two cultures concerned. I also argued that we cannot judge the future; that in our own culture we do not know if we are half way through, or near the end, of a particular line of thought. Although I argued that our neo-Epicureans adopt their attitudes by contrast to our immediate past, I also pointed out that they represent a very old story in the history of our culture. I bring these strands of argument together at this moment in order to emphasise what it is we do learn from history. We do not learn what is going to happen next; in that sense the lesson of history would indeed be that we cannot learn from history. What we do learn is about possibilities. It is an important part of knowledge to be able to measure one's ignorance. History teaches us that we are wrong to assess our own future as all of us constantly do; and above all that the future is open, not only to new cultural developments in the 'West', but to a large variety of different developments in different cultures.

We have the right to be hopeful; but, for our hopes to be satisfied, all the cultures must have confidence. Those that will survive will have unity and determination, courage and conviction and pertinacity; if not, they will pay a price in corruption, the decay of old growth without organic replacement. Corruption that matters is not venality; it is the loss of direction and the dissipation of energy. It is not always easy to recognise. The withering of a culture may be hidden by its success, if its success is the product of its past; growth must be at the roots. Conversely, political divisions, and even political uncertainties, may mask cultural conviction. The outer appearance is no sufficient guide to the health of the root. The developing world can have the necessary confidence and other qualities that make it up, but there is a pre-condition. It must develop in its own way, at its own speed, under its own control and in its own chosen direction — and not following the way, the speed, control and direction of foreign experts, whose function ought to be only to answer questions. If it can do this, it can modernise without loss of the separate identities that make it up. Where mediaeval Europe was so successful was in maintaining its identity. It built up confidence and cohesion and passed them on as a legacy to posterity. This was a source both of good and of bad. It made an important contribution to subsequent European aggression, as well as supplying the motive power for immediate action. Those who resist imperialism should first recognise its strength. Imperialism took courage and confidence, not just as personal qualities in each adventurer, traveller, soldier, administrator, missionary, in himself, but also as derived by him from the solidarity of the society from which he came. His strength was in his sense of the moral demands his country and religion made on his performance and in the support he was conscious of receiving when he did his duty. If he failed in loyalty, he was punished, usually not by execration, but by oblivion. This powerful social cohesion was the unremitting creation of earlier centuries and especially of those periods that we lump together as mediaeval. It is correspondingly more difficult for the other ecumenes now to set up an effective cultural filter; their immediate past is not one of self-confidence. They have a history of unwilling submission to foreign rule which was at first often divisive; finally it was unifying. A common struggle against an intruder, a mere sense of struggle, a mere awareness of intrusion, certainly the resentment of alien domination: all these tended to unite. They are unhappily negative, but they may be capable of holding societies together while more positive forces are nurtured. This is why anti-imperialist sentiment, even when it is excessive, or extravagant, can serve a useful purpose. Imperialists who feel that they are abused unfairly should swallow their annoyance for the sake of the greater public good.

It is because the worst pressures are universal, and consist largely of the effects upon us all of the increasing population, that a yearning, often violent, for small communities erupts, and indeed that the usefulness of such communities becomes visible. A community is defined by its separate existence; by having its own customs. Universalism was the dream of humanity when people were divided; a new Roman Empire was Dante's infinitely remote dream, and Dante was the citizen of a sovereign city-state. Today we find that the Catholic church itself is breaking up the celebration of its liturgy, not indeed by countries, but by each linguistic sub-culture; and many people feel the appeal of loyalty to a small nation barely viable in modern terms, to Scotland or Wales or to a Basque land, all nations which Leviathan would have to vomit back. Men also create tiny little sub-cultures for themselves, specially formed societies with their own rituals and obligations, created just so that people can belong to them, so little do they feel they belong to the greater groupings to which they owe formal allegiance. It seems likely that the reason for this is not the mere magnitude of the official community, but rather its amorphous character; the same need is felt now as by those who preserved a civilised if Stoic life in religious Houses during the centuries of barbarian invasions. If we have to recognise a need to strengthen group identities — to belong to a culture of some character — would it not be folly to spread our present culture out even more thinly than it already is? Should we possess anything of value after further dilution? The most likely result of more dilution would be the growth of new varieties of concentration within it; in fact, the destruction of the hypothesis.

This is why we should not resent the varieties that already exist, and why we should hope to preserve them. Certainly we should never object if our techniques are plundered while our culture is despised. A little contempt between cultures is normal; we see it everywhere, it is a universal human experience, past and present, and it even brings advantage to all concerned. It really is important to see, and to consent with heart and soul, that it is to our advantage not to impose our way of life on other people. Of course, there is no doubt that people will always be irritated to find other people behaving differently from themselves. Everyone who goes abroad is irritated by the silly way the people of other countries carry on; this is general experience, and the most sophisticated and the most tolerant feel it sometimes. It is nothing whatever to do with the developmental level of either host or guest. How deep is this notion that our own way of life ought to suit everyone else, if only other people knew what was good for them? We should be odd if we did not feel this way sometimes, but of course it is only a manifestation of ordinary cultural xenophobia. It is true that the French have opened their total culture to any stranger willing to forego his own, and painfully to train in theirs; and it is true that some Americans have found it impossible to believe that any way of life but their own is tolerable, or that they could make the world any more valuable gift. To these forms of arrogance we may add the British conviction that no one can share in their culture unless brought up in it from childhood. Two contrary beliefs, that everyone ought to share our own culture, or that no one is capable of doing so, spring from the same root, that sense of superiority of which I have spoken at length. On the contrary, every member of the human race ought rightly to say: 'our culture is for us and other people's cultures are for them'.

What is not going to improve anything is a vague good will; it has failed to produce communication in the past, and it is more than likely to fail again. A vague good will is a disposition in the subject, not an illumination of the object in any clarity of detail. A vague good will disappears under the strain of any difference, difference of interest, or even difference of behaviour. Communication requires precision; communication requires something to communicate. The reason why techniques and methods are relatively easily transmitted is that they require a technical background, which is tiresome or delightful to acquire, according to temperament, but never as difficult, if we suppose intelligence and determination, as a cultural background. To teach book II algebra, it is necessary only to have completed book I (and to share a language); we pre-suppose a common purpose or motivation. Real communication is necessary both to commerce and to politics. It is specifically in our Western interest that all countries should reach a point of technological development where they can derive maximum benefit from our economy and we, without inequality, from theirs. It is in our political interest that they should not forever suspect everything we may want to do; the social benefits of anti-imperialism have a limit. The only way to avoid a reaction is not to provoke it; it goes without saying, not to exploit the economies of weaker countries to their disadvantage, but also not to expect them to behave in our way rather than their own. In a word, we must not deserve a penalty we wish to escape. We have to recognise reality, and then to accept it, not to wish in vain that things were different. This is true of international politics, and it is also true of commerce. Some business interests would prefer to change the market than to modify their business; but even they must learn to adapt to changing realities, as the biggest business, oil companies, for example, has already done. There is nothing in the least funny, when we stop to reflect, in the joke about selling refrigerators to Eskimos: the perfect salesman is the perfect cultural imperialist, imposing his product where it is least appropriate. Communication itself depends on the principle, 'ours for us and theirs for them'.

Once communication is established, we can even think of going beyond mere borrowing of techniques into the field of an actual cultural interchange. I have talked at length of the need to divest technical borrowings of their cultural accretions, but this is not absolutely to preclude some give and take of cultural accretions. Again, however, 'culture-transferability' applies: what is borrowed must be transmuted in the process of migration. This is clear enough in the case of art forms — painting, ceramic, literary, architectural. Moreover, the situation may vary, not only according to the thing borrowed, but also according to the lending and borrowing cultures. When the consumption of coca-cola spread in Europe after the second world war, it was seen to bring a measure of American culture with it, because there was no local tradition of consuming such kinds of liquid, and it went with American manners. In the Middle East, coca-cola (succeeded by pepsi-cola) was just another kind of sherbet, and absorbable without a cultural tremor.

The situation of the world is complex. Our one world is made up of an infinitely graded series of different units, all possessing a little more or a little less of that desirable commodity, economic development, with all its related developments, not least the educational. In this great series of larger and smaller cultures, of ecumenes and their dependences, countries and regions and families, all with different shares in development, the last unit is the individual. Cultures draw their shape and their vitality from the sum of the acquired characteristics of the individuals who compose it, habits largely acquired in childhood and transmitted to children, so that in the last resort the only unit is the individual, and the only sum of individuals is the human race. It is in no way inconsistent with the reality or force of different cultures to recognise that there are world trends: for example, the destruction of privilege seems everywhere today to be consistent and universal; it is combined perhaps with the re-allocation of privilege; it may be that it is only that privilege is shifting to new centres. It is not always associated with a party revolution, and we cannot be quite sure what it is, or at all sure how it will end, but the chief point of difference from one place to another seems to be the stage reached in a process we can see to be everywhere similar. This and other common factors are bound to affect the interaction of different cultures; but they are neutral factors, because, as with a technology, we can all do different things with them, and they can lead in different directions.

It is more necessary to preach the independence of cultures than the inter-dependence of all human beings, because the latter is in no danger; if we are concerned with the welfare of human beings, then we must be concerned with the welfare of their various cultures. Communication links the cultures, but it also preserves them, provided it be true communication. Diplomatic relations between States are a microcosm where we can see the pattern of all wider kinds of inter-cultural relation. If two countries can communicate, they can discuss their areas of common interest and their conflicts of interest, and hope to adjust them appropriately; but if they are not really communicating (and speaking the right languages is the least part of communication) diplomacy is reduced to posturing, to acting tough, or being haughty, or condescending, but in any case to playing a part. The pity is that we have too often taken communication for granted, or have believed that we were in communication, when we were merely exchanging courtesies — have mistaken the necessary preliminaries for the final achievement. In any relation of richer with poorer, each side has its peculiar problems, but both must exercise endless patience. If countries do not put real communication high among their priorities, virtual isolation must result. At the extreme there is the danger of a self-generating culture in a state of progressive deterioration. The Merovingian Franks developed their culture of hermits, saints and relics, but they barely preserved their great literary inheritance. In the case of modern England, only communication prevents it from becoming Little England; and communication with the outside means, first, with Britain outside England, and then with Europe outside Britain, and in turn with the developed world beyond Europe, and finally with the rest of the world outside that. I take these in turn, but the order in which I do so is only a logical order; all come together in importance. If diplomatic relations are a microcosm, academic exchange and educational aid are one stratum of the macrocosm; and it is the importance of communication which explains the State interest in these things, which are apparently peripheral to politics. We always come back to the fact that the one clear interest common to all the states of the world, all the people, all the classes, and to every size and shape of culture, is communication.

A family may be quite sure that its own ways are best, and yet tolerate the absurd ways of the family next door, because the cultural links are much greater than the differences. It is harder to tolerate other peoples' ways of doing things, when we are thinking on the scale of whole cultures. It is mutual jealousy and dislike which have kept them separate; but the instinct to resist domination and to dominate, to defend and to attack, is all one. We are in the paradoxical situation that for our own sake we must hope that our almost involuntary attempt to dominate will fail, and that the people of other cultures will not be dazed by the glamour of our technological achievements, or by temporary advantages which our cultural uncertainties have not yet nullified, into stopping their resistance. If they do, there will be no more communication, because there will be nothing to communicate. In the last resort, one single culture is impossible; it could only be formed to break up again into smaller loyalties and associations. The choice may be between variety based on traditions which inherit a past, and variety based on new divisions more or less spontaneously invented. If so, the choice is between the whole of humanity and a part; between all those who, from the beginning of the human race, in such changing circumstances have been, have thought, have felt, have done, and have died —

and this will soon include ourselves—and, on the other hand, just ourselves alone. We might choose, with monstrous egoism, while closing our own minds to the past, to try to impose our present pattern on the future—a future for which we can only be the past. What reason is there why our present should not be soon forgotten? And with it our idea of what the future will be like? These very generations which feel themselves now in some important kind of conflict with each other, may well be confused by popular writers and slipshod historians of the future. If we deliberately reject our past we deserve no better. Yet this choice does not in fact exist. However hard we may try, we can never cut ourselves off from the past of which we are made up.

Practica

PRACTICAL RULES IN any kind of personal relation are elusive. They are not like practical rules of medicine or engineering. We can say that some things are not helpful, some things do not matter, or do matter; we can talk about things that are cultural, not personal, that belong to our environment, not to ourselves. Where the two meet is an area that needs great delicacy in treatment; and yet, out of our various theoretic conclusions, does no practical conclusion result? One trouble about practical rules of behaviour is that they are by definition insulting. We do not like, very naturally, to be taught our manners. Yet experience is worth something. Anyone with long residence overseas has made so many mistakes, and watched others make the same or other mistakes so often, that he may feel encouraged to write down the obvious, and risk causing offence. Let us imagine that we are giving ourselves advice; we may be going to teach or to study in a strange country; we may be going to give expertise, or to seek it; we may be travelling as planners and administrators of education, either to give our services as experts, or to become more expert through in-service training; any one person may do all of these in a lifetime. This chapter, then, is a chapter of self-advice, and all of it is based on the need to enjoy cultural differences. Ibn Khaldūn, speaking of a society very differently organised from ours, said that it is 'absolutely necessary for the acquisition of useful knowledge' to travel in pursuit of it. The purpose was to learn from a variety of teachers, and in our quite different situation this still has some relevance. 'Meeting scholars and having many authoritative teachers', he continued, 'enables the student to notice the difference in the terminologies used by different teachers and to distinguish among them. He will thus be able to recognise the science itself behind.'[1] Obviously good advice to the modern intending student, this has its application also to the itinerant teacher, if it will dispose him to see through the differences of cultural terminologies to the real knowledge behind.

We cannot today think simply of a few wandering scholars, such as were common in either the Arabic or the Latin ecumene of seven or eight hundred years ago. Such people exist today, and are to be found in most of the universities of the world, but they are not part of the special pattern of education aid that exists today. They may easily fulfil the ideal of ibn Khaldūn; they belong to the concept of equal interchange; good or bad, they are examples of the normal situation that there ought to be, and we trust one day will be. Meanwhile the characteristics of the situation now are those that we examined, if not analysed, in the early chapters of this book: many of those teachers and students in strange countries live an uncertain and unsettled life for want of a familiar background, of known ways of life, of their own community to which they are sure they belong. The process of transmitting techniques is relatively uncomplicated, considered by itself, and it is necessary and inescapable; but it becomes complicated because there is a positive social advantage in the separation of cultures. This means that teachers abroad must expect to meet, and students here are likely to offer, technical co-operation combined with cultural resistance. This is a situation bound to cause individual unhappiness, especially loneliness. Up to a point the reluctant traveller who goes overseas, not because he likes it, but because he has to, to do some particular job, can join with compatriots to form a community of their own, for their hours of relaxation at least. This is easier for those whose reasons for travelling are nothing to do with learning; they can congregate for much of their time, and pretend that the country in which they are living is not there. Teachers are least easily isolated and least successful when they act in this manner. They must be constantly in touch with their hosts, if in fact any learning is to be done. For them there must be other solutions. The most obvious would be better selection of those who are to go; but the techniques of selection for this purpose are undeveloped; the students are chosen because they are needed to practise some technique, not because they are good at living abroad, and there simply are not enough people willing to go abroad to teach for it to be practicable to weed out the plants that will never do well, even if we knew how to do so. Good advice is all that we have to fall back on.

The briefing of the overseas student and of the travelling teacher before they leave home sometimes fails to warn them what to expect, although this is precisely what it sets out to do. Most of us expect that some sort of interest will attach to us just because we come from another culture; but in practice we shall find few who will do more than they must to make room for us. People will usually be kind, but kindness is often negligent, and through a failure of imagination may not be available when it is most needed. It is a guest who best learns how to be a good host, but most of those who receive students in this country have never been students abroad, and most of those overseas who ask for foreign teachers and experts to be sent to them have not themselves the experience of arriving in a strange culture as experts. The 'expert' in particular is apt to feel that he has something rather special to offer — why should he otherwise be invited at all? — and it is natural that he should feel that he is hedged by a little divinity. Somehow the briefing has got to put over the idea that we can be needed, perhaps quite desperately needed, but that we have still got to fit into a society that is already in existence and cannot be changed to suit us; we have to slip into our jobs unobtrusively, giving as little trouble as possible. Most of us want a rest from the rat-race, but, although foreign expert status looks likely to give us that, we shall not escape being judged; in fact, we shall be seen and accepted for what we are, which may or may not be a consolation to us. I do not think that any briefing will be any good that does not include a thorough discussion of the principles of foreign educational aid; only a proper understanding of why and for what we are needed will enable us to travel in a useful frame of mind. In the reverse direction, the student may come to Britain expecting to be put on and should be warned that he is more likely to find himself ignored. If he is apprehensive, he may be reassured — for example, an African who is going to an advanced medical course in Birmingham and has been distressed by tales of colour discrimination. Reassurance can never be wholly effective, and in this situation an Englishman talking is the least credible witness; but there is a good chance that in the event the student will be agreeably surprised. In whichever direction we travel, the warning we need is not to expect things too good, and not to fear that they will be too bad. It seems obvious; and yet briefing has failed, again and again, to my certain knowledge, to induce this realistic state of mind.

It is even more difficult to devise a briefing that will teach the recognition and acceptance of cultural differences. How do we first learn that things that look strange and different are really the same as we are used to, but in a different cultural guise; or that what looks so much the same is different in its new context? Many people in practice find this recognition curiously difficult. It may be of some use to give examples to people who are going abroad, and suggest that they try to identify new examples themselves when they get there. Like everything else, this faculty requires exercise in order to develop. When we say of some other people that 'politics is their national sport', we are making the right kind of cultural transposition, although distinctly a patronising one; it must indicate that 'they' are taking their politics too lightly, unless at least 'we' admit to being too serious about sport. It is a proportionate relation: politics is to them as sport is to us. My A is x to you and your B is x to me, but my B and your A may be anything; conversely, A may be x to you and y to me. This is most obvious in words and idioms. For example, the phrase 'my dear' has (or had) a feminine or effeminate connotation in English, but in many languages has the same force as 'mate' or as, in a disappearing class, 'old boy', in English.

The person using 'my dear' in his own language and culture means neither more nor less than the Englishman using a phrase he supposes less effusive. It is a question of usage; even at the same date in English, 'my dear' and 'my dear fellow' have had quite different cultural implications. The direct translation of courtesies will usually result in something that seems rude or ridiculous or both. Most people realise that courtesies change from culture to culture, but many still suppose that there can be an objective judgement of the absolute quality of each; they need to be told that if they think that the other man is either absurdly demonstrative, or short and curmudgeonly, they are wrong; that two men who observe very different conventions are in fact alike in their conventionality. Of the convention itself there can only be a relative assessment. This is also obvious in the case of dresses or hair-style. Women's dresses today would have seemed ludicrous, unbecoming and indecent a hundred years ago; dresses of last century have the charm or glamour of nostalgia today that they certainly did not have at the time; but at any date the culturally comparable thing to do is to wear the fashion. The same thing applies across space as across time: the foreigner does not notice if a Sudanese girl slips her *tawb* back from the top of her head, but it is significant of a social and political attitude that she should do so (or it was at one time). These matters are fairly easy; it is indeed easy to step from one culture to another. An Indian girl might wear an English dress at the length fashionable in England, but it would not occur to her to abbreviate a sari; and if she could not bear to wear a dress of the length in fashion in England, she would not defy the English convention by wearing a dress of unfashionable length, but would escape altogether from English culture into her sari. Out of Europe, the traveller who sees two men holding hands in the street must not take it that they are effeminate any more than if he saw one man's arm over another's shoulder. This last used to be very common in Britain and had no implication beyond hearty good will. Different conventional ways achieve the same purpose. I pointed out earlier that one of the most frequently recurring of cultural misunderstandings is about cleanliness, and many people who think others of a different society dirty would be incredulous to realise that the others think that they themselves are. This is most applicable to different customs of lavatory cleanliness, but it applies also to showers and baths; some British people cannot accept that someone who does not take proper baths can be clean, and many, Asians for example, are horrified at the habit that the British have of sitting in the water they wash in. All these are easy ideas; they will do to tell learners what to look out for; the overseas resident will find many more, and more subtle, cases of the same thing.

Most important of all, perhaps, is to try to guard against the double standard of judgement. In the examples I have just given, 'we' infer something untrue about 'them' out of ignorance. Abroad, riots and revolutions are more disconcerting than at home, because it is difficult to assess the background. Do we judge like things alike? In day-to-day life this difficulty is most easily, but quite wrongly, resolved by attributing individual shortcomings specifically to the culture. In an example I gave earlier, a drunk proves that 'these people' drink (whoever these people may be), yet when our friend is drunk, we know why, and can excuse him. So with driving faults: 'these people' are terrible drivers, but the same fault at home shows that 'this individual' is a bad driver. Another example: bureaucracy has much the same faults everywhere and, *inter alia*, minor clerks like to keep the public waiting, especially when they get a chance to annoy the more affluent without themselves being penalised. Overseas students here often attribute such rudeness to hatred of foreigners. I have known Britons, other Europeans, and Americans abroad who boast of getting 'good results' from shouting at dilatory or impertinent officials, but I have never been able to establish that any one of them behaves in the same way to dilatory or impertinent officials at home. In this instance the double standard passes from the mental state to physical action; and we can at least make a firm rule for all: never to do anything away from home that we would not do at home. This rule used to be taught at some schools; 'would you behave like that at home?' we were asked. To unimaginative individuals this is difficult to put over. Some people, who have never had servants at home, will have servants abroad; they must ask themselves, not 'is this how I treat a servant at home?' but, 'is this how I *would* treat a servant at home?'. Those who come in the opposite direction must adjust to the reverse problem. It is easier to correct overt actions, harder to control the thoughts from which the actions spring. If in a strange culture our immediate colleagues behave in a way we do not like — they are excessive drinkers or druggers or players of cards or whatever it may be — it is a great temptation to conclude from a year to two of experience in a narrow range of contact that the behaviour we do not like is typical of and created by the culture. The only corrective is to imagine the foreigner coming to similar conclusions about ourselves at home. No one is free of this fundamental fault of false attribution of a characteristic to a culture. I remember once, in a certain country, a threatened strike was carried out, although the cause was removed and the remedy conceded before it was due to take place. I thought this must be a characteristic product of the culture in which I met it. I had occasion within a week to travel to England, where I immediately came across another example of the same thing. As soon as we attribute a fault to a culture we start on the road of blaming it, while excusing ourselves for the same offences, and soon we are behaving as we should emphatically not behave at home. Of course, academically we can say that cultures have their characteristic faults. I have said that it is good that cultures are different, and there will be good and bad differences; but the overseas resident should make a stern practice of not regarding the mote in the eye of his hosts.

Will all these examples serve to avert the constant repetition of the same mistakes? I am working through some of the kinds of behaviour that we noted in earlier chapters as inhibiting communication, and trying to think of ways in which to express a warning that will be sufficiently memorable to help those who go abroad. One of the barriers I discussed earlier was the tendency to be a missionary, and perhaps this is hardest of all to warn people against effectively. There really is a *ius gentium* and a kind of universal law, but it is for each people to defend the *ius* in its own place. What I am saying here applies more to outward than to inward traffic. We may be devoured by the need to take part in some universal struggle, but a foreigner must wait, and do so on local invitation, and in a way natural to the culture whose guest he is; this applies whether we are talking about cruelty to animals or Marxist revolution. There is a good practical reason for this; I have known a custom which no one would otherwise defend to be supported and maintained only because foreigners so strongly disapproved as to provoke a contrary reaction. Resentment at being found wrong can impair good taste and good sense and sound judgement. It is not only that foreign interference is likely to be counter-productive, although that is reason enough. It is also that the best way to get a universal idea accepted locally is to present it in local terms; and local people will know best how to do this. Simultaneously this enriches the universal idea; consider the different kinds of Marxism that exist today, and still more the different forms that Christianity has taken; remember, too, the temporary impoverishment of Christianity by forcing it over too much of the world into a European cultural mould. How do we prevent the young missionary of religion, or revolution, or his particular technology, from burying the universal and transferable under his Europeanism (or other culturalism)? He is carried away by the truth that he feels is in him, and cannot see what barriers he is throwing up all the time. If we disagree with local custom or local authority about something so strongly that we cannot keep quiet about it, then it is better that we should go away and indulge our principles somewhere else.

The revolutionary who ends by slipping cultural imperialism in under the guise of the newest and best idea is the extreme case; it is more often a matter of intolerance of local custom, especially if this involves 'hypocrisy'. It is one idea current in the West that, if there is a social convention or accepted ideal that is not observed in practice, it ought to be discarded; that a new ideal that conforms to the practice ought to be adopted; that anything else is 'hypocrisy'. This is just another attitude of Western culture, and need not and should not be for export. The older idea that the practice should conform to the ideal, although it has never perhaps been crowned by success, obtains very widely still. Most people will accept the necessity of conforming to the minimum standards of public behaviour required by a host culture; they will please themselves in private without feeling that they are hypocritical. This applies to traffic into as well as out of Britain. There is usually little difficulty in conveying this advice. A warning against the opposite extreme is equally easily intelligible. Dressing up in local costume is a kind of amateur play-acting, as is any unnecessary adoption of local ways; it will do nothing to further good understanding, if only because it looks like condescension. The line between sensible clothing for a hot (or cold) climate and dressing up may be delicate. When does an Englishman wear a kilt in Scotland? It may in rare circumstances be appropriate, but the answer must come from the hosts. We are giving advice to the foreigner who wants to live, and should do so, unobtrusively and sympathetically abroad; if he were absorbed into the host culture he would no longer be foreign and he would do nothing to help communication between different cultures. This is theoretic, but many people know it instinctively and do naturally what we find difficult to teach.

The advice I have been discussing has been generally applicable to overseas residence. There are a few points primarily applicable to those engaged in giving overseas aid which are very clear, and correspondingly easy to follow. People who are concerned with overseas aid, whether as teachers or as administrators, sometimes worry about keeping close to British cultural standards. In a former colony, for example, should the school system conform to the English one? Should the University administration remain what it was under British inspiration and rule? From the point of view of the local culture, it hardly needs to be argued that the system should be based on need rather than on an alien model; these may or may not coincide. It should be equally clear that there is no possible British interest in maintaining an unsuitable model that will not work and will only acquire odium for Britain to no purpose. The individual involved in giving aid should not keep in mind a model of his own culture by which to judge his own work. What he should hold always in mind is the main objective of all interchange: the aim is equal exchange, as we saw; this is too easily and too often forgotten. While we are actually working a system that is not and cannot be wholly reciprocal, while there is palpable inequality in giving more than we can take in obvious and immediate advantage, there is every chance that we shall forget where we are going. It is bad for the teacher to forget that he is doing his job only till someone comes back from study abroad to do it just as well as he had been doing it; or for any expert to forget that by definition he is a stop-gap, keeping things going for the man or woman who will be doing it permanently and properly, fitting into the culture as the outsider never can. It is only too easy for the foreign teacher to think that he brings something that the local man cannot supply; the reverse is the case, because the foreigner communicates with his students with more difficulty and at fewer points. It is only when most of the teaching is done by local people in the normal way that the insights of a foreigner, coming now as a supplement to the essentials, are valuable. This is why I believe that it is useful to counsel each individual donor of aid to remember all the time that the objective is his own departure. Very rightly this has always been one of the principles of UN aid, and, in general, of all aid; but it has not always been applied by individuals as a personal guide to their own everyday behaviour. It can even be taken a step further. There is so much to be learned from cultural differences, so much to stimulate, so much to analyse, that a very easy test suitable for self-application, is to ask oneself, 'am I gaining at least as much as I give?'; if the answer is 'no', or even if it is uncertain, it might be better to go back home. This is one of the applications of the remarks I quoted from ibn Khaldūn: teaching or learning in a new culture should increase our understanding of our subject.

The golden rule of reciprocity has two aspects, one subjective and one objective: whatever falls short of reciprocity falls short of our intention; and whatever falls short of reciprocity is also to the disadvantage of all concerned. One or two illustrations of the latter point, although they are of general import, rather than advice to intending experts, may be useful and practical. It applies, for example, to the politician, and to the diplomat who must do much of his work for him. International politics more than any other activity depends on communication; at the lowest, even hatred presupposes a measure of understanding, and a channel by which it may be expressed. For the politicians it is necessary that academics and others should be left free to develop non-political relations between cultures, because it is only in a total framework of understanding that they themselves can function freely. If they subordinate educational and generally non-political work to immediate political considerations — and politics is the art, not only of the possible, but also of the immediate — they destroy the conditions of their own work: you cannot crop a harvest where you first take away the soil. Nor is it on aid because it is a gift that politics depends; it does so in spite of the fact that aid (up to a point) is a gift. It is aid as a means of constructing an equitable cultural relationship that will make an intelligible political relationship possible. The need for reciprocity can be illustrated in quite a different way when we consider the planning of aid. The organisation-and-method attitude which envisages efficiency in a vacuum cannot see that efficiency calculated to the wrong end, or to no sufficient end, is a kind of inefficiency; in educational aid, where the donor is usually a government, an international agency, or a university, or some combination of these, the intentions of the recipient sometimes get forgotten; and when we have lost reciprocity of aim, we have quite lost sight of the end. It is useless, for example, to build a school not in the place where the local authorities think it should be. The most efficient thing to do is what will tend to achieve a purpose shared by donor and recipient. This may look less efficient to the idealists who think themselves realistic, but the realist (whom they accuse of idealism) knows that we can only give what others want to receive. It is true that a gift is rarely refused, but means are usually found to frustrate the intention of the donor if it is not acceptable.

Over-planning is another example of the failure in reciprocity. Economists, as we have seen, dislike education that does not lead to jobs; it ought to be vocational, and education for unemployment ('unemployable graduates') is uneconomic and politically unstable. In fact the only planning that one culture can do for another is at the purely technical level; the thinking and the policy must be home-grown. If a culture wants to over-educate, and by that we can only mean 'impart more knowledge than is necessary for production and employment', is that not a decision in which no one from outside should take part? Whether a policy is in accord with 'advanced thinking' among the experts of the world is not a question about what is right to do, because the fashions of 'advanced thinking' are scarcely more constant than those of haute couture. No man can say what is the right solution to a problem in a culture different to his own; still less can any man say that one solution is right in all cultures; least of all that anything can be right for recipients but not for donors. Admittedly it is anywhere absurd that a university graduate should insist on a highly paid job, if no such job exists; but, although the problem has universal validity, its solution must vary from each culture to the next.

Indifference to political solutions that are a local concern is right not only for the institutional donors of aid; it is right for the individuals who give the aid in person. Sometimes they may need to be reassured that they are not being disloyal to their own cultures in seeming indifferent to international happenings. It is an important part of their briefing to tell them that even the most generally accepted political ideas at home, if uttered abroad, may effectively block any sort of communication at all. On nearly all major international questions each culture is likely to have a prevailing opinion. It may be strongly held, and the contrary opinion prevailing in our own culture may be equally charged with emotion. The minority view in our culture may be the majority view in theirs; in that case, we may add to straight disagreement our additional contempt for attitudes we have already rejected at home. Anyone who feels strongly in such matters ought always to find out what view prevails locally, and keep silent if in his opinion it is the wrong one. If he feels that this is cowardly he should reflect that disagreement of this sort leads both sides to entrench themselves more deeply in their original positions. There is no converting; there is only obstinacy. A rise in temperature prevents future understanding at any level. Even if we say nothing, we may find that there is hostility towards us because our culture is under suspicion—especially of imperialism—and because some xenophobia is part of human nature. Patience will usually overcome this kind of hostility, which is often detached, and usually transferable from persons to principles.

A few practical reflections relate to our behaviour, not as guest experts overseas, but as British hosts, in Universities and elsewhere, to foreign students. How far is it useful to try to impose our own cultural ideas, while we are teaching techniques? And do we always know when we are doing it? We have to try to relieve, above all not to increase, the pressure of strangeness and isolation on the student. Loneliness cannot be abolished just by wishing. We should always be revising such technique as we have for finding out what foreign students need, a need that changes as years pass. Those who would never have left home, but for the necessity of learning, will obviously be happiest if they can organise themselves in national societies, and even the most adaptable students usually want at least some sort of national society, just as Europeans and Americans abroad organise national clubs, chiefly for purposes of amusement. Host authorities must welcome such groupings, although they measure a failure to assimilate; they do siphon off the unassimilable. Articulate unionism is useful also because it produces representatives who can be consulted. Personal relationships are less easily regulated; they are successful only if they are spontaneous. When formal hospitality is offered without genuine friendship, it is of little use to anyone. Friendship must spring up as it can, and foreigners, like everyone else, must themselves want it before they can find it. Cultural factors, such as not knowing how to behave (or even fearing not to speak correctly) may produce impossible shyness or unacceptable behaviour, and constitute a barrier that often discourages even the attempt to surmount it. No one can say how to make friends, but we can talk about cultural obstacles that can be removed. Diagnosis precedes treatment. As cultures best intermingle where there is a common purpose, so the friendships which intermingling makes possible most naturally arise in the course of a common occupation.

Some of the problems to which we referred earlier have solutions that are fairly obvious. We shall not be disturbed if students come to us in a spirit of criticism and resentment; we understand the reasons, and realise that we in our turn should be foolish to resent their hostility. Those whose job it is to look after students and professional visitors ought of course to try to extract their criticisms from them, however reluctant they may be to express them. In practice most people find it difficult not to react defensively and even resentfully to any criticism of their own manners and customs, or treatment of their guests. Some students simply ought to be discouraged from leaving home at all. It is almost universally agreed now that none should come who could be following equivalent courses at home. I am thinking here of ordinary degree courses; it is much better anyway for students to live abroad when they are older and more mature. The courses that some Universities offer at postgraduate or non-graduating level, designed only for foreign students, are sometimes good and sometimes bad; if standards are specially lowered, they are wholly bad. The opposite fault occurs when a supervisor undertakes a subject in which he is not really competent, perhaps because he fails to take his pupil seriously. The cure for such ills is obvious. The reverse of the incompetent teacher is the unteachable student. The 'compassionate PH. D' is disastrous; it is by definition well-meant in a paternalistic way, but it can contribute nothing to international understanding, and it devalues the degrees of those who have earned them properly. Universities should accept students only for subjects they can teach and the students can learn, and that will be taught and examined as advertised. Am I stating the obvious? There are many cases where these canons have not in practice prevailed.

I was young and inexperienced when I first came to adjust to living abroad, now many years ago; but I thought that the sensible assumption to try out, within myself and therefore also in public, was that people differ in quality, not as members of one society or another but only as individuals. I found in time that I had made a right choice, and I never had a moment's occasion to regret it. The opposite assumption, that inequality is created by cultural differences, does not work. It only creates perpetual new barriers. Naturally, patterns recur. People in the same situation, wherever it may be, tend to the same behaviour.

Travellers everywhere, to Britain or from Britain (or Europe or America) behave much alike; their hosts similarly act according to one pattern. Hosts tend to ignore their foreign guests, except when occasional conscience moves them. Guests tend to expect more attention as foreigners than they are ever likely to enjoy. The advice that in this chapter I have imagined giving to those who intend to live and work abroad has been primarily for those who go from the technically dominant culture to teach abroad, but much of it has applied equally to those who come in the opposite direction to learn. If it falls to us to give 'introduction' or 'orientation' courses to both kinds of traveller, we shall find that what we say is much the same in either case. 'And he would gladly learn and gladly teach!' Chaucer's scholar is the man that every traveller ought to be. The key to living successfully in a strange culture is always to be both teaching and learning, and, as ibn Khaldūn so clearly saw, identifying the same knowledge more precisely for seeing and hearing new ways of expressing it. Chaucer's theme is elaborated in part by Pope:

But where's the man who counsel can bestow,
Still pleased to teach, and yet not proud to know?

What Pope saw fit to admire in the individual critic applies so much more appositely to the meeting of cultures:

Who to a friend his faults can freely show,
And gladly praise the merit of a foe.

This is the imaginative leap that is the condition of living between two cultures. As hosts or as guests, there is really no better rule to follow than the old-fashioned golden rule, *do as you would be done by*; but the important word, in Pope as in Chaucer, is 'gladly'. We expect to find other cultures different; we shall get nowhere unless that is what we like about them. It is no good pretending. I have never known anyone succeed in being double-faced. A man who has one attitude for his own people and another for his hosts is always seen for what he is. Indeed, we are what we are, and cannot hide it. Those who do not like living in another world should not try to do so; they should finish what they have to do, and go; they are better at home. Sincere enjoyment of a different environment can only come out of ourselves, and we cannot change ourselves by travelling: *caelum non animum mutant qui trans mare currunt.*

CHAPTER ONE. *Conditions of Cultural Exchange*
1   *History and Anthropology* (London 1968) p. xv.
2   J. H. Griffin *Black Like Me* (London 1962).
3   'Some Reflections on "Negro History Week"' in *Malcolm X, The Man and His Times* (New York 1969) p. 330.
4   With A. Haley *The Autobiography of Malcolm X* (London 1966) pp. 417–18, 441–2, 451.
5   N. C. Chaudhuri *Autobiography of an Unknown Indian* (London 1951) p. 126.
6   *Disappointed Guests*, ed. H. Tajfel and J. L. Dawson (London 1965) p. 95.
7   Francis M. Deng in op. cit., pp. 88, 98.
8   C. Nwiariaku, in op. cit., pp. 83–4.
9   National Council of Social Service *Report of Review Committee* 1969 (London).

CHAPTER TWO. *Suspicion of the West*
1   'Telephone conversation' with Carlos Moore in *Malcolm X, The Man and His Times*, p. 210; cf. in op. cit., 'Islam as a Pastoral in the Life of Malcolm X', by Abdelwahab M. Elmessiri; and 'Malcolm X: an International Man' by Ruby M. and E. U. Essien-Udom; cf. also the latter's *Black Nationalism* (New York 1962) 'Conclusions and Trends'.
2   Engels to K. Kautsky, 12 September 1882 in *On Colonialism* (Moscow, Foreign Languages Publishing House, published in Great Britain 1960). Director of Studies: Tom Soper in *Lloyds Bank Review*, 'Western Attitudes to Aid', October 1969. Marx: articles dated September 1859 and June 1853, in *On Colonialism* (in the last quotation I have reversed the order of his phrases).
3   *Imperialism—A Study*, ch. VII (edition of 1905) pp. 316, 317, 321.
4   'Preliminary Draft of Theses on the National and Colonial Questions' reprinted from V. I. Lenin *Selected Works* (Foreign Languages Publishing House, Moscow 1952) vol. II, part 2, by Foreign Languages Press, Peking 1967.
5   *Neo-colonialism, the Last Stage of Imperialism* (London 1965) pp. ix, xi, 253.
6   'On National Culture (Reciprocal Bases of National Culture and the Fight for Freedom)' in *The Wretched of the Earth*, English translation 1965 (reprinted 1967) of *Les Damnés de la terre* (1961). An excellent short example of the traditional colonial policy towards a popular culture has been reprinted in two recent and easily accessible books, 'Civil Secretary's Policy Memorandum on Southern Policy' (in the Sudan 1930), appendix 1 in *The Southern Sudan* by Mohamed Omer Beshir (London 1968) and appendix VI in *Imperialism and Nationalism in the Sudan* by Muddathir Abd al-Rahim (Oxford 1969).
7   *The Times*, 10 November 1969.
8   Babikr Bedri, quoted to the writer by Sayed Yousef Babikr Bedri.
9   Moral superiority: e.g. al-Kawakibi 'The Excellence of the Arabs' in S. Haim *Arab Nationalism, an Anthology* (Berkeley and Los Angeles 1964); cf. Khaldun Sati' al-Husri *Three Reformers* (Beirut 1966) p. 60. In general, see A. Hourani *Arabic Thought in the Liberal Age* (London 1962). Lighted streets: al-Kawakibi, in al-Husri, op. cit., p. 74. Al-Tahtawi, in al-Husri, op. cit., pp. 16–18. Jamāl al-Dīn al-Afghāni, in N. R. Keddie *An Islamic Response to Imperialism* . . .

(Berkeley and Los Angeles 1968) 'Lecture on Teaching and Learning', Calcutta 1882.

10   Khayr al-Dīn al-Tūnisi *The Surest Path . . . to Knowledge concerning the Condition of Countries*, trans. and ed. L. C. Brown (Cambridge, Mass. 1967) pp. 78, 81, 151, 160; cf. Hourani, op. cit., p. 87 ff., al-Husri, op. cit., pp. 38–9.

11   Anwar al-Sadat on East and West, 'Mistaken Principles' in K. H. Karpat *Political and Social Thought in the Contemporary Middle East* (London 1968). Muslim Brothers: cf. R. P. Mitchell *The Society of the Muslim Brothers* (London 1969) p. 224 ff. Arab socialists: cf. Karpat, op. cit., e.g. Muhammad Hasanain Haikal 'Communism and Ourselves' p. 157, and Jamal Abd al-Nasser, p. 201. Civilisation of all humanity: Muhammad Wahbi 'The Arabs and the Civilisation of the Century' in Karpat, op. cit., p. 236.

12   Cameron Duodu *The Gab Boys* (London 1967, reprinted 1969) p. 200. K. A. Busia *African Search for Democracy* (London 1967) p. 16. J. Nyerere, quoted in Busia, op. cit., p. 76 and in W. Friedland and C. G. Rosberg, eds. *African Socialism* (Stanford 1964, also London and Nairobi) pp. 238–47. Camara Laye *The African Child* (London 1955 as *The Dark Child*, reprinted 1959, from *L'Enfant noir*, Paris 1954). African novels: C. Achebe *Things Fall Apart* (London 1962) and others in the same series.

13   Muhammad Iqbal, from M. Siddiqi *Image of the West in Iqbal* (Lahore 1956) pp. 61, 44. Gandhi *Autobiography*, trans. M. Desai (Ahmedabad, reprint of 1958) pp. 15, 56–7, 256. J. Nehru *Glimpses of World History* (1934, second edition, Bombay etc., 1962) p. 89; *The First Sixty Years*, vol. 2.

14   K. M. Panikkar *Asia and Western Dominance* (London 1953) p. 482. For the Arab world cf. Mustafa Khalidy and Omar Farrukh *Missionaries and Imperialism*, in Arabic (Beirut 1953). Raja Rammohun Roy 'The Brahmunical Magazine or the Missionary and the Bragmun' (Calcutta 1821) reprinted in *The English Works* part II (Calcutta 1946) p. 238. N. C. Chaudhuri, op. cit., pp. 117 ff., 313, 317.

15   Rammohun Roy, Letter to Lord Amherst 11 December 1823, *English Works* part IV (Calcutta 1946) pp. 106–7. S. Radhakrishnan *Indian Philosophy* vol. 2. (London 1927) p. 780. Swami Vivekananda *The Complete Works* vol. IV (7th impression, Calcutta 1955) 'Modern India', trans. from Bengali, March 1899, p. 477. Chaudhuri, op. cit., p. 456; he also quotes Bankim Chandra Chatterji, who, in an historical novel written about 1880, wants Hinduism to base a spiritual revival of something very un-English on 'physical or external knowledge' acquired from the English (op. cit., 427–8).

16   Lian Chi-Chao *Intellectual Trends in the Ch'ing Period*, trans. I. C. Y. Hsu (Cambridge, Mass. 1959) p. 123, and *History of Chinese Political Thought*, trans. and adapted L. T. Chen (London 1930) p. 13. Mao Tse-Tung: *Quotations from Chairman Mao Tse-Tung* (ed. of 1966) p. 194, giving the original references. My wife, M. R. Daniel, has pointed out the closeness of his views on the eight-legged essay to the Preface to the Lyrical Ballads.

17   Mohammad Ali 'Historiographical Problems' in Soedjatmoke *An Introduction to Indonesian Historiography* (Ithaca New York).

18   El Sir Hassan Fadl *Their Finest Days* (London 1969) p. 59.

CHAPTER THREE. *Academic Traffic*

1   *Times Educational Supplement*, 7 August 1970.
2   T. Nordenstam *Sudanese Ethics* (Uppsala 1968) p. 15.
3   Nordenstam, op. cit., pp. 67, 123–5.
4   *Advancement of Science* (*British Association*) 50 (September 1956) 136.
5   In this example, and throughout this and the next chapter, I write with both remembered experience and documented instances in mind; examples taken from countries with which I am not personally familiar are, of course, supported by documentary sources. My generalisations are based upon both documents and personal experience. In the previous paragraph the expert referred to was described to me by a colleague of his in the nation to which he was posted; this was not a country I know personally.
6   Example taken from a country which had not been the object of imperial rule.
7   Example taken from another country which was never imperially ruled.
8   Quoted by kind permission of the author.
9   Said in Bengal.
10 All these examples and those in the paragraphs following taken from actual cases.
11 Amya Sen *Problems of Overseas Students and Nurses* (Slough 1970). The failure rate for all foreign students is not likely to be any indication of the rate for selected students. Overseas universities and governments that send teaching staff to work for higher degrees would probably claim a negligible or non-existent failure rate.
12 Recent criticisms by British academics.
13 See the course prospectuses.
14 The product of discussions about the exact demand for these courses.
15 These passages also relate to particular cases.

CHAPTER FOUR. *Cultural Shock and Adaptation*

1   Nazeer Dafaalla, Sudan paper on 'Present State and Future Needs of Co-operation' in *International University Co-operation* Papers of the International Association of Universities, no. 9 (Paris 1969).
2   Ja'far Muhammad Nimairi to University of Khartoum on 5 December 1969, reported in local press.
3   The immediate source of these remarks is a discussion with a senior official of a country which is not known to the writer personally; they are confirmed by general experience.
4   The foregoing examples or case-histories are taken from the writer's personal experience; those following, from documentation.
5   Amya Sen, op. cit., for social failures attributed, whether rightly or wrongly, to racial prejudice; in the printed version pp. 80–1; but in the fuller version published earlier in stencilled form in greater detail, p. 169 ff., where several exceptionally interesting examples of student hostility are quoted.
6   The foregoing cases are summarised from documentation not selected by the writer, but collected, in order to illustrate difficulties, by case-workers unaware of the exact purpose for which they were wanted, and they simply represent the natural incidence of cases of this type. They are cited to indicate factors common to all cases irrespective of

origin, not to provide statistical information about the places of origin of the sufferers.

7   cf. Sen, op. cit.; part played by language is one of the main features of this study, especially chapters 8, 9 (part) and 10 (part) and tables (stencil version).

CHAPTER FIVE. *Techniques and Cultures*

1   Ja'far Muhammad Nimairi on the occasion already quoted (above ch. 4 n. 2).

2   p. 191 (London 1967, 1969).

3   1277: *Chartularium Universitatis Parisiensis*, ab anno M CC usque ad Philippum IV Reg. Franc. no. 473, p. 543 ff. References to mediaeval economic development: L. White *Mediaeval Technology and Social Change* (Oxford 1962).

4   *Analogy of Religion*, 'Advertisement to First Edition'.

5   Quoted in W. Hinton *Fanshen, a Documentary of Revolution in a Chinese Village* (New York and London 1966, reprinted Penguin 1972) p. 288.

6   Chaudhuri, op. cit., p. 48.

CHAPTER SIX. *Evaluation of Cultures*

1   Gordon Childe *Social Worlds of Knowledge*, Hobhouse Memorial Trust Lecture, no. 19 (London 1949) pp. 18, 22–3.

2   Liddell and Scott, s.v. *barbaros*.

3   Lewis and Short, s.v. *barbarus*.

4   Ducange, s.v. *barbarus*.

5   John of Salisbury *Letters*, ed. W. J. Miller, H. E. Butler and C. N. L. Brooke (London and Edinburgh, 1955) no. 87. Cordovans: e.g. Alvari Cordub. *Indiculus Luminosus*, Migne *Patrologia Latina*, 221, coll. 530, 542, 554; Eulogii Arch. Toletani *Memorialis Sanctorum*, Migne *Pat. Lat.*, 115, coll. 748, 761, 776, 793; *Liber Apologeticus Martyrum*, ibid., col. 862. *Eadmeri . . . vita S. Anselmi* cap. xxxiii, ed. and trans. R. W. Southern (London and Edinburgh 1962). Turci: e.g. *Gesta Francorum*, ed. L. Brehier, *passim*, but especially cap. IX (Paris 1924) p. 50 — 'who dare describe the shrewdness, the fighting qualities and the bravery of the Turks?'

6   Crusaders: Fulcher of Chartres *Historia Hierosolymitana* III.xxxvii.3. John of Salisbury: *Polycraticus* VIII.7. *Epinomis*: cf. the comments of A.-J. Festugiere *L'Astrologie et les sciences occultes* (Paris 1944) pp. 6–7.

7   Persian speaker: taken from a personal report, 1969.

8   Italian: *Pietro Casola's Pilgrimage*, trans. M. M. Newett, ch. XII (Manchester 1907) p. 257. Tenth century: Richeri *Historiarum libri IV*, ed. R. Latouche (Paris 1967) lib. I. 20.

9   Maundrell, letter of 10 March 1698, to Rev. Mr Osborn, Fellow of Exeter College, appended to *A Journey from Aleppo to Jerusalem* (1697). Lady Mary: letter dated 1 April 1717 (o.s.), to the Abbé Conti (Everyman edition, p. 106). Byron: Notes to *Childe Harold's Pilgrimage*, canto II (Oxford edition p. 865 col. 1; cf. p. 868, col. 1 'it is possible to live among them for twenty years without acquiring information'). See also my *Islam, Europe and Empire* (Edinburgh 1966) where all these are quoted.

10   Francis M. Deng: in *Disappointed Guests*, cited above p. 99.

CHAPTER SEVEN. *Past and Present*

1   Herodotus *History*, opening sentence, Book 1, chapter 1 ; Thucydides
     Peloponnesian War, Book 1, chapter 1 ; Xenophon *Hellenica*, 2.3.55–6,
     5.1.4, 7.2.1 (I owe the references in the Hellenica to a recent study of
     classical historians which I cannot now trace). Livy *Decades*, preface;
     Sallust *Cataline*; Tacitus *Agricola*, 46 ; Bede *Ecclesiastical History*, ed.
     B. Colgrove and R. A. B. Minors (Oxford 1969) preface; Procopius
     Anecdota, introduction.

2   William of Malmesbury *Liber de Gestis Regum*, praefatio, and ep.
     dedicat.; Liutprand *Antapodosis*, lib. III cap. 1 ; William of Tyre
     Historia Rerum in Partibus Transmarinis Gestarum, Migne *Pat. Lat.*,
     201, coll. 211–12, prologue. Ahmed Moussa and H. Altenmüller
     The Tomb of Nefer and Ka-Hay (Mainz-am-Rhein 1971).

3   Eadmer *Vita Anselmi*, ed. cit., praefatio. Gerald of Wales *Itinerarium
     Kambriae* (Everyman trans.) and *de Rebus a Se Gestis*, prologus
     (Rolls Series 21, vols. 1 and 6). John of Salisbury *Polycraticus*, ed.
     C. C. I. Webb (Oxford 1909) prologue. Richard of Bury *Philobiblion*,
     cap. 1, ed. E. Thomas (London 1888).

4   Thucydides, loc. cit. Traveller (below) : Ricoldo *Itinerarius* x, see
     ch. 9 n. 18.

5   In the translation by F. Rosenthal and abridgement by N. J. Dawood
     (London 1967), *The Muqaddimah*, opening (ed. cit., p. 11) and
     'Preliminary Remarks' (p. 39).

6   V. H. Galbraith *Introduction to the Study of History* (London 1964)
     p. 79. Arnold: in Galbraith, op. cit., p. 77.

7   R. G. Collingwood *Human Nature and Human History* (Proceedings
     of the British Academy 1936 xxii) pp. 123–5 ; *Autobiography*, chh. x
     and xi (London 1939); *The Historical Imagination* (Oxford 1935).

8   Sydney Smith *Selected Letters*, ed. N. C. Smith (London, World's
     Classics, 1956) to Lady Holland, 20 April 1819.

9   *The Parables of Jesus*, third English (sixth German) edition (London
     1963) p. 136.

10   *Semantics of Biblical Language* (London 1961) pp. 278–9 and index,
     s.v. *construct state*.

11   Marc Bloch *The Historian's Craft* (American edition printed Man-
     chester, England, 1954) tr. of *Apologie pour l'histoire ou métier
     d'historien*. Galbraith: op. cit., p. 13.

12   *The Carmen de Hastingae Proeli*, ed. C. Morton and H. Muntz
     (Oxford 1972) lines 371–2.

13   Bloch, op. cit., pp. 79, 95. John of Salisbury *Letters* (ed. cit.) nos.
     57, 67, 73 and 86.

14   Bloch, op. cit., pp. 43–5.

15   Childe, op. cit., p. 18.

16   Strickland, especially in *Plain Tales from the Hills*; Arbuthnot,
     especially in *Greenmantle*.

CHAPTER EIGHT. *Transmission of Ideas*

1   Venus: text in Levison *England and Europe in the Eighth Century*
     (Oxford 1946) p. 312. Neither these pages nor the early pages of
     chapter 10 below are intended even to suggest the total outline of the
     development of mediaeval learning, for which see, e.g., D. Knowles
     The Evolution of Mediaeval Thought (London 1962) and other
     writings; the writings of R. W. Southern and E. Gilson; and for

scientific development, A. C. Crombie *Augustine to Galileo* (London, 2nd ed., 1959) and other works. Nothing that I argue in the present book is intended to run counter to the positions adopted in these recent and accessible books by contemporary authorities. For mediaeval technology, cf. ch. 5 n. 3.

2   For the general impact of these translations and of false orientalism, see further my *Islam, Europe and Empire*, pp. 48 ff.

3   Lady Liston's diary, 17 August 1813, National Library of Scotland, MS 5709 fo. 64 r. and v. Dr Lorenzo: ibid., 20 January 1815, MS 5708 fo. 7 ff. Other references, Daniel, loc. cit.

4   My treatment of Napoleon here is also a summary of the argument in my *Islam, Europe and Empire*, pp. 96 ff, q.v. for full references.

5   Gordon: written at al-Fasher, 17 May 1879, BM Add. MS 40665, and his 'Foreigners in the Service of Oriental States', in *Colonel Gordon in Central Africa*, ed. G. B. Hill (London 1881). See also R. L. Hill 'The Gordon Literature' *Durham University Journal* XLVII, no. 3 (June 1955); and my 'Bishop Gwynne and General Gordon' *Sudan Notes and Records* XLVIII (1967).

6   For my views on Gladstone, especially in relation to Turkey and to Arabi Pasha in Egypt, see *Islam, Europe and Empire*. For references in this paragraph, see ibid. pp. 139, 270, 291, 340, 380, 396, 400. For Gladstone and Blunt consult also BM Add. 44110 fo. 94 ff.

7   Traveller's account of 1836, National Library of Scotland, MS 7183 fo. 84. Bowring: *Report on Egypt*, Parliamentary Papers XXI (1840).

8   Thackeray 'The Portfolio' *Punch* (1848) reprinted in Daniel, op. cit., pp. 360–1. Other references pp. 273, 534.

9   Op. cit., pp. 247, 258, 297, 326–7, 346, 380. Gwynne: Daniel *Sudan Notes*, cit. n. 5 above. Panikkar, op. cit., pp. 481–2. Rammohun Roy, op. cit. (ch. 2 n. 14 above) part II, p. 137.

10   Ambassador: Sir Robert Liston, National Library of Scotland, MS 5572, fo. 141. Indian visitor: Mirza Abu Taleb Khan *Travels in Asia, Africa and Europe* (London 1810).

11   Engels to E. Bernstein on 9 August 1882, in *On Colonialism* (ch. 2 n. 2 above). Other quotations in Daniel *Islam, Europe and Empire*, pp. 153, 345. Byron, loc. cit., p. 868, col. 2.

12   Dumas *Impressions de voyage — Le Veloce* (Paris 1861) p. 270. Kipling *Ballad of East and West*.

13   Gervase Mathew *Byzantine Aesthetics* (London 1963) p. 135.

CHAPTER NINE. *A Cultural Filter in the Middle Ages*

1   The principal Latin sources for the martyrs movement have already been cited in ch. 6 n. 5. For the life of Eulogio see Alvaro's *Vita vel Passio Sancti Eulogii* in Migne *Pat. Lat.* 115, coll. 705 ff.

2   The story of Perfectus, John the merchant, and Ishaq, in Eulogio *Memorialis Sanctorum*, lib. II cap. 1, lib. I cap. 8, lib. II cap. 2 and lib. I praefatio; and Alvaro *Indiculus Luminosus*, coll. 518, 520, 527.

3   Eulogio's account of Flora and companion, *De Vita et Passione SS. Virginum Florae et Mariae*, in Migne *Pat. Lat.* 116, coll. 835 ff. and *Epistolae*, ibid., coll. 841 ff.; his exhortation to them, *Documentum Martyriale*, ibid., coll. 819 ff.

4   For cultural and psychological conflict: *Indiculus*, coll. 554–5, 527, 529, 518, 530; *vita S. Eulogii*, 712, 715 and scolium 726; *Memorialis*, coll. 735, 754–6, 761, 768, 770, 791, 794, 800, 811; *Epistolae*, 850;

and *Liber Apologeticus Martyrum* (a sequel to the *Memorialis*), ibid., 866 ; *Indiculus*, 523–4, 529 ; *vita S. Eulogii*, 717–18 ; *Memorialis*, 754–6, 759, 761 ; *Documentum Martyriale*, 823–4, 832 (*venite sorores sanctissimae ingredimini thalamum sponsi vestri* 'for—Song of Songs 2.11—now the winter is past').

For polemic– Pamplona document: *Liber Apologeticus*, loc. cit., coll. 859 ff. The main other apologetic matter occurs in the body of the *Indiculus*, e.g. 536–40, 546 and in the first book of *Memorialis*. Classicism: e.g. Eginhard's *Vita Karoli* and Richer's *Historiae*, modelled on Suetonius and Sallust, respectively. Isidore of Beja: Migne *Pat. Lat.* 96, col. 1253 et seq.

5   Descent of Ismail : Genesis 16 : 10 ff. For use of 'Saracen', etc., see my *Islam and the West* (Edinburgh 1966) pp. 14 and 79. The word 'Arab' is occasionally used in our sense, e.g. sometimes by Roderick of Toledo in *Historia Arabum*. 'Saracen' was used in pre-Islamic times by Greeks (e.g. Eusebius) and Latins (e.g. Ammianus) to mean 'Arab' but it lost all precision in the Middle Ages.

6   Sack of St Peter's: e.g. Hincmar in *Annales Bertiniani*, ed. G. Waitz (Hanover 1883) anno 846 ; a very colourful account in Benedict of St Andrew's at Monte Soracte, *Monumenta Germaniae Historica*, Scriptores III, *Chronicon*. Accounts of devastation: e.g. *Chronicon Salernitanum* (ibid.) ; *Chronica Montis Casinensis*, *M G H* VII ; *Epitome Chron. Heremperti* in Muratori V and Lupi Protospatae *Breve Chronicon*, ibid. Garigliano: Liutprand *Antapodosis* 2.46 ; African destruction: ibid. ; Arabs in Provence: ibid., 1.4. John of Gorze: *Vita* in *M G H* SS. IV, p. 369 et seq., and Liutprand *De Legatione* ; Aachen: *Annales Regni Francorum*, ed. G. H. Pertz (Hanover 1895) s.a. 817. Maieul: Raoul Glaber *Historia*, lib. I, *M G H* VII, p. 54 ; *M G H* IV, *Vita S. Maioli*, p. 652. John VIII: *Epistolae*, in Migne *Pat. Lat.* 101. Peter the Deacon: 'forged' martyrdom of St Placidus, *de ortu et obitu justorum Casin*, in Migne *Pat. Lat.* 173 col. 1070 ; his account of Constantine the African, ibid., *Liber de Viris Illustribus Casin*, cap. xxiii. For Salerno: A. Mieli *La Science Arabe* (reprinted Leiden 1966) pp. 219 ff. French jealousy: Richer, op. cit., ed. cit. (Latouche) lib. II, para 59 (vol. 1, pp. 224–6).

7   Daniel *Islam and the West*, pp. 243, 270, 271, pp. 195 ff., 255–65.
8   Lull *Life*, trans. E. A. Peers (London 1927) chh. IV, VI and VII.
9   Turpin Chronicle, cap. xv and xxi, *The Pseudo-Turpin*, ed. H. M. Smyser (Cambridge, Mass. 1937); cf. R. Dozy *Récherches sur l'histoire et la littérature de l'Espagne*, 3rd ed., vol. 2 (Paris/Leyden 1881) pp. 372 ff. and J. Bédier *Les Legendes Epiques*, vol. 3 (Paris 1929) pp. 42 ff.

10   Daniel, op. cit. ; cf. M. T. d'Alverny 'Deux traductions latines du Coran', in *Archives d'histoire doctrinale et littéraire* (Paris 1948) and with G. Vajda 'Marc de Tolède', in *Al-Andalus*, vol. xvi ; J. Kritzeck *Peter the Venerable and Islam* (Princeton 1964) ; R. W. Southern *Western Views of Islam* (Cambridge, Mass. 1962).

11   Aquinas *contra gentiles* l. vi ; al-Ghazāli *Réfutation excellente*, ed. and trans. R. Chidiac (Paris 1939).

12   References in *Islam and the West*, pp. 109–10, to restoration theory. Arab resentment: *Cafari Genuensis Liberatio Orientis*, cap. xv (*Recueil des historiens des croisades*). Right to conquest: Turpinus xv (ed. cit.).

13   Cronica: R. Dozy *Récherches sur l'histoire et la littérature de l'Espagne,*
      2nd ed., vol. 2, pp. 33 ff. The Cid: cf. ibid., pp. 109–213 and 214–53;
      and in *Poema de Mio Cid,* ed. R. Menendez Pidal (Madrid 1919);
      same writer, *La Espana del Cid* (Madrid 1929); *Cronica General,*
      same writer, ed. (Madrid 1955). For monastic landlords in Sicily, see
      Lynn White *Latin Monasticism in Norman Sicily* (Cambridge, Mass.
      1938); Frederick: J. L. A. Huillard-Bréholles *Historia Diplomatica
      Friderici Second* (Paris 1868–72). Translations: Mieli, op. cit., and
      Haskins, note below.
14   The locus classicus in Usama b. Munquidh: *Memoirs of an Arab-
      Syrian Gentleman,* trans. P. K. Hitti (Princeton 1929, reprinted
      Beirut 1966).
15   William of Tyre: Zangi, in *Historia* (ed. cit.) lib. 21 cap. 33. On
      Islam, the early chapters of book 1, and 19.20.
16   Richard of Devizes: *Chronicle,* ed. J. T. Appleby (London and Edin-
      burgh 1963) pp. 75 ff. Fidenzio *Liber de Recuperatione,* in P. G.
      Golubovich *Biblioteca Bio-bibliografica* (Quaracchi 1905–) p. 25.
17   William of Tripoli: *de statu Saracenorum* (printed by H. Prutz, *Kultur-
      geschichte der Kreuzzuege,* Berlin 1883) references to chapters xviii,
      xix, xxi, xiv, xiii, i-iv, xxv, xvii. Julius: most authorities have
      Julianus, surely in error?
18   *De Judaeis et Saracenis* in the canonical collections, *Sextus decretalium
      liber, Clementinae,* and *Extravagantes* (many editions); Raymund of
      Penaforte *Summa Sacrorum canonum* (Verona 1744) and *Ray-
      mundiana* in *Monumenta ord. Fr. Praed. Historica* (Rome and
      Stuttgart 1898); W. von Heyd *Histoire du Commerce du Levant au
      Moyen âge* (Leipzig 1885–6) Pilgrims: e.g. Simon Simeonis, in
      G. Golubovich *Biblioteca Bio-Bibliografica,* vol. 3; Jacopo da Verona, in
      Revue de l'Orient Latin, vol. 3 (1895); Ludolf of Sudheim, in *Archives
      de l'orient Latin,* vol. 2 (Paris 1884). Lull: *Life,* trans. E. A. Peers
      (London 1925) ch. 11. Trinity: Daniel, op. cit., pp. 176 ff. Ricoldo:
      Itinerarius, in J. C. M. Laurent *Peregrinatores medii aevi quatnor*
      (Leipzig 1864) chh. x, xiii, xvii, xx-xxix.
19   Heresy: mediaeval polemic, *passim*; refer Daniel, op. cit., pp. 184 ff;
      cf. N. Cohn *The Pursuit of the Millenium* (London 1957); Spain:
      refer H. C. Lea *The Moriscos of Spain* (London 1901) and H. Kamen
      The Spanish Inquisition (London 1965, reprinted 1968) ch. 6. Lepers:
      Confessio Guillelmi Agassa Leprosi, in *Registre d'Inquisition de
      Jacques Fournier,* ed. J. Duvernoy (Toulouse 1964). Wycliff: R. W.
      Southern *Western Views* (*supra*) pp. 79–82.
20   Paul Tannery *Mémoires scientifiques* x (supplément tome vi)
      (Toulouse and Paris 1930) no. 3, October 1900—'Histoire des
      sciences—mathématiques', p.25. Gerbert: Migne *Pat. Lat.* 139;
      operum pars prima, *de disciplinis mathematicis,* coll. 85 ff.
21   For Salerno and for Constantine the African see A. Mieli, op. cit.,
      52, and Peter the Deacon, *M G H* ss. vii, *Chronica Mon. Casinesis,*
      p. 728; Stephen of Antioch: his translation of 'Ali ibn al-'Abbās al-
      Majusi (Haly Abbas), editions and manuscripts, see C. H. Haskins
      Studies in the History of Mediaeval Science (New York 1924 and 1927,
      reprinted 1960) p. 131 (cf. Mieli, op. cit., 23 and 53). References
      here to printed text fo. 5r, cf. 136r (Lyons 1523); also Vat. lat. M s
      2429. Adelard of Bath: ed. M. Mueller *Die Quaestiones Naturales des*

Adelardus von Bath, Beiträge zur Geschichte der Philosophie und Theologie des Mittelalters (Munster 1934), esp. pp. 1, 5, 9, 12. (Virgil eclogue x, 490). The *de eodem* ed. Willner *Des Adelard von Bath Traktat De eodem et diverso*, in the same Beiträge series (Munster 1903) dedication, pp. 3–4. For Adelard's translations from Arabic, and in general, see Haskins, op. cit., pp. 20 ff.

22   Mark of Toledo, preface to the translation of the Qur'an printed by d'Alverny and Vajda, op. cit. Hermann: some passages printed by Haskins, op. cit., pp. 43 ff; Robert of Ketton: ibid., pp. 120 ff (under the name of Robert of Chester), and see Bibliander, loc. cit. Hermann's *de essentiis*: Bodley MS CCC 243; for Hermann, see R. Lemay *Abu Ma'shar, and Latin Aristotelianism in the Twelfth Century* (Beirut 1962). Al Khwarizmi: many MSS, e.g. Cambridge University Library Mm 3.11 (with commentary). Hugh of Santalla: passages printed by Haskins, op. cit., pp. 67 ff. Raymund of Marseilles, ibid., pp. 96–8 and Bodley MS cit. fo. 53 ff. Constantine: Peter the Deacon, cited note 21 above. See also Lemay, op. cit.

23   Karl Sudhoff 'Die Kurze "Vita" und das Verzeichnis der Arbeiten Gerhards von Cremona' (text, *Sicut lucerna relucens*, p. 75 ff.) in *Archiv fur Geschichte der Medizin*, Band VIII (November 1914). Karl Sudhoff 'Daniels von Morley Liber de naturis inferiorum et superiorum', pp. 7, 40, in *Archiv. f.d. Geschichte Naturwissenschaften u.d. Technik*, Band VIII. Unknown writer: text in Haskins, op. cit., p. 99. Gundisalvo: ed. Baur *Beiträge* IV (1903), *de divisone philosophiae; de scientiis*, ed. M. A. Alonso (Madrid and Grenada 1954).

24   The 'Romans': *Hunc librum intellexerunt romani*, in Cambridge U.L., MS Kk.4.7, fo. 122 r and v. *Pagani* in Crusading literature or *paien* in chansons de geste has the crudest sense of 'heathen'; in writers like Alan of Lille (*de fide catholica contra hereticos*) or St Bernard it has an equally pejorative but more sophisticated sense. See appendix A of my *Islam and the West* for the imputation of idolatry to Islam (p. 309).

25   Philip of Tripoli: examples in Cambridge U.L., MSS Mm.3.11 fo. 161v, Gg.4.25 fo. 13r, Gg.4.29 fo. 1r. Haskins says over 200 MSS, op. cit., p. 137. Bacon's edition printed in *Opera Hactenus Inedita* (fasc. V) ed. Robert Steele (Oxford 1920). Bacon: *The 'Opus Majus' of Roger Bacon*, ed. J. H. Bridges, vol. III (Oxford 1897) pp. 54, 55, 64, 66 (pars secunda, *philosophiae cum theologia affinitas*). *De viciis*, above, note 7.

26   Michael Scot: I have used Bodley MS 266 fo. 25 and Edinburgh University MS 132 fo. 34.v.

27   A useful summary of the Alfonsine translations in Mieli, op. cit., pp. 237 ff. Arnald of Villanova: *Opera Omnia* (Basle 1585) esp. coll. 245, 638–40, 691, 842, 1646. 'Adaptations': re-edition of Bacon *de conservatione juventutis*, see *de retardatione*, etc., ed. A. G. Little and E. Withington (Oxford 1928) (*opera hactenus inedita*). Hippocratic inheritance: pre-Arabic influence status, Richer *Historiarum libri*, ed. R. Latouche (Paris 1967) *passim*, and esp. lib. IV. 50.

28   Examples: Ketton's *Liber Algebrae et Almucabola* (as *Robert of Chester's translation of the Algebra of al-Khowarizim*, ed. L. C. Karpinski, New York 1915). For Ketton's practice see also 'd'Alverny 'Deux Traductions' (ch. 9 n. 10 above) and Bibliander's *Machumetis*

... *Alcoran* (Basle 1550). Others: Sahl ibn Bishr (who was known to be Jewish) Camb. Gg.6.3 fo. 154v. *Liber introductorius* ... *Alquindi* (Beiträge ed. cit.) p.41. Mark of Toledo, loc. cit., and in the Qur'an translation, Vienna cod. 4297. Other phrases quoted in Cambridge MSS, Kk.1.1 fo. 117v, 222v; al-Zarqali, ibid., fo. 125r. See also Ff,4.13 fo. 7r (cf. 8r); ibn Butlan *Tacuinum Sanitatis* (opening passage) printed with ibn Wafid *Liber Albenguefit de virtutibus medicinarum* (Strasburg 1531) and many MSS, and ibn Ridwan (e.g. BM Royal 12.F.VII). Al-Razi: Camb. Ff.6.50 fo. 39v. Scot's *de animalibus*, Camb. Dd.4.30 and Ii.3.16. Opening of ibn Sina's *Canon*, many printed editions and MSS. Philip of Tripoli's *secretum secretorum* in Steele's edition of Bacon's version, pp. 178, 36, 241, 146, 266, 175, 39. The MSS cited in this note are convenient examples of a widespread genre. 'After Compliments': regular East India Company practice.

29   Correction of tables: Haskins, op. cit., *Twelfth Century Writers on Astronomy*, pp.82 ff., and *Introduction of Arabic Science into England*, pp.113 ff; cf. also Tannery *Memoires Scientifiques* V, *Sciences exactes au moyen âge* (Toulouse and Paris 1922) and L. Thorndyke *History of Magic and Experimental Science* vol. 1 (London 1923); cf. Roger of Hereford, Haskins loc. cit., and Cambridge MS Ii.1.1. For the sociology of astronomy cf. F. Cumont *L'Egypte des Astrologues* (Brussels 1937). Abu al-Hasan 'Ali ibn abī Rijāl: printed text (Basle 1551); MS, Cambridge Mm.4.43. fo. 1 ff.; cf. Mieli, p.181. References to the Basle edition, pp. 1, 144, 296, 352, 410.

30   Aquinas citations, in C. Vensteenkiste 'San Tommaso d'Aquino ed Averroe', in *Rivista degli studi orientale* 32 (Rome 1957). Bacon: al-Farghani, in *Baconis Operis Majoris Pars Septeima sue Moralis Philosophia*, ed. F. Delorme and E. Massa (Zurich 1953) pp.22, 206–7; ibn Sina, ibid., pp.25–6 and 72, with al-Farābi, ibid., pp. 209, 210; and *de viciis*, loc. cit., p.36.

31   My *Arabs and Mediaeval Europe* (London 1975). A short introduction to the extensive literature of Arab influences is W. Montgomery Watt *The Influence of Islam on Mediaeval Europe* (Edinburgh 1972).

CHAPTER TEN. *A Cultural Filter in the Modern World*

1   Although this chapter does not quote cases, it can be said that the Afro-Asian countries, rather than Latin America, provide the material for generalisation.

CHAPTER ELEVEN. *Theorica*

1   13 August 1970.

CHAPTER TWELVE. *Practica*

1   Ibn Khaldūn, op. cit., p.426. (For any who have forgotten and wish to recall the contexts of the three quotations in the last paragraph of this chapter, they are: *Canterbury Tales*, Prologue, 308; *Essay on Criticism*, 631–2, 637–8; Horace, *Epis.* I.xi.27.)